DIGITAL IDENTITY IN THE AGE OF BIG TECH

An accessible introduction to the technical and social construct of digital identity, this book helps students understand how the data they generate through online activities and apps is used and the implications it can have.

Each of us has a digital identity, compiled of multiple identities, which has been built over the years as we have interacted with various technologies and apps. This book explores how the data generated through these online activities is used by third parties to form our digital identity and how this identity can then determine where we live, what job we have, what we buy, who we vote for, what healthcare we can access, and much more. Featuring real-world examples, discussion questions, and activities throughout, the book aims to help students understand the impact of their digital identity on everyday life. By understanding how technologies are used by apps, businesses, governments, and third parties, they can then begin to manage their digital identity and regain control of the way they are represented to the world.

An important guide to digital identity for undergraduate students, this book will be especially useful to those studying topics such as big data and society, digital literacy, media and communication, social media and society, and beyond.

Cynthia Tysick is the Innovative Pedagogy and Creative Spaces Librarian at the University at Buffalo as well as Adjunct Professor in their Interdisciplinary Social Sciences Department where she teaches a first-year seminar on digital identity. Cynthia's research explores the formation of digital identities and how individuals construct those identities through various landscapes, both physical and virtual.

DIGITAL IDENTITY IN THE AGE OF BIG TECH

Cynthia Tysick

Routledge
Taylor & Francis Group
NEW YORK AND LONDON

Designed cover image: Getty Images

First published 2026
by Routledge
605 Third Avenue, New York, NY 10158

and by Routledge
4 Park Square, Milton Park, Abingdon, Oxon, OX14 4RN

Routledge is an imprint of the Taylor & Francis Group, an informa business

ISBN: 978-1-032-88731-9 (hbk)
ISBN: 978-1-032-88729-6 (pbk)
ISBN: 978-1-003-53944-5 (ebk)

DOI: 10.4324/9781003539445

Typeset in Sabon
by KnowledgeWorks Global Ltd.

To my daughter, Mara, whose strength, insight, and encouragement have inspired every page and to my dearest friend, Kathy, whose unwavering support and belief in me never faltered.

This book would not exist without you both.

With love and gratitude.

CONTENTS

INTRODUCTION

Each of us has a digital identity. It has been built over the years as we interact with various technologies and apps. What most of us don't realize is that this identity can determine where we live, what job we have, what we buy, who we vote for, what healthcare we can access, and much more. This is because our digital identity is more than gathering data or tracking social media posts. Big Tech and corporations are in the business to make money from our daily activities. To do this requires the gathering of our data through text messages, emails, videos, social media posts, voting records, purchases, and health records. Complex algorithms are often used on these data sets to lure us into making decisions that, on the surface, seem autonomous, but are predicted based on manipulation.

Our digital identities, often invisible yet always present, represent the most significant social construction of the 21st century. Unlike the physical self, which is bounded by flesh and geographical location, our digital selves exist in a perpetual state of both presence and absence, simultaneously everywhere and nowhere. This paradox forms the foundation of what sociologists increasingly recognize as "digital ontology", a new way of being that transcends traditional boundaries of selfhood. The digital traces we leave behind, our searchable histories, our social media engagements, and our online purchases are not just records of our activities but constitute an alternative self that exists independent of our conscious awareness or consent. This digital doppelgänger lives in databases, traverses networks, and increasingly shapes our lived experience in ways both subtle and profound. It is a self we simultaneously create yet never fully control.

DOI: 10.4324/9781003539445-1

The transformation of personal identity into monetizable data represents one of the most consequential economic shifts in human history. Digital capitalism now monetizes human existence using our preferences, beliefs, relationships, and behaviors to manipulate what we consume. Our digital profiles have become the most valuable resource many of us possess. Data brokers have built empires not by selling products to us, but by selling us as products to advertisers, political campaigns, and other companies. The seemingly harmless "free" services we enjoy like social networks, search engines, and email providers operate on a business model where our attention and personal information serve as the true currency. This represents a fundamentally unequal power dynamic whereby corporations possess sophisticated tools to analyze and predict our behavior, while most individuals remain unaware of even the basic mechanisms by which their data is harvested and utilized.

The algorithms that process our digital identities don't merely observe; they shape, nudge, and constrain. They create what social theorists call "choice architectures" that guide us toward certain decisions while obscuring alternatives. These systems don't just predict what we *might* do; they actively influence what we *will* do. Consider how recommendation algorithms determine what news we consume, what products we see, what entertainment we enjoy, and even whom we might date. These systems create segmentation models that progressively narrow our experience and reinforce existing beliefs and behaviors. This digital curation of our virtual selves extends beyond individual choice to broader social dynamics, potentially reinforcing societal divisions and inequities. While we may believe ourselves to be acting autonomously, the reality is far more complex. Our apparent choices are frequently predetermined by invisible structures designed to maximize engagement, consumption, and data generation. What feels like discovery is often carefully orchestrated exposure.

Multifaceted Digital Self

In this book, we will break one's digital identity down into six aspects: social, financial, professional, health, civic, and consumer. These dimensions, while analytically distinct, operate in constant interplay, creating a complex web of data that defines our opportunities and constraints in contemporary society.

The social dimension encompasses our relationships, communities, and interpersonal communications. It includes not only explicit social media activities but also metadata about our connections – who we communicate with, when, and in what contexts. These interaction patterns reveal intimate details about our social location and networks of influence. Our financial identity includes not only official credit scores and banking records but also subtler indicators like spending patterns, payment timing, and financial app usage. These data points increasingly determine access to economic opportunities, from mortgages to employment, often through opaque algorithmic assessment.

The professional aspect extends beyond résumés and LinkedIn profiles to include digital work habits, communication styles, and professional network structures. Prospective employers increasingly deploy sophisticated tools to evaluate candidates based on digital footprints, sometimes unbeknownst to the individuals being assessed. Our health identity now transcends traditional medical records to include fitness tracking data, food delivery choices, search histories for symptoms, and even patterns of mobility that might indicate physical or mental health status. These dispersed health indicators create shadow medical profiles that may influence insurance rates, treatment options, and healthcare accessibility.

The civic dimension captures our political and community engagement, voting records, petition signatures, political donations, and the geographic metadata that places us within civic contexts. These digital traces increasingly shape political targeting and public resource allocation. Finally, our consumer identity aggregates purchasing patterns, brand affiliations, product searches, and review histories to create predictive models of our future consumption. These profiles determine what offers we receive, what prices we're shown, and what products are developed to target our predicted needs.

The Intersectionality of Digital Identity

The interconnectedness of these aspects is explored throughout the remaining chapters where we will discuss the use of AI and predictive analytics to drive individuals to action via data manipulation. The power of these systems lies precisely in their ability to cross-reference seemingly unrelated data points, connecting, for instance, social media activity with financial vulnerability, or consumer preferences with political susceptibility. This intersectional analysis reveals how digital identities don't merely reflect existing social inequalities but often amplify them. Algorithmic systems trained on historically biased data frequently reproduce and intensify patterns of discrimination along lines of race, gender, class, and other social dimensions. The actions resulting from these systems can lead to devastating results for individuals and groups. This will be explored in the chapter on doxing and cancel culture, phenomena that represent the weaponization of digital identity against individuals. When personal information is mobilized for harassment or public shaming, we see the darker potentialities of digital existence.

Reclaiming Your Digital Self

This book offers a pathway toward digital self-determination. Each chapter builds upon the other and offers you a framework to scaffold your authentic digital self. A case study is presented in each chapter to illustrate the main concepts discussed. Exercises at the end of each chapter ask you to consider the concepts as they relate to your own situation. These reflective exercises aim to transform abstract social theory into practical personal action. By understanding how your multiple identities are formed, you can begin to manage your digital identity and take back control of the decisions third parties are making for you.

This book was not written to instill fear or resignation, but to encourage you to understand the digital systems you interact with daily. Through this understanding, you will begin to take the first steps toward socially constructing a digital identity that represents you in equitable, humane, and transparent terms. Your digital self isn't merely a technological artifact; it's an organic extension of you. By approaching digital identity through a social sciences lens, we can move beyond technical discussions of cybersecurity and algorithms to address the fundamental questions of agency, equity, and humans flourishing in the digital age.

1

DIGITAL IDENTITY

What Is It and How Is It Formed?

Scholars define digital identity as a "set of digital data which represents an individual in a digital virtual world" (Laurent & Bouzefrane, 2015, p. 27). Your digital identity can span several activities and, by nature, be segmented and interconnected at the same time. It is these aspects of digital identity that this book will explore. Oftentimes, as you go about your day online, constantly connected through various devices, you don't consider the multifaceted identity you're creating and maintaining. Your identity is built as you buy merchandise with a credit card at a self-checkout terminal where your transaction is video-recorded. It continues to be built when you use GPS to navigate to a friend's house where you add to your identity with Instagram pictures and TikTok videos. In this short period of time, you've contributed to your consumer, civic, and social identities. All of which could look very different from each other and come with unique vulnerabilities.

Interconnected Identities

As we've alluded to, your digital identity is not just a one-dimensional representation of you. It's a faceted jewel with many sides. Your identities are built with the activities you do online through Internet searches, navigating various websites, creating your own content. It continues to form through engagement on your favorite applications like TikTok, YouTube, Reddit, or Uber. However, your digital identity is also subject to activities you don't perform, through third parties like your government, marketers, and "bad actors" (cybercriminals or hackers). Naturally, this leads to security and privacy vulnerabilities that you often have no control over, and when things go wrong, you

DOI: 10.4324/9781003539445-2

won't find out about it until it's too late. It's important to understand the various digital identities you have, how data about those identities is generated, who controls access to that data, and how that access could be compromised.

What are the various digital identities that make up you? They'll vary by individual, depending on their geographic location, lifestyle, and access to technologies. Sometimes they connect and sometimes they remain separate; it depends on how intentional you are in keeping them separate. People have been known to keep multiple aliases and accounts on social media and other online platforms to segment parts of themselves. For most of us, there are six core identities that are collected across our lifetime: Social, financial, health, professional, civic, and consumer.

Your social digital identity is perhaps the most visible and actively cultivated facet of your digital presence. It encompasses not just your explicit social media profiles but the entire ecosystem of your online social interactions. Your financial digital identity extends far beyond traditional credit scores and bank statements to encompass your entire relationship with money from accessing it to using it. Your health digital identity represents perhaps the most intimate data collection about your physical and mental functioning, extending far beyond traditional medical records. Your professional digital identity is more than your LinkedIn profile; it encompasses all digital traces related to your work life, skills, and employability. Your civic digital identity includes your relationship with governance systems, political engagement, and community participation in the digital sphere. Finally, your consumer digital identity represents your value as an economic agent in the data economy, encompassing all aspects of your purchasing patterns and preferences.

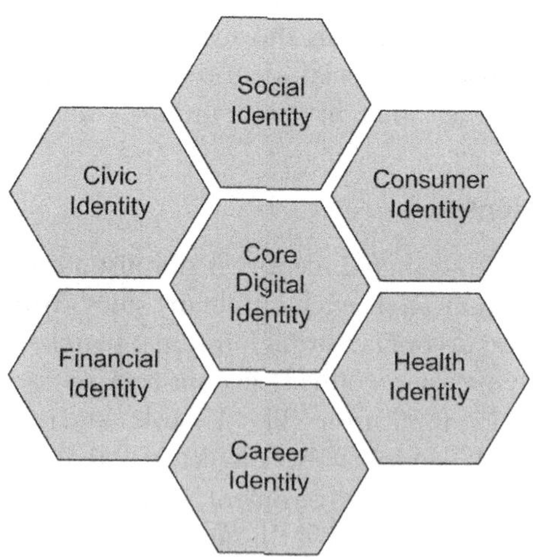

FIGURE 1.1 Your digital identities.

Digital Identity Formation

Your digital identity begins before birth. Happy parents share ultrasounds or test strips on Instagram. Grandparents post announcements on Facebook. The baby's social identity has begun. In the parent's womb the baby's life is being captured electronically through medical records and health insurance bills; their health identity has begun. Parents register themselves and the baby at local shops and online retailers for clothes, toys, and diapers, thus establishing the baby's consumer identity. It's important that parents consider this fact and limit the amount of personal information they post online about their children. That is because nefarious forces are always at work, using such information to build elaborate profiles of individuals for the purposes of identity theft, fraud, and other crimes. Furthermore, parents can find themselves being manipulated through algorithms to purchase items they may not have necessarily needed or wanted from companies driven purely by profit.

Once you're born, your digital identity begins in earnest. In most countries, a baby's birth is officially recorded with their government. Depending on the country, they will be issued some type of government identification, such as a social security number (SSN) in the United States or a civic identification number (CIN) in the European Union. These identification numbers become one of the first pieces of digital data recorded and trackable for an individual. The number tracks us for life, and as we go through our various online identities, it's one of the most used pieces of authentication information. As a result, these numbers become precious commodities on the criminal market because they can often be used to obtain credit, drivers' licenses, passports, and other goods and services.

As we age, our digital identity continues to grow, branch, and mature with us as we go to school, use the healthcare system, engage in extracurricular activities, build relationships, gain employment, vote, obtain loans or other forms of credit, and make purchases throughout our lifetime. In addition to forming our identity, these activities become part of our "digital footprint". Digital footprints are the data that exists about you because of your online activity. They're created by the websites we visit, the information we share with online and digital applications, and activities we post on social media or what others post about us. These footprints, when analyzed by computer algorithms, allow various commercial, medical, and government entities to build a profile of a person. With the help of an ever growing and sophisticated artificial intelligence network, these entities can predict and manipulate our actions.

It's important to understand the impact all the devices and tracking has on your digital identity and digital footprint. Currently, it's almost impossible to escape creating some type of digital footprint and digital identity.

However, there are ways to mitigate the impact external entities have on each of us as we go about our everyday lives. One of the easiest things to do is read and understand the terms and conditions of all digital tracking applications and interactions. How many of us read the terms of applications like TikTok or Snapchat? How many times have we gone about our days signing electronic documents without fully going through them? The answer for many of us is too many times. We want to access an app so we click "accept", we want to play the game our friends are playing, and we don't have time to waste reading a long document intentionally written in legalese. The temptation to ignore protecting ourselves both digitally and legally stems from the need to be part of something, to belong and participate.

As we begin to express ourselves online and engage with diverse communities, we inherently navigate complex issues of race, agency, and culture, which are grounded by the concept of kinship in shaping identity (Wilson, 2017). Therefore, recognizing the multifaceted nature of digital identity is crucial for fostering these kinships and promoting a healthy, positive engagement in digital spaces, which eventually influences personal and communal identity formation. It cannot be overstated that your digital identity is formed through various channels, including civic participation and consumer behavior, underscoring the need for you to critically navigate your online presence and begin to understand why you engage the way you do in these digital spaces.

Participatory Culture

In 2006 the MacArthur Foundation funded a project, led by Dr. Henry Jenkins, to explore the ways digital technologies were impacting young people both socially and emotionally. The team developed the concept of participatory culture theory to explain why youth were compelled to utilize these technologies (Jenkins et al., 2006). The theory suggests people desire to become part of a culture through activity rather than observation. To engage in this digital, online culture, they must become producers of content rather than mere consumers. The attraction of online engagement is its relatively low barrier to artistic expression and creative engagement. Once a person is in this online, digital culture, there is strong support for them to create and share their work in communities. The communities have various hierarchical structures, but they will all have some type of mentorship scheme where more experienced members pass along knowledge and advice to newer members. This type of culture is one where the members believe their contribution matters and they feel some degree of connection to one another. The community, rather than the individual, becomes the focus.

There are some flaws in this theory. It ignores the fact that most of the world lives on $22,000 USD per year and access to unlimited data on smartphones is beyond the reach of many (World Economic Forum, 2024). Second, there are still remote areas of the globe, like central Africa and Asia, where the internet and cell towers haven't been established. Therefore, we must acknowledge the social inequity of participatory culture. However, once "online", anyone can begin connecting with like-minded people through artistic expressions, collaborations, or information sharing. People are more likely to stay engaged in these digital communities as long as they perceive their participation adds value, they are forming meaningful relationships, and/or they give or receive mentoring within the community. Here, we must acknowledge that interactions may not be supportive or artistic expressions celebrated. Unfortunately, people do experience bullying or hate speech in these online forums and fake or altered images are created as ways to manipulate members.

If one does decide to engage in online communities, there are four main methods to participate: Affiliations, expressions, collaborative problem-solving, and circulations. Each method has its own audience and community. As we review each method, consider which digital applications and platforms might be more conducive to these community builders. Ask yourself, which methods am I more likely to engage in and why am I drawn to them? We are often drawn to communities and desire to participate in a culture due to a host of emotional, psychological, and possibly spiritual reasons.

Affiliations

Affiliations are a form of participatory culture through memberships. These affiliations can be formal, as in the case of professional-related groups, or informal. We tend to gravitate toward informal affinity groups to establish a link with like-minded people, seek membership, and pursue validation. At any given time, we are given the freedom to post or comment on content and begin navigating through the online community upon membership. All our activity becomes part of our digital footprint but predominantly falls under our social or civic identities.

Each affiliated community usually focuses on one theme or topic like a favorite movie, travel, or hobby. Examples of affiliations would be online fan sites and Facebook groups. Swifties would be an example of affiliations. These fans don't just have one online location to participate; they usually use platforms such as TikTok or Instagram to express their appreciation for their favorite singer. Their interactions range from selfies with the singer or memorabilia, videos at concerts, or reactions to her latest album. There are Reddit sites like r/TaylorSwift and Facebook pages like https://www.facebook.com/TaylorSwift/ that have millions of followers. To signal member affiliation, we can add tags or emojis in our social media bios or notes in our messaging identities.

Expressions

Expressions allow those with artistic talents to mix their work with those of whomever or whatever they follow. Fan fiction around a favorite movie or book series is a prime example of expressions. Here, one can weave in AI generated content with actual movie footage or images, overlay with music and text to create a backstory or predict the future of favorite characters. Archive of Our Own, https://archiveofourown.org/, is a fanfiction website dedicated to individuals who would like to express their appreciation for books, movies, characters, musicians, and video games through the remixing of storylines, lyrics, scenes, etc. Fans on the site can rate each other's work, offer feedback to improve, and post their own fan work in written or media form. The site is open to all and includes a "terms and conditions" clause expressly stressing that all activity within the site can be viewed by anyone who accesses the site. Another example of expressions would be stitching in social media applications like TikTok. TikTok is famous for encouraging various trends that community members try to follow like copying dance moves by actor Will Smith and asking your Gen Z parents to dance. While these examples aren't nods to a specific group or communities, it's a way for someone to connect to others over social, political, or other issues.

Collaborations

Collaborative problem-solving is a type of participation whereby members work together to solve a problem that they are passionate about. An example of these communities are video game platforms like Minecraft and Fortnite where players can work in real-time, multiplayer environments to achieve goals within the game. Not only players are required to have a certain level of knowledge and experience in the game to be helpful, but they must also communicate effectively in the jargon of the game to meet their objectives. Because Minecraft is an evolving game, without end, players are encouraged to be creative in solving various game challenges. Another example of community collaboration is Wikipedia. Wikipedia has an extensive behind-the-scenes editing operation of Wikipedians, volunteers with a passion for writing, editing, a specific topic, or teaching. New writers/editors are welcomed to the community after successfully completing Wikipedia training. Editors have background conversations around entries and provide feedback and suggestions on text edits (Wikimedia, 2023). Collaborating is such a valuable "real world" skill that educators often use challenges within Minecraft and group course assignments in Wikipedia to teach students to work together (Andersen & Rustad, 2022).

Circulations

The final method of participating in online culture is through circulation. Here, people engage through the various affordances offered in an application or platform, such as sharing, forwarding, reposting, liking, or side-by-sides (aka Duets). This type of participation often revolves around social issues. One of the earliest online examples was the "Arab Spring" of 2010–2011. During this period, youth from Middle Eastern and North African (MENA) countries capitalized on the technological and social media inexperience of older government officials to coordinate a series of uprising across the region (Grinin & Korotayev, 2022). Using primarily text messaging and Facebook posts, they were able to advertise the day, time, and location of protests across major cities throughout the MENA. The overthrow of Tunisian and Egyptian dictators was facilitated through circulations of mass protests during this period. Yemen, Syria, and Libyan opposition forces also launched efforts against their governments with differing levels of success. Circulating TikToks, Tweets, and YouTube mashups surrounding the 2022 footage of Iranian Mahsa Amini sparked a yearlong series of unrest and protests in both Iran and abroad. Amini was seen being dragged, semi-conscious, into an Iranian police station and charged by the morality police for failure to properly wear a hijab (United States Commission on International Religious Freedom, 2022). She was later filmed in a hospital room with facial bruises, in a coma and on a ventilator. It was rumored she had been beaten in the van both on the way to the police station and to the hospital. She later succumbed to her injuries. Social justice minded community members on X, YouTube, and TikTok posted footage, created their own duets, and circulated various letters to government officials demanding justice for Amini.

Online Persuasion

In the digital landscape, persuasion operates as a powerful undercurrent shaping our online behaviors in ways both subtle and profound. The ever-present smartphone cameras that accompany nearly every social interaction have transformed ordinary moments into potential performances. This phenomenon creates what sociologist Erving Goffman might recognize as an expanded "front stage" where we increasingly engage in impression management not just for immediate audiences, but for potential future viewers across digital spaces (Cole, 2024).

The knowledge that our actions may be recorded, shared, and preserved indefinitely introduces a new dimension to social psychology. This awareness of potential surveillance significantly alters our behavior, making us hyperaware of our surroundings. As a result of having a potential audience, we adjust our actions accordingly. We may perform more cautiously, self-censoring controversial opinions or avoiding behaviors that might be damaging. The smartphone camera has emerged as perhaps the most potent tool of social persuasion. Its mere presence, or even the possibility of its presence, can dramatically alter social dynamics. Consider how behavior changes in public protests, police interactions, customer service disputes, or even casual social gatherings when recording begins. The camera becomes not just a documentation tool but an active participant in the social situation, persuading participants to modify their behavior based on how they wish to be perceived by the invisible digital audience.

This persuasive power operates through several means. First, it activates what psychologists call the "spotlight effect", the tendency to overestimate how much others are noticing our behavior. Second, it triggers identity protection, where people become more concerned with preserving their public image. Third, it introduces social proof dynamics, where people look to others' reactions to determine appropriate behavior when uncertain about social norms. The mechanisms of digital persuasion can be understood through four primary dynamics that shape online behavior: Amplification, bonding, positivity, and conformity.

Amplification operates through the promise of expanded reach and influence. Users are persuaded to modify their behavior by the potential to reach audiences far beyond their immediate social circles. A young artist posts their work on TikTok and sees a video unexpectedly gain thousands of views and shares. Encouraged by the potential for increased visibility, they start tailoring their content to trends and popular hashtags in hopes of reaching even wider audiences. Here, the promise of amplification persuades the user to adapt their behavior to maximize reach.

Bonding functions through the digital simulation of intimacy and connection. From superficial relationships with influencers to community building in niche forums, users are persuaded to engage through promises of belonging. Fans of a popular YouTuber feel deeply connected to them, even though the relationship is entirely one-sided. The influencer refers to followers as "friends" or "fam", creating a sense of closeness. In niche Reddit communities, users bond over shared interests and feel part of a digital "family", persuading them to return, post, and interact regularly. This simulated connection drives engagement through a sense of belonging.

Positivity persuades through the neurochemical rewards of social validation. The dopamine release triggered by likes, shares, and positive comments creates powerful behavioral reinforcement. An Instagram user posts a carefully edited photo and receives a rush of likes and heart emojis. This positive reinforcement triggers a dopamine reward, encouraging them to post more frequently and seek out similar social validation. Over time, their behavior becomes increasingly shaped by what content earns praise.

Finally, conformity operates when we align our behavior with perceived group standards to avoid rejection. The fear of social exclusion persuades users to conform to the digital norms. On Twitter, a user hesitates to express a controversial opinion because they fear backlash or losing followers. Instead, they retweet popular opinions even if they privately disagree. Here, the fear of exclusion and desire to be accepted persuade users to align with dominant digital norms.

These persuasive forces, amplification, bonding, positivity, and conformity, not only shape how we interact online but also play a critical role in constructing our digital identities. Every post, like, or retweet becomes a data point that contributes to defining who we are in digital spaces. However, the same systems that reward our engagement can also harm us, especially when our personal data is mishandled or our digital identities are misrepresented.

Emotional Consequences

As you build and manage your digital identity, it's important to recognize that this process extends beyond information management and into the realm of emotional and psychological well-being. What you post, how others respond, and how often you compare yourself to others online all shape your sense of self. Your collective online identities, social, consumer, and professional, often become so interwoven with your offline identity that separating the two becomes emotionally taxing. This convergence can affect your self-esteem, create feelings of disassociation, and increase your risk for social anxiety and burnout.

While you navigate through digital spaces it's easy to fall victim to making social comparisons (Festinger, 1954). When you scroll through Instagram, TikTok, or LinkedIn, you are constantly exposed to curated representations of others' lives. What you see are filtered bodies, idealized achievements, and polished personas. When you compare your own life against these highlight reels, it can leave you feeling inferior or inadequate. This constant comparison, especially in spaces where metrics like likes and followers are public, can diminish self-esteem over time (Appel et al., 2020). You might start to believe that others are more successful, more attractive, or more socially connected than you are, even when that perception is based on heavily edited or fictionalized content.

This leads to another major issue: The fear of missing out or FOMO. FOMO is the persistent concern that others are having rewarding experiences that you are not part of. It's a byproduct of seeing friends on vacation, at concerts, or engaging in trending challenges while you are at home or at work. Social media platforms are designed to amplify this effect, using algorithms that prioritize popular content to keep you engaged. Research shows that FOMO can lead to compulsive checking behaviors, disrupted sleep, and symptoms of anxiety and depression (Roberts & David, 2020). You might even feel pressured to participate in activities or purchase products, not because you want to, but because you fear being left out of the digital narrative.

Over time, these pressures can lead to disassociation, where you begin to feel disconnected from your true self. When your digital persona becomes too carefully curated, you may experience a sense of alienation or internal conflict. This is especially common when people maintain multiple identities across platforms, professional on LinkedIn, humorous on TikTok, and politically engaged on Twitter/X. While some level of identity shifting is normal, constantly toggling between these personas can erode your sense of authenticity. You may feel like you are performing rather than living. This psychological distance between your online and offline selves can lead to emotional exhaustion and self-doubt (Diefenbach & Christoforakos, 2019).

Further complicating the matter is the rise of burnout associated with social media use. Originally a term used in workplace settings, burnout now increasingly applies to digital life. It manifests as emotional fatigue, cynicism, and a reduced sense of personal accomplishment due to sustained online engagement. If you are constantly trying to keep up with trends, respond to comments, or maintain a presence across platforms, your mental resources become depleted. This can lead to withdrawal, anxiety, and in extreme cases, depressive symptoms. Importantly, this kind of burnout isn't just emotional; it can affect your academic performance, interpersonal relationships, and physical health.

The emotional consequences of online identity formation are particularly acute for adolescents and young adults, but they can affect anyone.

Younger users may be more susceptible because they are still in the process of developing a stable sense of self. Teens who aren't sure of who they are or what they stand for are more likely to compare themselves to others online and often end up feeling worse afterward (Valkenburg et al., 2021). Professionals who constantly self-brand on platforms like LinkedIn may experience similar stress from maintaining a "perfect" career narrative. Even parents may feel pressure to present the "ideal family" online, leading to heightened stress and guilt when real life doesn't match the digital portrayal.

Managing Your Digital Identity

How do we manage our digital identities in a landscape where influence, exposure, and risk are so deeply intertwined? The intricate landscape of digital identities reveals significant vulnerabilities that arise from mismanagement, posing risks to individuals and organizations. As our digital identities evolve through various online interactions, they create extensive digital footprints susceptible to exploitation by malicious actors, particularly when organizations fail to protect personally identifiable information effectively. For example, millions of digital records are exposed annually, often due to inadequate organizational practices by both private companies and governments. This emphasizes the critical need for effective data governance at both the country and international levels. Additionally, proper data management within sensitive sectors, such as healthcare, is needed where mismanagement can lead to severe legal and financial repercussions (Faridoon & Kechadi, 2024). This complexity demonstrates the need for all of us to comprehend the nuances of our digital identities.

How we curate our online personas plays a pivotal role in shaping our self-perception and ensuring our mental, emotional, and physical security. With the rise of mental health issues, particularly among youth, the influence of social media on self-esteem and anxiety becomes increasingly evident. Recent research has linked increased anxiety, stemming from various social, cultural, and political factors, to the pressures of maintaining an idealized digital image (Bell et al., 2019). Digital identities are not merely a reflection of online behavior but are intricately woven into the fabric of our social interactions, consumer habits, and even civic engagement. Characteristics such as community memberships, access to education, and the implications of digital media practices fundamentally contribute to identity development, emphasizing the need for awareness when we engage in these digital spaces either in groups or alone.

BOX 1.1 CASE STUDY

On November 27, 2023, the sports outlet Deadspin posted an article criticizing the NFL for allowing Native headdress and "culturally insensitive" face paint to be worn by fans (Phillips, 2023). The author included a picture of nine-year-old H.A. with the following caption: "It takes a lot to disrespect two groups of people at once. But on Sunday afternoon in Las Vegas, a Kansas City Chiefs fan found a way to hate Black people and Native Americans at the same time". H.A. was wearing a headdress with feathers in the KC Chief's colors and the part of his face facing the camera was painted black. The story was immediately flagged by X for misinformation because it did not show his whole face, which had been painted half black and half red in the colors of the KC Chiefs. Furthermore, a few days later his mother responded to the author on X, calling him out for trying to create divisiveness in America by showing half his face and not knowing or asking that her son is Native American.

The young man's affiliations were as a football fan AND a Native American. The circulation of a biased image of him will forever be online, through various websites and apps, to frame his digital identity without context.

Conclusion

Digital identity is not a static or isolated concept; it's a dynamic, lifelong process shaped by our everyday interactions with digital technologies. From before birth through every stage of life, we continuously create, modify, and expose aspects of our digital selves. These identities are shaped both by what we share voluntarily, such as photos, preferences, and social connections, and by what is recorded without our active awareness, such as location data, purchase history, or government documentation. As this chapter explored, digital identity is multifaceted, composed of six key dimensions: Social, financial, health, professional, civic, and consumer. Each facet reflects a unique set of data relationships and vulnerabilities, all of which interact to form a person's full digital footprint.

Understanding the structure of digital identity is especially important in an era shaped by algorithmic systems and data-driven decision-making. Participatory culture theory helps us see why we're drawn into digital platforms, not just for consumption, but to contribute, collaborate, and express ourselves. However, these engagements are influenced by persuasive platform designs that reinforce social norms, amplify conformity, and reward behaviors that may not always reflect our true selves. Furthermore, the risks associated with mismanaging digital identities from privacy violations to identity theft highlight the urgent need for users to become more digitally literate and ethically aware.

Ultimately, the responsibility of managing one's digital identity falls to each of us as active digital citizens. Recognizing how our identities are formed, monitored, and monetized allows us to engage more intentionally with digital platforms. It also positions us to advocate for stronger protections and more humane technologies. As we move further into a connected future, digital identity will remain central to how we define ourselves, how others perceive us, and how we navigate the world.

Exercise

Search through the social media account you are most active in. Answer the following:

1 Who is your affinity group or groups?
2 What are the top two ways you participate in the social media platform?
3 Are there any interactions or posts you feel might misrepresent you?
   a If so, what are your concerns? How might you be looked at from just the post or comment?
   b Will you delete the post or comment?
4 How has your digital identity shaped what you believe about yourself?
5 Do you feel your contributions to the social media platform add value?
   a If so, how?
   b If not, why stay on the platform?

References

Andersen, R., & Rustad, M. (2022). Using Minecraft as an educational tool for supporting collaboration as a 21st century skill. *Computers and Education Open*, 3, 100094.

Appel, H., Marker, C., & Gnambs, T. (2020). Are social media ruining our lives? A review of meta-analytic evidence on the relationship between social networking use and well-being. *European Psychologist*, 25(4), 263–277.

Bell, J., Reid, M., Dyson, J., Schlosser, A., & Alexander, T. (2019). There's just huge anxiety: Ontological security, moral panic, and the decline in young people's mental health and well-being in the UK. *Qualitative Research in Medicine and Healthcare*, 3(2), 87–97.

Cole, N. (2024). Goffman's front-stage and backstage behavior: Understanding a key sociological concept. ThoughtCo. https://www.thoughtco.com/goffmans-front-stage-and-back-stage-behavior-4087971

Diefenbach, S., & Christoforakos, L. (2019). The selfie paradox: Nobody seems to like them, yet everyone has reasons to take them. An empirical analysis of psychological functions of selfies in self-presentation. *Frontiers in Psychology*, *8*(7), 1–14.

Faridoon, A., & Kechadi, M. T. (2024, February). Healthcare data governance, privacy, and security – A conceptual framework. In *EAI International Conference on Body Area Networks* (pp. 261–271). https://doi.org/10.1007/978-3-031-72524-1_19

Festinger, L. (1954). A theory of social comparison processes. *Human Relations*, 7(2), 117–140. https://doi.org/10.1177/001872675400700202

Grinin, L., & Korotayev, A. (2022). The Arab Spring: Causes, conditions, and driving forces. In J.A. Goldstone, L. Grinin, & A. Korotayev (Eds.), *Handbook of revolutions in the 21st century*. Societies and Political Orders in Transition. Springer

Jenkins, H., Clinton, K., Purushotma, R., Robison, A. J., & Weigel, M. (2006). *Confronting the challenges of participatory culture: Media education for the 21st century*. The MacArthur Foundation Digital Media and Learning Initiative.

Laurent, M., & Bouzefrane, S. (2015). *Digital identity management* (pp. 595–624). Elsevier Science.

Phillips, C. J. (2023). *The NFL must ban native headdress and culturally insensitive face paint in the stands*. Deadspin.

Roberts, J. A., & David, M. E. (2020). The social media party: Fear of missing out (FoMO), social media intensity, connection, and well-being. *International Journal of Human–Computer Interaction*, *36*(4), 386–392.

United States Commission on International Religious Freedom (2022). USCIRF condemns Iran's government for killing of young woman with "improper hijab". United States Commission on International Religious Freedom, United States.

Valkenburg, P. M., van Driel, I. I., & Beyens, I. (2021). Social media and adolescents' self-esteem: Heading for a person-specific media effects paradigm. *Journal of Communication*, *71*(1), 56–78.

Wikimedia (2023). Wikipedia training for students. https://dashboard.wikiedu.org/training/students

Wilson, G. (2017). Fictive kinship in the aspirations, agency, and (im)possible selves of the Black American art teacher. *Journal of Social Theory in Art Education*, *37*(1), 49–60.

World Economic Forum (2024). What is the average wage around the world? *Economic Growth*. https://www.weforum.org/stories/2015/06/what-is-the-average-wage-around-the-world/

2

EXTERNAL INFLUENCE

The Tools to Mold You

The rise of machine learning and advanced analytics has transformed consumer behavior analysis by integrating insights about both "what one does" and "who one is" (Kotras, 2020). This enables businesses to craft highly personalized marketing strategies that align closely with our preferences, psychological traits, and behavioral patterns. While this approach can enhance our experience by delivering tailored content and recommendations, it also introduces ethical concerns around privacy, data protection, and manipulation. For instance, knowing a person's car type, hometown size, political affiliation, and age can allow marketers to accurately predict lifestyle choices such as gym memberships, restaurant preferences, or beverage habits. Algorithms, programs designed to collect and analyze our data, are not just tools for efficiency; they are powerful instruments for predicting and shaping our behavior. Their influence raises critical questions about consent, autonomy, and the responsible use of personal data in an increasingly surveilled digital environment.

Predictive analytics has emerged as a powerful tool businesses use to understand and influence our consumer behaviors. Predictive analytics leverages statistical techniques, machine learning algorithms, and data mining to forecast future trends and individual preferences with remarkable accuracy. Experts have suggested that predictive analytics needs to only be 10% greater than a chance guess to yield millions in profit for companies. Predictive analytics can be applied to virtually any field including medicine, finance, agriculture, retail, hospitality, automotive, aerospace, neuroscience, and weather forecasting (Rustagi & Goel, 2022).

DOI: 10.4324/9781003539445-3

The data-driven insights afforded by predictive analytics enable businesses to anticipate our needs, personalize product recommendations, and optimize marketing campaigns with unprecedented precision (Zulaikha et al., 2020). For example, retailers can leverage predictive models to identify customers who are likely to purchase specific products based on their past purchases, browsing history, and demographic information, allowing them to target these people with tailored advertisements and promotional offers (Sarker, 2021). This level of personalization can be highly effective in driving sales and increasing customer engagement; however, it also raises concerns about privacy and autonomy, as consumers may feel that their choices are being subtly guided or even manipulated by unseen forces.

Behavioral Analysis

The intricate interplay of data analytics and understanding customer behavior reveals significant insights into purchasing decisions. As data aggregating techniques evolve, they facilitate a nuanced comprehension of consumer behavior, encompassing not just patterns of online engagement but also offline activities. This is particularly important as marketers use location analytics to track and analyze our movement, creating a synthesized profile that informs targeted marketing strategies. The implications of such practices often raise concerns regarding privacy and surveillance, as evidenced by the tension between the benefits of broadband access and the threats to personal privacy (Gangadharan, 2017). The sociological dimensions of these analytical strategies underscore the potential for reinforcing existing socioeconomic stereotypes, creating situations whereby consumer relevance is shaped by biased algorithmic systems.

The evolution of these analytic capabilities has transformed the methods companies employed in analyzing potential customer behavioral patterns. Enhanced data aggregation techniques now allow researchers and organizations to merge information from disparate sources, thereby enriching the context in which individual behaviors are understood. For instance, the integration of online and offline tracking creates a comprehensive view of consumer habits, revealing patterns that traditional methods might overlook. However, this vast data landscape also raises critical concerns regarding privacy and ethical considerations, particularly in relation to the potential misuse of sensitive information. As the location analytics industry continues to grow, it requires discussions about the socioeconomic implications of data classifications and how algorithmic developments reshape our understanding of community dynamics (Smith et al., 2020).

As a result, these methods not only inform predictive profiling but also challenge our notions of privacy and ethical data use in an increasingly surveilled environment.

Data Aggregating

The proliferation of digital devices and the expansion of the Internet of Things (IoT) have triggered a surge in the methodologies employed for data aggregating. As diverse devices continuously generate a plethora of data points, the aggregation process becomes pivotal in constructing predictive profiles that inform decision-making across various domains. This practice hinges on the synthesis of both macroscopic behaviors and service-specific data, employing techniques such as artificial intelligence (AI) to enhance accuracy and efficiency. For instance, frameworks like **PRIMATE** (PRofilIng MechAnism Based on ConTExt) demonstrate how data-driven classification can "capture the complex interactions within network environments, thereby enabling better management of resources in industrial settings (Koursioumpas et al., 2022, p. 1046)." As a result of such work, ethical considerations emerge when analyzing data aggregating, particularly regarding transparency and privacy, which must be balanced against the benefits to the targeted audiences (customers).

Predictive profiling relies on a wide range of data sources collected from different platforms and technologies, each adding depth to the overall dataset. As people interact more online through e-commerce, social media, and other digital services, they generate large amounts of data that offer insights into their behaviors and preferences. However, collecting and combining data from many places raises serious ethical concerns, especially about privacy. For example, in areas like homeland security, using multiple databases can help with security goals but may also risk exposing personal information. Tools like PRIMATE show how AI can be used to analyze complex data in ways that are efficient and scalable. These technologies help identify patterns and behaviors across networks without always needing heavy computing resources. While such innovations improve how we understand and use predictive profiling, they also highlight the need to balance data use with privacy and ethical responsibility (Koursioumpas et al., 2022).

Click Farms

Click farms are organized operations designed to artificially inflate digital engagement metrics, often by employing low-paid workers or automated bots to generate fake clicks, likes, views, followers, and ratings across platforms such as social media, search engines, and e-commerce sites (Varian, 2019). These tactics are used to manipulate algorithms and deceive us into perceiving a product, person, or campaign as more popular or trustworthy than it is. For example, on Amazon, it's not uncommon to see products with thousands of five-star ratings but very few written reviews. This discrepancy is often a red flag, suggesting the involvement of click farms. While generating fake star ratings requires minimal effort, writing convincing text reviews remains more complex, though advances in AI are quickly closing that gap.

FIGURE 2.1 Young woman working at an Asian click farm.

Click farms are typically located in developing countries, where low labor costs, high levels of digital connectivity, and weak regulatory oversight make these operations both profitable and difficult to monitor. Nations such as Bangladesh, India, China, the Philippines, and Indonesia serve as major hubs for these activities due to their large populations of digitally literate workers willing to perform monotonous tasks, such as liking posts, clicking ads, or following accounts, for extremely low wages (Shao et al., 2018). These digital laborers often operate in informal economies, where employment is precarious and wages fall well below international standards. In many cases, click farm work is one of the few viable income-generating options available in under-resourced communities.

While many click farms support commercial marketing strategies, others serve more controversial or covert purposes. Eastern European countries, particularly Russia and Ukraine, have been identified as sources of click farm activity tied to political manipulation and disinformation campaigns (Bradshaw & Howard, 2019). These operations have been linked to efforts to distort democratic processes by artificially amplifying certain political messages, spreading propaganda, or flooding platforms with coordinated misinformation. In this context, click farms are not just tools for commercial deception but instruments of geopolitical influence.

The global distribution of click farms underscores a troubling digital divide: Economically disadvantaged regions often become digital labor zones for the benefit of wealthier nations and corporations. This exploitation raises important ethical questions about labor rights, digital governance, and the global inequalities embedded in the architecture of online influence.

Beyond manipulating engagement, click farms contribute to the larger problem of data aggregation-based profiling. The manipulation of engagement data undermines the authenticity of digital ecosystems and challenges the validity of profiling practices. As platforms increasingly rely on predictive analytics to personalize user experiences, the presence of falsified signals raises concerns about data integrity, digital trust, and algorithmic fairness. Combating this issue requires not only improved detection mechanisms but also greater transparency in how profiles are constructed through aggregated data streams.

Tracking

As we navigate online spaces, we inadvertently leave behind digital footprints that can be meticulously tracked and analyzed. This tracking is facilitated by various technologies, such as cookies, browser trackers, cross-device trackers, and tokens, each serving as critical tools for predicting user behaviors and preferences. When you go on your cellphone and order from the Amazon app, then go to a Chrome browser and read a news article, these applications talk to each other. The trail you left on Amazon carries over to the news site in the form of targeted ads on the page.

This level of data collection raises significant privacy concerns. As you navigate an increasingly complex web of tracking practices, understanding the implications of such technologies becomes essential. In addition, behavioral and cognitive biases show that without intervention, we may remain unaware of the risks associated with digital tracking, thus necessitating a thoughtful examination of these technologies (Zimmerman, 2021). Understanding how these tools all work together is vital for grasping the broader implications of digital surveillance and privacy. You must be empowered to recognize when these tracking tools are being used and how to disable them, if you desire.

Cookies

Aside from being something you eat, a cookie serves a pivotal role in tracking by storing small packets of data on your device, allowing websites to remember your past activities and preferences. This functionality enables a more personalized user experience, which can lead to increased engagement and potentially higher conversion rates for online retailers. Their goal is always to keep you on their platforms and potentially make a sale. However, the use of cookies also raises significant privacy concerns. Users often express apprehension about being monitored and profiled through online behavioral advertising (OBA), where the relevance and utility of ads can unwittingly compromise their privacy (Aiolfi et al., 2021). As interactions within the digital ecosystem evolve, particularly with the emergence of advanced technologies, understanding the impact of cookies becomes essential.

Cross-Device Tracking

Cross-device tracking enables advertisers and service providers to gather data on our behavior across smartphones, tablets, and computers, creating a comprehensive digital profile. Unfortunately, this method often occurs without explicit user consent, allowing for the potential misuse of personal information. Unlike cookies, which must be disclosed and approved, cross-device trackers are part of the terms of service on many applications, under the heading of third parties. For example, imagine you research running shoes on your smartphone, then see ads for orthopedic insoles on your work laptop the next day. The ad broker, through your login data, email, or IP address, has associated your devices and assumed a potential injury or age-related health issue. This inference can lead to more invasive profiling, such as targeting you for pain medications or life insurance products. Recent studies indicate that first-party cookies are commonly exploited by advertisers to facilitate cross-device tracking, despite attempts to limit third-party cookie use through enhanced privacy policies (Munir et al., 2023). Such practices not only compromise user privacy but also lead to user experience issues when privacy protections are implemented, as highlighted in research comparing browsers like Chrome and Brave (Berham & Morris, 2022). Consequently, understanding the implications of cross-device tracking is vital for personal awareness in a digitally interconnected world.

Online to Offline Tracking

In the increasingly interconnected landscape of consumer behavior, the transition from online interactions to physical engagements has garnered significant attention from marketers and data analysts. This phenomenon, known as Online to Offline (O2O) tracking, employs a sophisticated methodology to bridge the digital and physical realms, enhancing the predictive profiling process. By utilizing data garnered from various online platforms, companies can effectively tailor their marketing strategies to influence in-store purchases, thus maximizing consumer engagement and sales. However, the implications of such tracking extend beyond mere commercial advantage; they raise critical concerns about privacy and data security. As noted in recent literature, such as the challenges associated with managing diverse databases and maintaining confidentiality (Yao et al., 2022), the ethicality of O2O Tracking must be scrutinized. Moreover, innovations in AI, like those discussed through PRIMATE, offer promising frameworks for navigating these complexities (Koursioumpas et al., 2022), ensuring a balance between effective marketing and consumer protection.

As the landscape of digital interaction evolves, so too do the technologies employed to track user behavior, fundamentally shaping predictive profiling methodologies. Advanced systems utilize the Industrial Internet of Things (IIoT) to monitor devices and user equipment (UEs) within complex networks, allowing for the real-time aggregation of data that fuels behavioral analysis. These frameworks, exemplified by the PRIMATE system, integrate AI to classify the networking behaviors of diverse entities, enhancing resource management through a holistic understanding of user interactions (Koursioumpas et al., 2022). In the realm of e-commerce, companies harness clickstream data to decode shopping patterns, balancing the push for tailored experiences against the imperative of user privacy. This duality highlights the necessity of employing sophisticated technologies that not only enhance business performance but also navigate the ethical implications of data collection and user consent in an increasingly data-driven world.

As technology continues to advance, mobile devices have become indispensable tools for tracking, significantly enhancing predictive profiling capabilities. The pervasive use of smartphones enables continuous data collection on user behaviors, preferences, and locations, creating a wealth of information that can be analyzed for marketing and security purposes. As highlighted in the ongoing development of integrated sensing and communications (ISAC), the potential of mobile networks to support complex applications is increasing, allowing for enhanced tracking precision in real-time environments (Liu F et al., 2022). The ability to track us through our mobile devices not only facilitates tailored experiences but also raises important ethical considerations regarding privacy and data usage in the realm of predictive profiling.

Predictive Profiling

The growing need for effective data management and analysis in various fields has resulted in the emergence of predictive profiling as a critical tool. Predictive profiling integrates advanced analytics and machine learning techniques to forecast individual and group behaviors and preferences based on historical data. Predictive profiling hinges on the aggregation of vast amounts of diverse data sources, which enables various organizations to create comprehensive profiles of users and entities. The insights garnered from these profiles create tailored experiences, optimizing the decision-making processes across industries, from marketing to cybersecurity. Furthermore, the birth of technologies such as AI has revolutionized the field of predictive analytics. For instance, frameworks like PRIMATE highlight the potential of a big data-driven classification approach, which models networking behaviors in a nuanced manner, emphasizing both macroscopic and service-specific perspectives (Koursioumpas et al., 2022). PRIMATE is an AI-driven framework for collecting, analyzing, and profiling the connected behavior of users through their various interconnected devices.

The rapid technological advancement and integration of predictive profiling into societal structures has become increasingly significant. This evolution not only facilitates enhanced decision-making processes within businesses and governments but also raises critical ethical considerations regarding individual privacy and autonomy. Predictive profiling employs data aggregation and behavioral analysis to generate insights that can streamline operations and personalize services, thus reflecting the principles of the platform economy. However, the implications of such technologies, particularly in the context of civic engagement, health, and personal security applications, are profound, as algorithms automate and redefine everyday activities and personal routines. Our growing reliance on technologies that put information at our fingertips highlights the need for AI and algorithms that are context-aware and can cater to our specific user needs (Iqbal et al., 2015). Hence, while offering numerous advantages, predictive profiling demands a careful examination of its ethical ramifications and societal impact.

Predictive Profiling in Marketing

In the evolving landscape of digital marketing, the integration of predictive profiling serves as a transformative strategy for enhancing consumer engagement and brand loyalty. Employing data aggregation and behavioral analysis, marketers can leverage detailed consumer profiles to tailor their advertising strategies effectively. Streaming platforms like Spotify and Netflix offer compelling examples of predictive profiling in marketing. These services analyze user behavior like listening history, time of day, skipped songs, and binge-watching patterns to predict mood, habits, and preferences with high precision. For instance, Spotify may detect that you tend to listen to acoustic playlists on weekday mornings and begin suggesting wellness podcasts or mindfulness content during that window, subtly guiding your routine. Similarly, Netflix uses complex machine learning algorithms not only to recommend shows based on viewing history but also to curate thumbnails, descriptions, and categories tailored to your profile, thereby increasing engagement and viewing time (Gómez-Uribe & Hunt, 2016). These personalized recommendations are not simply responsive; they are predictive, anticipating emotional and contextual states to shape future behavior. While this creates a more seamless user experience, it also raises concerns about how much influence these platforms wield over personal choices and how invisibly our digital habits are being profiled and monetized.

Predictive Profiling in Law Enforcement

In the evolving landscape of law enforcement and security, significant advancements hinge on the strategic use of predictive profiling. Techniques involving data aggregation and behavioral analysis facilitate the identification of potential threats by linking various sources of information. Notably, data-oriented systems now infer relationships based on genetic material and shared behaviors, raising ethical questions regarding the implications of such associations.

In the United Kingdom, the National Data Analytics Solution (NDAS) project exemplifies the growing use of AI in law enforcement. Launched as a pilot initiative involving West Midlands Police and other regional forces, NDAS aimed to harness machine learning to identify individuals at risk of committing violent crime or becoming victims themselves. By analyzing data from crime reports, custody records, and social services, the system attempted to flag high-risk individuals for early intervention. However, the project quickly drew criticism for its lack of transparency, ethical oversight, and potential to infringe on civil liberties, particularly through profiling based on opaque risk scores. The UK Information Commissioner's Office (ICO) raised serious concerns about the project's legality and accountability, ultimately recommending a moratorium on its wider rollout (ICO, 2021). NDAS highlights the tension between technological innovation and the preservation of fundamental rights in predictive policing.

As law enforcement increasingly adopts these methodologies, it's crucial to address privacy concerns, particularly regarding how personal data from disparate databases can be linked to build comprehensive profiles while safeguarding individual rights (Rosenblat et al., 2014). Furthermore, in the wake of heightened security measures post-September 11, 2001, the government's expanded data mining activities, which incorporate both public and private databases, amplify the dialogue surrounding privacy erosion and the need for regulatory frameworks that balance security with personal privacy (Fienberg et al., 2006).

Ethical Implications and Concerns

The potential for misuse of predictive analytics highlights the need for greater transparency and accountability in data collection and usage practices, as well as robust regulatory frameworks to protect consumer privacy and prevent unfair or discriminatory practices (Mühlhoff, 2023). Transparency is critical in AI, algorithms, data, and data usage to improve accountability and effectiveness (Kaplan, 2020). The absence of transparency can lead to a loss of control by people regarding how their personal information is collected and used (Gambs, 2019). Concerns have also been raised regarding the algorithms' potential to solidify discrimination or inequality (Ibrahim et al., 2020). Transparency can allow for an analysis of potential bias. One potential area of concern lies in the perpetuation of existing biases and inequalities using biased data or flawed algorithms (Price & Cohen, 2018). For instance, if a predictive model is trained on historical data that reflects discriminatory lending practices, it may inadvertently perpetuate these biases by denying loans to people from marginalized communities. Companies must be transparent about the data they collect, how it's used, and the algorithms that drive their predictive models, allowing consumers to make informed decisions about whether to share their data and engage with their services. The process of data processing is often opaque to us, leading to a lack of control and oversight.

Addressing these ethical considerations requires a multifaceted approach that involves collaboration between researchers, policymakers, and customers to develop and implement ethical guidelines and best practices for the use of predictive analytics in consumer-facing applications. The issue of medical predictive analytics highlights the importance of transparency (Calster et al., 2019). Greater emphasis should be placed on openness and accountability in data collecting and usage to avoid ethical issues. This includes establishing clear standards for data privacy, security, and anonymization, as well as mechanisms for auditing and monitoring the performance of predictive models to identify and mitigate potential biases. Organizations must ensure that those responsible for developing and deploying algorithms are accountable for their decisions and actions (Dhopte & Bagde, 2023). Additionally, it's essential to empower consumers with greater control over their data by providing them with the ability to access, correct, and delete their personal information, as well as opt out of data collection and targeted advertising. It's imperative to engage multidisciplinary teams to co-develop algorithmic decision-making processes designed to maximize fairness, transparency, and accountability (Lepri et al., 2021; Patel, 2024).

BOX 2.1 CASE STUDY

In recent years, law enforcement agencies across the United States have increasingly adopted predictive policing technologies to anticipate where crimes are likely to occur and who might commit them. These systems use historical crime data, arrest records, and behavioral analytics to generate risk assessments and allocate police resources. One notable example is the Los Angeles Police Department's (LAPD) use of the

"PredPol" algorithm, which aimed to forecast future crimes based on past patterns.

PredPol (short for Predictive Policing) analyzed three main data points: Type of crime, location, and time. While the system claimed to help reduce crime rates by pre-positioning officers in high-risk areas, critics argued it disproportionately targeted minority communities, reinforcing existing biases in policing. A 2016 study by the AI Now Institute found that predictive policing often relies on flawed and racially biased data, leading to over-policing in neighborhoods already burdened by heavy surveillance (Lum & Isaac, 2016).

Civil liberties advocates, including the Electronic Frontier Foundation (EFF) and the American Civil Liberties Union (ACLU), have raised significant concerns about the lack of transparency and accountability in these systems. They warn that predictive policing may erode trust in law enforcement and lead to a "pre-crime" model of justice reminiscent of science fiction, where people are monitored or punished based on what they might do rather than what they have done.

In 2020, after intense public pressure and evaluation of its effectiveness, the LAPD officially ended its use of predictive policing tools, citing concerns about racial profiling, lack of oversight, and questionable outcomes (Miller, 2021).

Conclusion

This chapter has explored the powerful role predictive analytics, behavioral profiling, and data aggregation play in shaping our digital identity and consumer behavior. Through tools such as cookies, cross-device trackers, click farms, and AI-driven algorithms, corporations and institutions can collect, analyze, and act on massive datasets to influence our decisions in both subtle and overt ways. While these technologies can improve our experiences and business performance, they also raise pressing ethical questions about privacy, autonomy, and algorithmic bias.

We have seen how data gathered across platforms and devices is merged to construct detailed profiles, often without explicit consent. These profiles influence what products we see, what content we engage with, and even how law enforcement or healthcare providers assess risk. The use of click farms and surveillance technologies further highlights the global inequalities and manipulative tactics embedded in digital economies.

Exercise

As we've learned, our every move online is being tracked, analyzed, and manipulated in some way. Companies, third parties, and even governments are using predictive analytics and tracking to understand our online behaviors. It's important that you uncover the hidden surveillance infrastructure that follows your digital footprint by using the Brave browser's built-in tracking prevention and reporting tools.

Download and install the Brave browser (available at brave.com):

- Configure Brave's Shield settings to block trackers but record them
- Open Brave and click on the Shield icon in the address bar
- Ensure "Trackers & ads blocked" is set to "Aggressive"

Use Brave as your primary browser for 3–5 days of normal browsing. Visit at least 15 different websites across these categories:

- News/media (at least three sites)
- Shopping/retail (at least three sites)
- Social media (at least two sites)
- Entertainment (at least two sites)
- Education/research (at least two sites)
- Other sites you regularly visit

From your collected data, identify the three most common tracking companies. For each tracking company, research and document:

- Company name and ownership
- Business model and how they monetize data
- Types of data they typically collect
- How this data is likely to be used
- Any privacy controversies associated with the company

Personal impact:

- How do you feel about the level of tracking you discovered?
- What specific types of personal data might these trackers be collecting?
- How might this data be used to influence your behavior?
- What privacy protection strategies will you implement going forward?

References

Aiolfi, S., Bellini, S., & Pellegrini, D. (2021). Data-driven digital advertising: Benefits and risks of online behavioral advertising. *International Journal of Retail & Distribution Management*, 49(7), 1089–1110.

Berham, S., & Morris, S. (2022). A critical comparison of Brave Browser and Google Chrome forensic artefacts. *The Journal of Digital Forensics and Security Law*, 17(4), 1–25.

Bradshaw, S., & Howard, P. N. (2019). *The global disinformation order: 2019 global inventory of organized social media manipulation*. Oxford Internet Institute.

Calster, B. V., Wynants, L., Timmerman, D., Steyerberg, E. W., & Collins, G. S. (2019). Predictive analytics in health care: How can we know it works? *Journal of the American Medical Informatics Association*, *26*(12), 1651–1654.

Dhopte, A., & Bagde, H. (2023). Smart smile: Revolutionizing dentistry with artificial intelligence. *Cureus*, *15*(6), 2–10.

Gambs, S. (2019). Privacy and ethical challenges in big data. *Lecture Notes in Computer Science*, *11358*, 17–26.

Gangadharan, S. P. (2017). The downside of digital inclusion: Expectations and experiences of privacy and surveillance among marginal Internet users. *New Media & Society*, *19*(4), 597–615.

Gómez-Uribe, C. A., & Hunt, N. (2016). The Netflix recommender system: Algorithms, business value, and innovation. *ACM Transactions on Management Information Systems (TMIS)*, *6*(4), 1–19.

Ibrahim, S. A., Charlson, M. E., & Neill, D. B. (2020). Big data analytics and the struggle for equity in health care: The promise and perils. *Health Equity*, *4*(1), 99–102.

Information Commissioner's Office (ICO) (2021). The use of AI in the NDAS project: Investigation report. https://committees.parliament.uk/writtenevidence/38632/pdf/

Iqbal, R., Grzywaczewski, A., Halloran, J., Doctor, F., & Iqbal, K. (2015). Design implications for task-specific search utilities for retrieval and re-engineering of code. *Enterprise Information Systems*, *11*(5), 738–757.

Kaplan, B. J. (2020). Seeing through health information technology: The need for transparency in software, algorithms, data privacy, and regulation. *Journal of Law and the Biosciences*, *7*(1), 1–18.

Kotras, B. (2020). Mass personalization: Predictive marketing algorithms and the reshaping of consumer knowledge. *Big Data & Society*, *7*(2), 1–14.

Koursioumpas, N., Barmpounakis, S., Stavrakakis, I., & Alonistioti, N. (2022). AI-driven, context-aware profiling for 5G and beyond networks. *IEEE Transactions on Network and Service Management*, *19*(2), 1036–1048.

Miller, L. (2021, April 21). LAPD will end controversial program that aimed to predict where crimes would occur. *Los Angeles Times*

Lepri, B., Oliver, N., & Pentland, A. (2021). Ethical machines: The human-centric use of artificial intelligence. *iScience*, *24*(3), 102249.

Liu, F., Cui, Y., Masouros, C., Xu, J., Han, T., & Eldar, Y. (2022). "Integrated Sensing and Communications: Toward Dual-Functional Wireless Networks for 6G and Beyond," IEEE Journal on Selected Areas in Communications, *40*(6), 1728–1767.

Lum, K., & Isaac, W. (2016). To predict and serve? *Significance*, *13(5)*, 14–19.

Mühlhoff, R. (2023). Predictive privacy: Collective data protection in the context of artificial intelligence and big data. *Big Data & Society*, *10*(1), 1–14.

Munir, S., Siby, S., Iqbal, U., Englehardt, S., Shafiq, Z., & Troncoso, C. (2023). Cookiegraph: Understanding and detecting first-party tracking cookies. In *Proceedings of the 2023 ACM SIGSAC Conference on Computer and Communications Security*, 3490–3504.

Patel, K. (2024). Ethical reflections on data-centric AI: Balancing benefits and risks. *SSRN Electronic Journal*, *2*(1), 1–17.

Price, W. N., & Cohen, I. G. (2018). Privacy in the age of medical big data. *Nature Medicine*, *25*(1), 37–43.

Rosenblat, A., Kneese, T., & boyd, d. (2014). Predicting Human Behavior. 10.31219/osf.io/dpvyp

Rustagi, M., & Goel, N. (2022). Predictive analytics: A study of its advantages and applications. *IARS International Research Journal*, *12*(1), 60–64.

Sarker, I. H. (2021). Data science and analytics: An overview from data-driven smart computing, decision-making and applications perspective. *SN Computer Science*, *2*(5), 1–22.

Shao, C. et al. (2018). The spread of low-credibility content by social bots. *Nature Communications*, *9*(1), 4787.

Varian, H. R. (2019). The economics of fake engagement. *Journal of Economic Perspectives*, *33*(4), 217–232.

Yao, P., Osman, S., Sabri, M. F., & Zainudin, N. (2022). Consumer behavior in online-to-offline (O2O) commerce: a thematic review. *Sustainability*, *14*(13), 7842. https://doi.org/10.3390/su14137842

Zimmerman, S. (2021). Exploring strategies to prevent harm from web search (Doctoral dissertation, University of Essex). https://repository.essex.ac.uk/29762/

Zulaikha, S., Mohamed, H., Kurniawati, M., Rusgianto, S., & Rusmita, S. A. (2020). Customer predictive analytics using artificial intelligence. *The Singapore Economic Review*.0(0), 1–12. https://doi.org/10.1142/S0217590820480021

3

YOUR VALUE

Know the Power of Your Data

Globally, approximately 402.74 million terabytes of data is created each day. That equates to 146 GB per Internet user per day (Beamer, 2024). The sheer volume of digital data being generated daily, with 90% of the world's data created in the past two years alone, has transformed it into the "new oil" of the digital era (Tawil et al., 2024). In this new digital economy, personal data, ranging from browsing habits and purchase history to biometric information and social media activity, has become a highly valuable commodity. All the data that forms a core part of your digital identity is collected, analyzed, and monetized by a vast ecosystem of technology companies, advertisers, and data brokers. These third parties profit by using the data to target ads, optimize algorithms, and develop consumer profiles, often without direct compensation to you, the individual who generates the data in the first place. Tech philosopher Jaron Lanier has argued that this dynamic contributes to growing inequality and proposes a more equitable model in which individuals are paid for the data they produce. In his book *Who Owns the Future?* (2013), Lanier envisions a digital economy where crypto payments for data could serve as a form of universal basic income, potentially lifting individuals out of poverty by turning their data production into a source of personal wealth. This model challenges the current model of surveillance capitalism and opens possibilities for more ethical and inclusive digital economies around the world. Other experts have highlighted the need for a "digital commons" that would empower individuals to exercise greater control over their personal data and participate in the value creation process (Morrison

DOI: 10.4324/9781003539445-4

& Charbonneau, 2006). Consequently, there have been calls for a more balanced and ethical approach to data governance, one that recognizes the fundamental rights of individuals and ensures a fair distribution of the economic and social value generated by their data.

Data Extraction

Our digital footprints, comprising search histories, social media interactions, location data, and consumption patterns, constitute a comprehensive behavioral profile that holds tremendous economic value. This value emerges through several mechanisms:

- Predictive analytics enables corporations to anticipate consumer behavior with remarkable precision, thereby optimizing what they spend on marketing campaigns and maximizing the return on investment. The ability to forecast customers' purchasing decisions based on historical data patterns transforms these data points into valuable commercial intelligence.
- Personalization algorithms leverage individual behavioral patterns to customize experiences, creating digital environments where customers engage longer and purchase. This significantly enhances platform fidelity and increases advertising revenue streams.
- Risk assessment frameworks utilize an individual's digital identity profile to evaluate creditworthiness, insurance eligibility, and other economically significant determinations. These algorithmic judgments shape individual economic opportunities.

Capitalizing on You

Despite the immense economic value generated from our personal data, most individuals remain unaware of its full monetization potential. A global study revealed that fewer than 300 million people understand that their data is being collected, traded, and used to generate profit and that they themselves could benefit from these transactions. This widespread lack of awareness contributes to a persistent power imbalance, where corporations and data brokers accumulate vast revenues while the individuals producing the data receive little to no compensation or control. As a result, personal data becomes a lucrative asset for institutions, but a missed opportunity for the people behind it.

The extraction of value from digital identity has become foundational to the business models of major technology platforms. Shoshana Zuboff

(2019) identifies this phenomenon as surveillance capitalism, a system in which personal experiences become a commodity through continuous data capture. Leading corporations such as Meta have developed advanced infrastructures for harvesting, analyzing, and monetizing user data. In 2024 alone, Facebook generated approximately $118 billion, primarily through advertising revenues that rely on highly granular user targeting. Beyond these platforms, an entire ecosystem of data brokers thrives on the resale of aggregated personal data, often without users' knowledge or consent. These intermediaries operate across industries, enabling secondary markets where digital identities are repackaged and sold as economic commodities.

A variety of emerging models seek to return some of this value to individuals by enabling direct participation in the data economy. Data cooperatives are one such approach, offering a collective framework in which individuals can pool their data and negotiate fairer terms for its use. These cooperatives enhance individual bargaining power and provide transparency in data transactions. Personal data marketplaces, like DataWallet https://www.datawallet.com/, are also growing in popularity, allowing users to selectively sell access to their data on their own terms. These innovations aim to establish the technological foundation for data sovereignty, the right of individuals to own, control, and benefit from the digital assets they produce.

However, the vision of widespread individual data monetization remains difficult to realize due to several systemic challenges. First, assigning fair market value to isolated data points is complex. Second, creating and running the systems needed to safely manage and control personal data. Third, there is an unequal balance of power between regular people (individual users) and large companies that collect and control data (like Google, Meta, or Amazon). Even in systems that claim to reward people for their data, individuals still often have very little real power or control. Some systems pretend to give people control over their data by offering small payments, but those people still don't have the knowledge, power, or choice to make it truly fair.

Nonetheless, the idea that individuals can and should monetize their personal data is gaining public traction. A recent survey found that 53% of consumers consider their personal information an asset that could be used to negotiate better deals with companies (Stein, 2023). The proliferation of data marketplaces is helping shift perceptions of data from being passively extracted to being actively managed as personal property. As this paradigm gains strength, data sovereignty emerges as a vital principle, one that moves beyond compensation to demand control, consent, and transparency in how digital identity is used. In this evolving landscape, recognizing and securing personal agency over data is not just a matter of economics, but of digital citizenship and equity.

Algorithmic Discrimination and Risk

As digital identity becomes increasingly central to economic decision-making, algorithmic systems are playing a larger role in evaluating individuals for loans, jobs, housing, and insurance. These systems rely heavily on data derived from personal digital footprints, yet they often operate without transparency or accountability. When algorithms process biased or incomplete data, they can reproduce and even amplify existing social inequalities. This phenomenon, known as algorithmic discrimination, poses a significant risk to individuals whose data is used to make economically consequential decisions.

For instance, algorithmic credit scoring systems may penalize individuals for behaviors associated with poverty, such as irregular income patterns or frequent address changes, even if those behaviors do not indicate financial irresponsibility. These decisions are often made without the individual's knowledge, and the rationale behind them may be impossible to challenge or appeal (Eubanks, 2018). In effect, digital identity becomes a tool not only for opportunity but also for exclusion. Those already marginalized by race, gender, class, or geography may find themselves further disadvantaged in data-driven systems.

Predictive policing algorithms, which use historical crime data to forecast future criminal activity, have been shown to disproportionately target communities of color. These models are based on flawed assumptions and biased datasets that reflect structural inequalities in law enforcement practices. When incorporated into decision-making frameworks, such as employment background checks or housing eligibility, they extend the consequences of discrimination into new domains (Noble, 2018). This results in a cycle where past disadvantages are perpetuated and reinforced by automated systems.

The problem is compounded by the lack of oversight mechanisms and explainability in many algorithmic tools. Individuals are rarely told which data points influenced their evaluation, nor are they given access to meaningful channels for recourse. This lack of transparency creates what some scholars describe as a "black box" effect, where individuals are affected by decisions they cannot understand or contest (Pasquale, 2015). As a result, algorithmic risk frameworks often operate in ways that are opaque, unregulated, and resistant to challenge.

Moreover, because digital identity is now a commodity through the data collected, it creates financial incentives to maintain these opaque systems. The more granular and precise a data profile, the more valuable it becomes to corporations and institutions that depend on automated decision-making. Consequently, there is little motivation to question or reform systems that systematically disadvantage certain populations. Unfortunately, algorithmic discrimination is both widespread and largely unchecked.

To mitigate these risks, there is growing advocacy for algorithmic accountability and fairness in data-driven systems. Researchers and civil society groups have called for algorithmic audits, greater transparency in model development, and the inclusion of affected communities in governance processes (Dobson & Fernandez, 2023). For example, in the past it had been the practice to devalue the homes of families of color. Some jurisdictions are beginning to implement legal safeguards, such as New York City's law requiring bias audits for home valuations during mortgage applications. However, these efforts remain fragmented and are often reactive rather than proactive.

In the context of digital identity, algorithmic discrimination underscores the urgent need for equitable data governance. Protecting individuals from harm means not only ensuring data privacy but also challenging the assumptions and structures embedded in algorithmic technologies. Fair compensation for data use must be accompanied by ethical standards that safeguard against economic and social exclusion. Only then can digital identity become a tool for empowerment rather than a mechanism of control.

Developed and Developing Countries

The economic value of personal data is influenced by a variety of factors, including cultural norms, legal frameworks, technological infrastructure, and economic conditions. Developed countries, such as those in North America and Europe, generally have more advanced data protection laws and higher levels of digital literacy, which can influence how individuals value their personal data. In contrast, developing countries often face challenges related to limited infrastructure, weaker data protection laws, and lower levels of digital literacy, which can affect the economic value of personal data in these regions.

Research has shown that individuals in developed countries tend to place a higher economic value on their personal data compared to those in developing countries. For example, studies have found that Germans value privacy more than people in the United States and Latin American countries, with individuals in Argentina, Colombia, and Mexico even willing to pay to avoid receiving ads (Koch, 2022; Prince & Wallsten, 2020). This suggests that in developed countries, where privacy is often prioritized, individuals are more likely to demand higher compensation for their personal data.

In contrast, in developing countries, the economic value of personal data may be lower due to a variety of factors, including limited awareness of data privacy issues and the perceived benefits of sharing personal data for access to digital services. For instance, in some developing countries, individuals may be more willing to trade their personal data for access to financial services, such as credit, due to the lack of formal credit histories (Kemp & Buckley, 2017).

Economic factors, such as GDP per capita, also play a significant role in determining the economic value of personal data. Research has shown that wealthier countries tend to have higher levels of digital literacy and greater awareness of data privacy issues, which can lead to higher valuations of personal data (van Herk & Poortinga, 2024). In contrast, in developing countries, where economic conditions are often more challenging, individuals may be more willing to trade their personal data for access to digital services or financial opportunities.

Furthermore, the economic value of personal data can be influenced by the level of competition in digital markets. In developed countries, where digital markets are often more competitive, individuals may have more options for managing their personal data, which can lead to higher valuations. In contrast, in developing countries, where digital markets may be less competitive, individuals may have fewer options, leading to lower valuations of their personal data (Martens, 2021).

The economic value of personal data differs significantly between developed and developing countries, influenced by a variety of factors, including cultural norms, legal frameworks, technological infrastructure, and economic conditions. Developed countries generally place a higher economic value on personal data due to stronger privacy protections, greater digital literacy, and higher levels of awareness about data privacy issues. In contrast, developing countries may place a lower economic value on personal data due to limited infrastructure, weaker data protection laws, and a focus on accessing digital services and financial opportunities.

To address these differences, policymakers in both developed and developing countries must work to create legal and regulatory frameworks that protect individuals' rights while promoting economic development. This includes strengthening data protection laws, improving digital literacy, and ensuring that individuals have greater control over their personal data. By taking these steps, policymakers can help to create a more equitable digital economy where the economic value of personal data is recognized and respected.

Global South

While much of the discourse around data valuation and digital identity has been shaped by perspectives from the Global North, the reality in the Global South often reflects different socioeconomic imperatives. In developing regions, individuals frequently engage in "data-for-access" exchanges, offering personal data in return for access to essential digital services such as banking, education, or social media (Kemp & Buckley, 2017). These transactions typically occur without meaningful consent or a clear understanding of how the data will be used or monetized. The imbalance in digital power between users and platforms exacerbates vulnerabilities and diminishes opportunities for individuals to participate equitably in the data economy.

Consider the case of Ahmed, a 24-year-old university student in Lagos, Nigeria. Like many of his peers, Ahmed relies heavily on his smartphone for everyday activities, from mobile payments and online coursework to social engagement and financial services. One of his most-used applications is a mobile lending app, which provides short-term credit without requiring a formal banking relationship or credit history. In exchange, the app gains access to a wide range of personal data on his device, including call logs, SMS messages, geolocation information, contact lists, and social media activity (Privacy International, 2021).

Although Ahmed finds the app helpful for managing short-term expenses, the data practices behind the scenes raise concerns. The behavioral data collected from his device is aggregated and analyzed to build predictive profiles that determine his creditworthiness and eligibility for other digital services. These data profiles may be shared or sold to third-party brokers and advertisers, often operating outside Nigeria's regulatory environment. Despite contributing valuable data daily, Ahmed receives no financial benefit or insight into how his digital identity is being monetized.

Nigeria's data protection framework, the Nigeria Data Protection Regulation (NDPR), was introduced to establish legal protections for digital privacy. However, enforcement remains weak, and public awareness of data rights is limited. In contrast to frameworks like the GDPR in the European Union, NDPR lacks strong accountability mechanisms and comprehensive public education efforts. As a result, individuals like Ahmed are left with little control over their data and minimal avenues for redress when harm occurs (Paradigm Initiative, 2022).

The economic value of Ahmed's digital identity is shaped not only by his demographic profile young, urban, tech-savvy but also by his lack of negotiating power in a digital marketplace dominated by multinational platforms. His data is transformed into an asset that generates revenue for others while he remains excluded from the value chain. Companies benefit from the extraction and resale of his personal information without reinvesting in the local digital ecosystem. This power asymmetry reflects a broader pattern of data colonialism, where developing regions serve as data sources without reaping commensurate benefits (Zuboff, 2019).

Furthermore, the structural limitations of the digital infrastructure in many parts of the Global South exacerbate these inequalities. Many users rely on low-cost smartphones with limited security features and use internet connections that are vulnerable to surveillance and data breaches. Cybersecurity risks are heightened in environments with weak enforcement of digital rights, increasing the likelihood of identity theft and unauthorized profiling. Public campaigns to promote data literacy and privacy awareness remain underfunded and underdeveloped in most regions (Dobson & Fernandez, 2023).

Despite these challenges, signs of innovation and resistance are emerging. Nigerian startups are beginning to explore privacy-preserving technologies, including blockchain-based credit scoring systems that limit invasive data collection. Platforms like Africa Data Consensus and initiatives such as MyDataRightsAfrica https://mydatarights.africa/ are advocating for models in which users can co-own and profit from their data. These approaches seek to embed equity, transparency, and consent into the data economy from the ground up (Stein, 2023). Civil society organizations such as Paradigm Initiative continue to push for stronger legal protections, user empowerment, and ethical data governance frameworks (Paradigm Initiative, 2022).

Ahmed's story illustrates the complex dynamics of digital identity in the Global South. Every day, millions of individuals generate data of substantial economic value, yet remain largely excluded from the systems that profit from it. Addressing this imbalance requires not only more robust legal protections and improved infrastructure but also the development of inclusive digital economies. Empowering individuals through data literacy, cooperative models, and rights-based governance is essential for creating a fairer and more equitable future in the global digital landscape.

Demographics and Valuation

In the world of data economy, personal data is not valued uniformly; rather, its worth can be determined by a range of demographic attributes. This process of determining value to personal data is called data valuation; it assigns monetary value to our personal information based on the perceived need from third parties like advertisers, data brokers, and strategists. The value of this data is often measured through a platform's average revenue per user (ARPU). For example, Facebook reported an ARPU of $58 in North America in 2022, compared to just $4.47 in the Asia-Pacific region (Statista, 2023). This contrast demonstrates how location-based economic profiles directly influence the value of user data to advertisers.

The economic value of personal data is not distributed equally. As shown in Table 3.1, certain demographic characteristics, such as geographic location, age, profession, gender, and religion, can significantly influence the market value assigned to an individual's digital identity. These estimates are not neutral; they reflect the interests and biases of advertisers, data brokers, and political strategists who determine which populations are most valuable for commercial or political targeting (Datacoup, 2021; Stein, 2023). Consequently, individuals in higher-income urban areas or in sought-after professions like finance or technology often command higher data valuations than those in rural areas or less commercially attractive demographics.

These valuation patterns introduce a subtle but powerful form of bias into the data economy. For example, the higher estimated value of data from women in certain age groups is linked to their perceived consumer behavior, especially in retail and lifestyle markets, rather than their autonomy or interests (Zuboff, 2019). Similarly, religious affiliation, such as identifying as Evangelical, can increase data value for political advertisers, particularly in election cycles where targeted messaging is profitable (Prince & Wallsten, 2020). This reinforces the commodification of identity traits in ways that may not align with an individual's own values or intentions. In such cases, people are not being valued for who they are holistically, but for how profitable their traits appear to data buyers.

These economic differentials reflect and deepen existing social inequalities. Groups that are already marginalized, whether due to geography, race, socioeconomic status, or limited digital access, are often valued less

TABLE 3.1 Data Valuation by Demographic Characteristics

Demographic factor	*Example*	*Estimated value (USD) (per month)*
Geographic Location	Urban (New York, London)	$0.80–$1.50
Age Group	25–34 years old	$0.50–$1.20
Profession	Finance or Tech Sectors	$1.00–$2.00
Gender	Female (for targeted retail ads)	$0.30–$0.90
Religion	Evangelical (for political targeting)	$0.40–$0.75

in data markets, which limits their visibility and economic participation in the digital economy (Koch, 2022). At the same time, their data may still be collected and used extensively, just without the same level of compensation or targeted benefits. This dynamic mirrors broader patterns of digital discrimination, where marginalized populations are more likely to be surveilled but less likely to benefit from the technologies that monitor them (Eubanks, 2018). For example, in Kenya, many low-income individuals rely on mobile lending apps for quick, short-term loans. These apps are popular because they provide access to credit without requiring formal employment, bank accounts, or credit histories. However, to assess eligibility, these apps collect massive amounts of personal data, such as call logs, contact lists, mobile money transactions, GPS location, and even social media behavior.

The individuals using these services, often from underserved or rural communities, are highly surveilled, yet the data extracted from them is not valued equally compared to that of wealthier, urban users. Their data is used to refine credit models, but they're typically offered small loan amounts at high interest rates and receive no compensation for the commercial value their behavioral data generates. Meanwhile, they have little to no control over how their data is stored, analyzed, or sold to third-party brokers (Kemp & Buckley, 2017).

Such disparities also raise serious questions about fairness and consent in data-driven systems. If certain groups are routinely assigned lower data values, it becomes easier for platforms and policymakers to overlook their interests in the design of algorithms, platforms, and data governance structures. The result is a feedback loop: Undervalued data leads to underrepresentation in technological systems, which in turn leads to less favorable outcomes in areas like access to financial products, healthcare, and education (Pasquale, 2015). These biases are not accidental; they're built into the economic logics of platform capitalism and surveillance-based profit models (Noble, 2018; Zuboff, 2019).

Addressing these inequalities requires a commitment to equitable data governance and a deeper understanding of how bias operates in the data economy. Mechanisms such as data cooperatives, value-sensitive design, and algorithmic audits can help identify and challenge these disparities (Dobson & Fernandez, 2023). Moreover, frameworks grounded in data sovereignty, the right of individuals and communities to control their own data, offer a pathway to resist devaluation and exploitation (Makulilo, 2023; Paradigm Initiative, 2022). As we move toward more participatory models of data ownership and compensation, ensuring that marginalized voices are centered in policy and platform design is essential. Only then can we reshape the digital economy into one that values all individuals fairly, not just those deemed most profitable by opaque and biased algorithms.

These valuation patterns illustrate that certain identities are rewarded while others are marginalized, reinforcing socioeconomic divisions in the digital economy. Moreover, this imbalance highlights the need to develop mechanisms for developing more equitable data governance and fair compensation models in the future.

BOX 3.1 CASE STUDY

Mia, a 32-year-old graphic designer from Chicago, often scrolls through her favorite lifestyle blog during her morning coffee. One day, she clicks on an article titled "10 Best Indoor Plants for Small Apartments". Unbeknownst to her, that single click sets off a cascade of data transactions behind the scenes.

The blog is embedded with multiple tracking pixels and cookies from third-party advertisers and data aggregators. These tools collect information on Mia's browsing behavior, device type, IP address, and even her location. Within milliseconds, this behavioral data is matched with other data points like her online purchases, social media likes, search history, and geolocation patterns. All compiled by data brokers such as Acxiom, Oracle, or Experian.

Soon, Mia is categorized into high-value consumer segments: "Urban Millennial Homeowner", "Sustainable Living Enthusiast", and "Premium Shopper". This composite profile is sold to advertisers for targeted ad campaigns. Companies pay a premium to access users like Mia, whose detailed digital footprint enables precise microtargeting for everything from eco-friendly furniture to boutique insurance plans.

According to industry reports, Mia's aggregated data profile might be sold and resold dozens of times, earning data brokers upward of $0.50 to $5 per transaction, depending on its specificity. While that may seem trivial, when multiplied by millions of users, these seemingly mundane data exchanges form a multibillion-dollar industry.

Mia, meanwhile, remains unaware of the true value of her digital self. She receives more personalized ads but never sees a share of the profits generated from her own behavior. This asymmetry exemplifies the core issue at the heart of the digital economy: Individuals generate valuable data every day, but third-party aggregators are the ones capitalizing on it.

Conclusion

As this chapter has illustrated, digital identity is no longer merely a representation of who we are online; it's a source of economic value that fuels an expansive and largely opaque data economy. From targeted advertising and algorithmic credit scoring to predictive policing and political profiling, our personal data is continuously extracted, analyzed, and monetized. Yet, despite the central role individuals play in generating this data, they remain structurally excluded from the systems that profit from it. This exclusion is intensified by disparities in digital literacy, legal protections, geographic location, and demographic profiling, resulting in an unequal and often exploitative digital landscape.

Emerging frameworks such as data cooperatives, blockchain-based marketplaces, and privacy-preserving technologies offer glimpses of more equitable alternatives. Central to these models is the concept of data sovereignty, the right of individuals and communities to own, control, and benefit from the data they produce. Achieving true data sovereignty, however, requires more than technical innovation. It demands ethical data governance, policy reform, algorithmic accountability, and a cultural shift that re-centers human dignity in the digital economy.

Ultimately, recognizing the economic value of personal data is not only about compensation but also about justice, transparency, and inclusion. As the digital world continues to evolve, so too must our understanding of rights, risks, and responsibilities within it. Only by equipping individuals with the tools, knowledge, and agency to control their digital identities can we create a more balanced and equitable digital future, one in which the value of data is shared, not hoarded, and the power of identity is reclaimed by those to whom it truly belongs.

Exercise

In today's digital economy, your personal data has become a valuable commodity that companies collect, analyze, and monetize. This assignment challenges you to investigate the economic value of your own digital footprint across platforms you regularly use and understand how your online activities translate into monetary value for businesses.

Select three digital platforms you use regularly.

- Choose from social media, shopping, entertainment, or productivity applications.
- At least one platform should be primarily social and one primarily commercial.

- For each platform, locate and analyze the following documents:
  - Privacy Policy
  - Terms of Service
  - Data Policy (if separate from Privacy Policy)
  - Advertising Policy
- Research the economic value of personal data:
  - Find at least three credible sources (industry reports, academic studies, market analyses)
  - Document current market rates for different types of personal data
  - Identify factors that influence data valuation
- Estimate your personal data value:
  - Based on your research, estimate the approximate annual value of your data to each platform
  - Consider factors such as:
    - Your demographic profile
    - Engagement level
    - Purchasing behavior
    - Content creation activities
    - Influence on other users

References

Beamer, T. (2024). 402.74 million terrabytes of data is created every day. *Tech Business News*. https://www.techbusinessnews.com.au/blog/402-74-million-terrabytes-of-data-is-created-every-day/

Datacoup. (2021). Sell your data and earn cash. https://www.datacoup.com/

Dobson, D., & Fernandez, A. (2023). IDSov and the silent data revolution: Indigenous peoples and the decentralized building blocks of web3. *Frontiers in Research Metrics and Analytics*, *8*, 1–11. https://doi.org/10.3389/frma.2023.1160566

Eubanks, V. (2018). *Automating inequality: How high-tech tools profile, police, and punish the poor*. St. Martin's Press.

Kemp, K., & Buckley, R. P. (2017). Protecting financial consumer data in developing countries: An alternative to the flawed consent model. *Georgetown Journal of International Affairs*, *18*(3), 35–46.

Koch, E. (2022). How much is privacy worth around the world and across platforms? *Journal of Economics and Management Strategy*, *31*(4), 841–861.

Lanier, J. (2013). *Who owns the future?* Simon & Schuster.

Makulilo, A. B. (2023). Privacy as a human right in Africa and the global Internet. In H. Dube & L.A. Abdulrauf (Eds.), *The Internet, development, human rights and the law in Africa* (pp. 53–64). Routledge.

Martens, B. (2021). Data Access, Consumer Interests and Social Welfare: An Economic Perspective. Social Science Research Network. https://doi.org/10.2139/SSRN.3605383

Morrison, H., & Charbonneau, O. (2006). Creating a Digital Commons. http://summit.sfu.ca/system/files/iritems1/442/BCLA-HeatherOlivier.pdf

Noble, S. U. (2018). *Algorithms of oppression: How search engines reinforce racism*. NYU Press.

Paradigm Initiative. (2022). Digital Rights in Africa Report 2022. https://paradigmhq.org/

Pasquale, F. (2015). *The black box society: The secret algorithms that control money and information*. Harvard University Press.

Prince, J., & Wallsten, S. (2020). How much is privacy worth around the world and across platforms. *TPRC48: The 48th Research Conference on Communication*. McKinney, TX, USA.

Privacy International. (2021). The lending trap: How loan apps are exploiting mobile phone data in Kenya and Nigeria. https://privacyinternational.org

Statista. (2023). Meta: ARPU by region 2022. https://www.statista.com/statistics/234056/facebook-average-revenue-per-user-worldwide-by-region/

Stein, L. (2023). What your data is actually worth. Datapods. https://www.datapods.app/blogs/what-your-data-is-actually-worth

Tawil, A. R. H., Mohamed, M., Schmoor, X., Vlachos, K., & Haidar, D. (2024). Trends and challenges towards effective data-driven decision making in UK Small and Medium-sized Enterprises: Case studies and lessons learnt from the analysis of 85 Small and Medium-sized Enterprises. *Big Data and Cognitive Computing*, *8*(7), 79.

van Herk, H., & Poortinga, Y. H. (2024). Economic factors outweigh cultural values in explaining country variance: The limited role of value dimensions after accounting for GDP. https://osf.io/hr5bg/download

Zuboff, S. (2019). *The age of surveillance capitalism: The fight for a human future at the new frontier of power*. Profile Books.

4

SOCIAL IDENTITY

Your Friends Tell Us Who You Are

Globally, we spend approximately 2 hours and 23 minutes on social media (Kemp, 2024). In the United States, young people can spend up to 4 hours a day on social media (Rothwell, 2023). What are they doing online? The desire to contribute and be part of a community is a driving force in developing one's social identity. Is everyone creating content? The pressure to conform to peers for likes or shares makes demands on us to create content that may not accurately represent us in the "real-world". What ways are we participating in this online culture? If we're anxious or hesitant to engage in content creation, are there opportunities for us to like, share, and comment? Are there any harms to our social identity that can happen because of interacting? The people you interact with online may not be you see in their daily lives; therefore, you must be extremely cautious about how you react to content. Sometimes, these interactions have a direct, tangible impact on your "real-world" life.

Before we delve into the sociological and psychological formation of your social identity, it's important to understand the foundational elements of social media use. Social media applications like Snapchat, Instagram, and TikTok exist to sell a product or products. Sometimes it's hard to see what the product is and sometimes the product is you, in the form of your time, data, and money. Social media applications and platforms like Spotify, iTunes, YouTube, Twitch, and Vimeo bury media rights and privileges into their terms of service (ToS) to censor, brand, and market content people create. To actively and ethically engage with social media, it's important to understand the this is known as affordances. We use these affordances as signals, a shared language, to the groups we attempting

DOI: 10.4324/9781003539445-5

to enter. We maintain our relevancy within the groups by properly using them to conform, amplify, bond, or encourage as we participate. Finally, we need to acknowledge the psychological and cognitive impacts of using social media applications on ourselves, youth, and children.

Terms of Service

Many users engage with digital platforms without fully understanding the legal and ethical implications of their participation. A common example is the widespread habit of downloading mobile applications and mindlessly clicking "accept" on the terms and conditions without reading the document, formally known as the end user license agreement (EULA). This act reflects a broader pattern of trust-based engagement, in which users assume that technology companies operate in good faith and would not engage in harmful or illegal behavior. However, this assumption often ignores the asymmetric power dynamics between users and platforms, particularly regarding data ownership, usage rights, and surveillance.

By agreeing to these terms, we unknowingly grant corporations access to a wide range of our personal data, including behavioral patterns, location tracking, contact lists, and even biometric identifiers. These agreements often employ dense legal language, intentionally confusing us and upending the basic principles of informed digital participation. From the perspective of participatory culture theory, the urge to belong or keep up with peers can override cautious behavior, especially when popular applications are involved. Digital persuasion mechanisms, such as positivity (the thrill of accessing a new app) and conformity (not wanting to be left out), reinforce the tendency to ignore these legal agreements.

Some companies have taken creative approaches to highlight just how few users read EULAs. These legal documents, often dismissed with a quick click, can contain unexpected clauses. For example, Apple's iTunes includes a clause explicitly forbidding the use of its products for developing nuclear weapons, stating: "You also agree that you will not use these products for any purposes prohibited by United States law, including, without limitation, the development, design, manufacture, or production of nuclear, missile, or chemical or biological weapons" (Apple Music, 2024). While the clause is clearly a legal safeguard, it also reflects the absurdity that such language could go unnoticed by most users.

In another case, a software company called PitStop inserted a hidden clause in its EULA terms and conditions under which you enter into an agreement with these applications. It's also paramount to know the tools these applications provide you for interacting with other users in meaningful ways; offering a $1,000 reward to anyone who actually read it. One customer, Doug Heckman, did and was promptly rewarded for his diligence. Tumblr, too, adds levity to legalese, warning users against "squatting, hoarding, accumulating, accruing, racking up, trading, selling, laundering, ingesting, getting drunk on, cybering with, groping, or jealously guarding" usernames (Tumblr, 2024). Though comical, these examples underscore a serious issue: EULAs are contracts, and users often agree to them without understanding the rights they surrender or the responsibilities they accept. The consequences may extend beyond humor, particularly when digital identity, privacy, and even personal property, such as usernames, are at stake.

While these EULAs are absurd or humorous, they mask a more serious issue: Our digital identity has become a commodity. As discussed earlier, our digital identities are constantly shaped by the platforms we engage with, and agreeing to EULAs without scrutiny enables the unchecked harvesting and monetization of our social, financial, health, and civic data. In this light, EULAs are not just mundane legal documents; they're gateways that fundamentally affect our autonomy, privacy, and how we are perceived in digital spaces. Understanding and critically evaluating EULAs is, therefore, a key component of digital literacy and citizenship. To participate responsibly in digital culture, you must not only learn to read these documents but also develop a deeper awareness of how your social identity is shaped by the platforms you trust.

Affordances

When we engage with social media applications, our goals are not limited to passive browsing; rather, they often involve actively forming and performing aspects of our identity within digital communities. One of the key concepts for understanding how users interact in these spaces is affordances. In digital contexts, affordances refer to the design features of a platform that enable, guide, or constrain user behavior. Originally rooted in ecological psychology the term has been adapted in media and communication studies to describe the possibilities for action provided by technological environments (Lüders et al., 2022). Affordances are not merely technical tools; they're socially and psychologically meaningful because they shape how we engage with content and with each other.

There are several types of affordances that commonly shape social media interactions. Expressive affordances include the ability to post photos, write status updates, or upload videos, functions that allow users to share thoughts, emotions, and experiences. Interactive affordances involve tools like "like" buttons, emojis, comments, or shares, which enable users to respond to others and signal alignment, disagreement, or interest. Associational affordances allow users to form networks by following, friending, or joining groups and hashtags. Anonymity affordances, such as the option to post without revealing one's identity, can influence the tone of discourse and the willingness to express controversial or vulnerable opinions.

These features play a central role in how users construct their social identity online. For example, a user hesitant to create original content may still actively participate through comments, likes, or sharing, all of which are forms of identity signaling. On platforms like Instagram or TikTok, interactive affordances such as heart reactions or duets reinforce in-group belonging and shared emotion. Using a particular emoji or hashtag can indicate group affiliation, political stance, or cultural preference. In the end, affordances are the digital scaffolding upon which social interaction, community formation, and identity performance are built.

To build these communities within social media applications, algorithms send us suggested posts that we can choose to either accept (like, share, remix) or ignore (swipe right). They also send affinity groups suggestions to join (Facebook groups). When we join a group, we inherently accept the type and tone of content that will be allowed to be posted and shared. Unfortunately, disagreements can arise in these interactions. If large enough numbers of users form on either side of a disagreement, new communities can emerge. A recent example would be the move by some away from X, after the second election of Donald Trump as the 47th U.S. president, to BlueSky or the launch of Threads after the selling of Twitter to Elon Musk. One of the most common affordances utilized in community building is resharing content within the community.

When a contentious or controversial issue emerges within our online communities, members must navigate the complexities of responding and form their own opinions on the matter. This process often involves informal deliberation, where we seek input from trusted members within the community before engaging in broader discussions that could be fraught with social dangers. Digital affordances, such as private messaging applications like WhatsApp or Facebook Messenger, enable us to gauge the attitudes of close acquaintances, fostering a sense of security before publicly expressing our stance. These side conversations serve as preliminary spaces for testing opinions, refining arguments, and assessing potential social repercussions.

As an issue gains traction within our online communities, we may employ hashtags as a means of organizing discourse, signaling affiliation, and amplifying collective narratives. Hashtags such as #MeToo, #BLM, and #Trump2024 illustrate how digital activism and identity formation occur through this mechanism. By tagging a post with a widely recognized hashtag, we contribute to a growing storehouse of dialogue, effectively forming relationships between advocates and adversaries. This digital practice not only facilitates the creation of perspectives but also enables us to align ourselves within the broader conversation, building ideological boundaries and reinforcing group identities within the online platform.

As one reacts to posts, videos, "tweets", and images, they begin to affiliate themselves with groups. One of the easiest ways for someone to begin to form their social identity within an application is through the affordance of emojis or other emotion representations. Sharing one's emotions regarding a story leaves you vulnerable to a small degree. In some applications, the viewers are unable to see exactly who shared a heart or an angry face, so one can be an anonymous member. Applications that do not display user information afford users a greater level of honesty when engaged in the community. It has been proposed that it's one reason YouTube is the top social media application year after year. One can give a simple thumbs up or down and one will never know it was you. Recently, social media applications like Facebook and Instagram have instituted an anonymity feature for posting and comments. A final consideration regarding the use of emojis within shared online communities is their role in shaping collective perception and reinforcing group consensus. When viewing a video or image, the immediate visibility of a disproportionate number of dislikes compared to likes serves as a visual cue that reflects the prevailing sentiment within an affinity group. This real-time feedback mechanism allows us to quickly assess the dominant perspective within their community, reinforcing the ever-crucial social cohesion and guiding our own engagement with the content.

Understanding affordances is crucial because they do not exist in a vacuum; they're engineered choices made by platform designers to influence how users behave. These choices can guide users toward deeper engagement but also raise ethical questions about persuasion, privacy, and autonomy. Recognizing the affordances at play in any given platform allows you stop, think and be more reflective and intentional about how you interact, and acknowledge how your behavior contributes to the ongoing construction of your digital identity.

Psychological Impacts

Our engagement with social media is predicated on several assumptions, as we discussed in the Participatory Culture Theory. We engage in social media use because we believe we are adding value to the conversation and are creating meaningful relationships. There are also the psychological benefits one receives that need to be explored. The ability of our interactions to help us create meaning about ourselves and the world around us is something many of us probably don't consider when we are doom scrolling through TikTok. According to researchers, social engagement is "a holistic psychological state in which one is cognitively and emotionally energized to socially behave in ways that exemplify the positive ways in which group members prefer to think of themselves" (Lüders et al., 2022, p. 531). Being involved in the social media application fulfills some type of personal need; this could be emotional, relational, or transactional. The degree to which one engages is dependent on the satisfaction one receives when in the social media application. Therefore, it becomes extremely important for social media companies to ensure their applications are using every tool, affordance available to keep one in the application and engaged for as long as possible.

Applying the theory of *Social Media Engagement* (SME) developed by Di Gangi and Wasko, we find there are two psychological components to user engagement: Individual involvement and personal meaning (2016). User engagement will subsequently influence usage behavior. If interactions cannot be personalized, the filtered content is not seen as meaningful, or few social acquaintances are members, then one usually has limited engagement with a social media application. However, if there are a critical mass of acquaintances, if the application allows one to personalize their feed, and the application evolves over time, then most users are inclined to remain in the application. We can take Facebook as an example. When it started, there were very limited ways in which to show support for our friends. We could only make our posts public for all to see. Advertisements were sometimes irrelevant to us as individuals. When emojis came out, they were limited to thumbs up, thumbs down, and a heart. For example, Facebook has evolved to provide us with more expressive emojis like the hug or angry face, but as of this writing, many of us are eagerly waiting the yuck emoji as a reaction option.

Personality Traits

Your public image is shaped by your unique responses to social stimuli and your ability to adapt to the social features of your environment. These responses influence patterns of behavior and thought, often operating at an unconscious level, making aspects of your identity hidden or unknown even to yourself. Your identity is not static; it evolves dynamically and continuously. This evolution is influenced by distinct traits and characteristics, as well as experiences and interactions both online and in-person. As a result, identity formation is an ongoing process shaped by both internal dispositions and external social engagement.

There is a close interconnection between social engagement and personality traits, with some traits affecting how socially more than others. But what do we mean when we say personality? Personality refers to the unique set of characteristics, traits, and patterns of thought, emotion, and behavior that define a person and influence how they interact with the world. It's relatively stable over time and shaped by both genetic and environmental factors. Psychologists usually refer to the Big Five Personality Traits of openness, extraversion, conscientiousness, agreeableness, and neuroticism. Recent research has shown they have an immense impact on social media use and engagement (Lampropoulos et al., 2022). Openness and extraversion emerged as the two most significant positive predictors of social media use, while conscientiousness, agreeableness, and neuroticism were also considered important but to a lesser degree.

Openness reflects an individual's willingness to engage in new experiences, their creativity, and their ability to think in complex and abstract ways. Openness people tend to be curious and imaginative. People who are high in openness are more likely to explore diverse perspectives, engage with new ideas, and follow a wide range of content creators. Conscientiousness measures a person's level of organization, discipline, and goal-directed behavior, often associated with reliability and a strong work ethic. Conscientious people are careful about what they post and often curate their online presence to reflect professionalism and reliability. Extraversion describes sociability, energy levels, and assertiveness, with extraverted people being more outgoing and expressive. Extroverts thrive on social interaction and tend to be highly active on social media, frequently posting updates, engaging with comments, and initiating conversations. Agreeableness refers to a person's friendliness, compassion, and ability to connect with others, often characterized by kindness and altruism. Agreeable people prioritize harmony and positive social interactions, often using social media to support others and spread kindness. Finally, neuroticism reflects emotional stability, with higher levels indicating tendencies toward anxiety, insecurity, and stress. Those with high neuroticism may experience heightened emotional responses to online interactions, such as anxiety over likes and comments or sensitivity to negative feedback.

These traits collectively shape an individual's personality and interactions with the online world. Extraversion and openness traits impact social media interactions the most. If you are high in these two traits, you tend to engage more actively online, forming friendships, joining discussions, and expressing yourself freely, both offline and in digital spaces. You might frequently share articles on cutting-edge technology, engage in discussions about philosophy, or participate in niche online communities. If you're extroverted, you might livestream events, frequently post selfies or group photos, and interact with many followers through comments and reactions. On the other hand, if you are lower in extraversion and openness, you tend to struggle with online interactions. You might avoid engaging in online arguments to maintain a peaceful environment. Conscientiousness is a predictor of responsible social media use, while neuroticism can lead to addictive or abusive online interactions. A highly neurotic person might delete posts if they don't receive enough engagement, frequently check for reactions to their content, or feel overwhelmed by online criticism (Lampropoulos et al., 2022).

Ultimately, your purpose for using social media shapes your engagement, regardless of personality traits. However, emotional stability also plays a role in your social engagement, as emotionally stable people spend less time on social media, while those feeling lonely or isolated may seek social connections online. Given the strong link between personality and online behavior, researchers have increasingly explored how digital footprint, ranging from social media activity to browsing history, can be used to infer personality traits. By analyzing the types of content people engage with, the frequency and style of their interactions, and the language they use in posts or comments, predictive models can accurately assess personality characteristics based on frameworks such as the Big Five Personality Traits. This ability to predict personality through digital behavior has interesting implications for areas such as targeted advertising, mental health assessments, and even recruitment processes. However, it also raises ethical concerns regarding privacy and the potential misuse of predictive analytics. As artificial intelligence and machine learning models continue to advance, the balance between personalization and privacy in the digital space remains a critical issue.

Persuasion and Participatory Culture

To better understand the psychological mechanisms involved in the formation of our digital social identity, it's useful to connect the four persuasive mechanisms we discussed earlier. They're amplification, bonding, positivity, and conformity. Participatory culture, as Jenkins et al. (2006) describe it, emphasizes active engagement, low barriers to artistic expression, and a sense of belonging. Amplification, for example, directly supports participatory culture by encouraging us to share content widely to gain recognition and status in our digital communities. The wider the reach, the greater the perceived influence, which fulfills the participatory culture motive of "making one's voice heard". Understanding these links highlights how persuasive digital experiences are not accidental but designed to increase social dependency and content engagement. Recognizing this structure empowers us to make more informed, intentional choices about how and why we engage.

Bonding overlaps significantly with participatory culture's emphasis on shared purpose and mentoring. Digital affinity groups often provide emotional reinforcement, advice, and belonging, reinforcing community participation. Expressions, one of the four modes of participatory culture, are enhanced by bonding mechanisms, which give us emotional validation for our creativity or self-representation. For example, TikTok users often join challenges or remix videos (#duet or #stitch), participating in ongoing creative dialogue. When a user receives comments like "I feel this" or "You're so talented", it reinforces not only their participation but also their identity within that digital space. These interactions illustrate how bonding is not just emotional; it's cultural scaffolding that supports continued creative expression and mutual recognition within participatory networks.

Positivity and social validation, through likes, shares, and emojis, work as reinforcement loops. These loops tap into the intrinsic reward systems described by Jenkins and Di Gangi and Wasko (2016), strengthening both individual involvement and personal meaning in digital communities. For instance, on Instagram and TikTok, creators often report a "dopamine rush" from seeing their content go viral, driven by hundreds or thousands of likes and comments. This feedback not only boosts visibility but also reinforces the motivation to continue creating similar content, even adjusting tone or aesthetic to maximize engagement. Influencers and everyday users alike may begin to adapt their identities based on which posts receive the most validation, illustrating how social rewards shape self-expression and perceived value within a digital community.

Conformity pressures align with participatory culture's circulation function, where people share existing ideas and memes to signal alignment with dominant group norms, often suppressing dissenting views to avoid exclusion. For example, during major social movements, such as #BlackLivesMatter or #FreePalestine, many users reshared trending posts or changed their profile pictures to show solidarity. While some were deeply engaged, others may have felt compelled to participate to avoid being perceived as silent or indifferent, especially within activist-oriented circles. This behavior aligns with Jenkins's notion of circulation, where ideas, memes, and calls to action are rapidly reproduced across networks. On platforms like X and Facebook, dissenting or critical takes on dominant narratives are often met with backlash, silence, or even cancellation, demonstrating how conformity can suppress nuance to maintain group cohesion.

Right to Privacy

The persuasive pull of social engagement raises serious questions about our privacy and autonomy. While we willingly share aspects of our identity online, often for belonging or validation, the consequences can be far-reaching. From data tracking to facial recognition, the privacy rights of digital citizens are increasingly under pressure.

In the European Union, privacy is a legal right protected under the General Data Protection Regulation (GDPR), which includes the "right to be forgotten", a user's right to request the deletion of personal data (Voigt & Von dem Bussche, 2017). This regulation acknowledges that people should have the power to control how their digital identity evolves and how it's remembered. It serves as a safeguard against the perpetual presence of outdated or harmful content.

France has taken privacy even further with laws that prevent the public filming of individuals without consent, especially in public spaces (CNIL, 2023). This legal stance respects the idea that just because technology allows recording, it doesn't give one the right to infringe on another's private life. The CNIL (Commission Nationale de l'Informatique et des Libertés), France's data protection authority, underscores that personal image is protected under privacy rights, even on the street. There have been instances whereby doorbell ring cameras on homes have had to be removed because facial recognition of passersby is considered an invasion of their privacy.

These policies challenge the current norms of surveillance-based platforms that profit from constant sharing and visibility. In contrast to American standards, where public behavior is often assumed to be fair game for digital capture, the European model asserts a more human-centered digital ethic. These laws affirm that privacy is not simply about data security, but about dignity, autonomy, and the right to control one's representation in digital spaces. Whereas American platforms tend to operate under the assumption that content captured in public or shared online is fair game for commercial use or algorithmic analysis, European standards emphasize personal consent and the minimization of unnecessary data collection. This shift reframes digital citizenship as an active right to be protected, informed, and respected.

Ethics of Social Engagement

As digital citizens, it's essential to critically examine whether our online interactions contribute to a healthy, just, and inclusive digital environment. Participation in digital spaces should not come at the cost of personal dignity, privacy, or autonomy. The integration of participatory culture with ethical reflection challenges us to rethink the underlying design and governance of social media platforms. These systems must prioritize consent, personal control, and respect for your privacy rather than relying solely on persuasive algorithms that exploit our unconscious biases. Stronger advocacy is needed to push for policies that uphold digital rights, especially for vulnerable populations such as minors, racialized groups, and those with limited access to digital literacy education.

Education in this context must go beyond functional skills to include digital ethics, creating an awareness of how our personal data is collected, how interface design can manipulate our behavior, and how structural inequalities are reproduced and reenforced in digital environments. Recognizing the interplay between psychological persuasion, participatory norms, and legal/ethical protections enables a more comprehensive understanding of the social identities we construct online. Protecting those identities, and the rights that come with them, should be central to how we define responsible and empowered digital participation.

BOX 4.1 CASE STUDY

The psychological impacts of using social media at a young age have been the topic of debate for years. A 2021 Wall Street Journal article by Wells, Horwitz, and Seetharaman exposed *internal* research by Facebook (now Meta) revealing they knew for years that Instagram has a toxic impact on teenage girls, particularly concerning body image and mental health (Wells et. al, 2021). The company's internal studies found that Instagram exacerbates body dissatisfaction, with one in three teenage girls reporting that the platform made them feel worse about their appearance. The app's algorithm-driven content, which often promotes unrealistic beauty standards, leads to increased anxiety, depression, and self-esteem issues. Additionally, affordances such as likes, comments, and filters create social comparison pressures, making young users more vulnerable to negative self-perception and eating disorders. Despite being aware of these harmful effects, Facebook continued to expand Instagram's reach among teenagers, prioritizing engagement over well-being. The findings suggest that social media intensifies existing insecurities, making adolescent girls particularly susceptible to its psychological harms. Currently, there is a push across the globe to ban the use of cellphones by children and young adults as the psychological impacts are being realized.

Conclusion

This chapter explored the dynamic relationship between social media use and the formation of digital social identity. Social identity online is not a passive byproduct of participation; it's something actively shaped by the platforms we use, the affordances they offer, and the psychological mechanisms they employ. Social media platforms like Instagram, TikTok, and Snapchat are not neutral tools; they're structured to maximize engagement through features that influence how we express ourselves, connect with others, and perceive social norms. Through design elements such as likes, shares, emojis, and follower counts, collectively known as affordances, we communicate our belonging and align ourselves with digital communities. These interactions serve as social signals, influencing how we are perceived and how we internalize our identity over time.

This chapter emphasized how digital engagement is shaped by persuasive mechanisms of amplification, bonding, positivity, and conformity, which map directly onto Henry Jenkins's theory of participatory culture. Amplification enables us to share content widely for visibility and recognition. Bonding strengthens the community through emotional reinforcement and shared purpose. Positivity fosters engagement through social validation, while conformity encourages us to adopt dominant group norms, sometimes at the expense of our own voice. These forces reveal that social media is not simply about self-expression but about navigating a carefully constructed environment of influence.

Additionally, the chapter addressed the significant role of ToS and EULAs, showing how legal agreements that most of us overlook play a vital role in shaping our digital identity. By clicking "accept", we often give away rights to our personal data, which may be monetized or repurposed without full understanding or control. These contracts highlight an imbalance of power between users and platforms, reinforcing the need for greater digital literacy and personal awareness.

Personality traits, particularly extraversion and openness, were discussed as important predictors of online engagement. These traits help explain why some of us are more expressive, active, or vulnerable in digital spaces than others. The chapter also explored how predictive analytics and behavioral algorithms are increasingly used to infer personality from digital footprints, raising ethical concerns around privacy and consent.

Finally, this chapter highlighted important global differences in approaches to digital privacy. While American platforms often operate under surveillance-capitalist models, European frameworks like the GDPR and

France's street photography laws reflect a more human-centered digital ethic, one that prioritizes dignity, consent, and the right to control one's digital representation.

Exercise

Over a 24-hour period, analyze your own social media usage and identity formation. Answer the following:

- What types of interactions did you have over a 24-hour period (i.e., posting, sharing, commenting)?
- What applications did you use regularly?
- How many hours were you on all social media?
- Did one type or application dominate your usage?
- How many times did you share something someone else created?
- Review your interactions
    - How many positive affordances did you use?
    - How many negative affordances did you use?
    - Briefly describe these interactions
- What do these results say about your social identity and social affiliations?

References

Apple Music. (2024). Apple Media Services Terms and Conditions. Apple Inc. https://www.apple.com/legal/internet-services/itunes/us/terms.html

CNIL. (2023). Filming in public spaces: What are the rules? https://storiprotection.fr/en/2024/03/29/cnil-and-gdpr-regulation-of-videosurveillance-for-companies-in-france/

Di Gangi, P. M., & Wasko, M. M. (2016). Social media engagement theory: Exploring the influence of user engagement on social media usage. *Journal of Organizational and End User Computing (JOEUC)*, *28*(2), 53–73.

Jenkins, H., Clinton, K., Purushotma, R., Robison, A. J., & Weigel, M. (2006). *Confronting the challenges of participatory culture: Media education for the 21st century*. The MacArthur Foundation.

Kemp, S. (2024). Daily Time Spent Using Social Media. *Digital 2024: Global Overview Report*. https://datareportal.com/reports/digital-2024-global-overview-report.

Lampropoulos, G., Anastasiadis, T., Siakas, K., & Siakas, E. (2022). The impact of personality traits on social media use and engagement: An overview. *International Journal on Social and Education Sciences*, *4*(1), 34–51.

Lüders, A., Dinkelberg, A., & Quayle, M. (2022). Becoming "us" in digital spaces: How online users creatively and strategically exploit social media affordances to build up social identity. *Acta Psychologica*, *228*, 103643. doi.org/10.1016/j.actpsy.2022.103643.

Rothwell, J. (2023, Oct 13). Teens Spend Average of 4.8 Hours on Social Media Per Day. *Gallup*. https://news.gallup.com/poll/512576/teens-spend-average-hours-social-media-per-day.aspx.

tumblr. (2024, Oct 21). User Guidelines. tumblr. https://www.tumblr.com/policy/en/user-guidelines

Voigt, P., & Von dem Bussche, A. (2017). *The EU general data protection regulation (GDPR): A practical guide*. Springer International Publishing.

Wells, G., Horwitz, J., & Seetharaman, D. (Sept. 14, 2021). Facebook knows Instagram is toxic for teen girls, company documents show. *The Wall Street Journal*, https://www.wsj.com/tech/personal-tech/facebook-knows-instagram-is-toxic-for-teen-girls-company-documents-show-11631620739?mod=Searchresults_pos12&page=1

5

FINANCIAL IDENTITY

The Power of Your Social Credit Score

Your financial identity determines more than just what you can buy; it defines where you can live, how you move through the world, and the opportunities you can access. Being unable to board a subway train without a linked digital wallet, qualify for a mortgage, or apply for student loans are all examples of how deeply embedded your financial identity is in everyday life. Despite its significance, financial identity remains one of the most overlooked aspects of digital identity, second only to health identity in terms of its vulnerability and impact. It's also disturbingly easy to compromise. Children and the elderly are especially at risk, as they often lack the digital literacy or institutional safeguards needed to detect fraud. A stolen financial identity can lead to long-term consequences, ruined credit, denied housing, and exclusion from the banking system.

Components of Financial Digital Identity

In today's increasingly digital world, the components of your financial identity are essential for building trust and ensuring security in financial transactions. These components include personal identifiers, transaction histories, and behavioral analytics, all of which shape how people interact with financial institutions and online platforms. The robustness of a financial digital identity can significantly influence access to credit and other financial services, shaping economic opportunities for users. Moreover, the inherent risks associated with financial identity, such as fraud and privacy breaches, underscore the necessity for enhanced security measures within digital frameworks. Effective strategies for bolstering financial identity

DOI: 10.4324/9781003539445-6

must consider the unique affordances of the technologies employed, as highlighted by Bryce (2015). Thus, understanding the intricacies of financial digital identity becomes crucial for both users and service providers to navigate the evolving landscape of digital finance and mitigate associated threats to security and privacy, as pointed out by Combe and Hasbullah (2017).

Personal Identification Information

The significance of personal identification information (PII) in shaping financial digital identity cannot be overstated, as its integrity is essential for both security and privacy in the digital landscape. Increasingly, data breaches threaten the confidentiality of PII, exposing consumers to identity theft, which aggregates distrust in financial systems. Institutions handle massive amounts of PII, and their vulnerabilities have led to calls for stronger regulatory frameworks. As noted, data breaches are an increasingly common part of consumers' lives and current legal mechanisms are insufficient to protect against these threats (Marcus, 2018). Moreover, with the rise of biometric authentication technologies, the paradigm for securing identity is shifting. Such innovations could enhance digital security but also necessitate careful regulatory oversight to ensure that the collection and use of PII do not inadvertently compromise personal privacy (Desmarais, 2000). Thus, a multifaceted approach to PII management is crucial in safeguarding financial digital identity.

Financial History and Credit Scores

Understanding the evolution of financial history and credit scores is essential in the context of financial digital identity. Historically, credit scoring relied heavily on traditional financial indicators, such as credit card usage and payment history, which marginalized people, particularly in emerging markets. Recent advancements introduced by technology companies have begun to disrupt this paradigm, revealing that alternative data sources, like social media activity and mobile phone usage, can significantly enhance credit assessments for previously ignored populations (Deb et al., 2015). This shift not only democratizes access to credit but also raises critical questions regarding privacy and data security. In industries such as iGaming, the lack of a standardized identity management framework poses risks related to identity theft and financial fraud, illustrating the importance of establishing secure digital identities in modern finance (George, 2018). Thus, the interplay between credit scores and financial history continues to reshape the landscape of personal and commercial lending.

Chinese Social Credit Score

The Chinese social credit system (SCS) is a state-led initiative designed to monitor, assess, and regulate the behavior of individuals, businesses, and organizations based on a scoring mechanism. First announced in 2014, the system aims to enhance trustworthiness and compliance with laws and regulations by rewarding good behavior and penalizing misconduct. Although often compared to a Western-style credit rating system, the SCS extends beyond financial transactions to encompass social, political, and ethical behavior, making it a unique and controversial governance tool.

At its core, the SCS functions through the collection of vast amounts of data from government agencies, private companies, and digital platforms. Surveillance technologies, including facial recognition, big data analytics, and artificial intelligence, facilitate real-time monitoring of citizens' activities (Agarwal & Chakraborty, 2018). People and businesses are assigned scores based on compliance with laws, fulfillment of contracts, and adherence to social norms. Those with high scores may receive benefits such as streamlined bureaucratic processes, preferential access to loans, or enhanced career prospects. Conversely, those with low scores may face restrictions, such as travel bans, higher loan interest rates, or exclusion from certain job opportunities.

Companies, particularly in sectors such as finance, e-commerce, and transportation, contribute data to the system, enabling a more comprehensive assessment of individuals' behavior. For example, platforms like Alibaba's Sesame Credit provide users with ratings based on financial responsibility, shopping habits, and even social interactions. This integration of private-sector data with state surveillance has led to concerns over privacy, data security, and the potential for misuse. While supporters argue that the SCS fosters a culture of trust and accountability, critics highlight its risks to civil liberties and individual autonomy. One major concern is the system's potential to enforce political compliance. Reports suggest that citizens engaging in dissenting activities, such as protesting or criticizing government policies, may receive lower scores and suffer societal repercussions (Yang, 2022). This raises ethical questions about the balance between governance and personal freedom, particularly in an era where digital surveillance is increasingly pervasive. The potential for algorithmic bias further complicates the issue, as automated decision-making can reinforce existing inequalities without clear avenues for appeal.

Internationally, the SCS has sparked debates about the role of technology in governance and social control. Some analysts warn that similar models could be adopted by other authoritarian regimes, while others note that elements of social scoring exist in democratic societies through corporate reputation scores, credit histories, and online behavior tracking. The ethical and political implications of such systems remain a critical topic for scholars, policymakers, and human rights advocates.

Digital Payment Methods and Platforms

The evolution of digital payment methods and platforms has revolutionized financial transactions, drawing increased scrutiny regarding financial digital identity. With platforms like PayPal, Venmo, and digital wallets gaining prominence, consumers now enjoy the convenience of instantaneous transactions and enhanced accessibility. However, the proliferation of these services also presents considerable risks, including identity theft and fraud. To mitigate such risks, financial institutions are adopting comprehensive Know Your Customer (KYC) policies to verify user identities and monitor transactions rigorously. This proactive stance not only combats financial crimes but also fosters trust in digital platforms, ensuring user data integrity and security (Zentoni et al., 2025). Furthermore, the application of machine learning in fraud detection enhances the efficacy of these measures, adapting to evolving threats while optimizing transaction safety (Jeyachandran et al., 2024). Consequently, the integration of robust identification and security frameworks is paramount for the sustained growth of digital payment ecosystems.

Social Media and Its Impact on Financial Identity

The increasing prominence of social media platforms has transformed the landscape of financial identity, enabling individuals and businesses to create and manage their digital personas effectively. This shift is particularly notable among women entrepreneurs, who leverage these platforms to foster community engagement, receive timely feedback, and facilitate growth in their ventures. As noted in studies, the adoption of social media has catalyzed a revolution in digital entrepreneurial culture, shifting mindsets from job-seeking to job-creating (Slabbert et al., 2014). Furthermore, the integration of national digital IDs with private identities, such as social media accounts, underscores the importance of digital platforms in accessing financial services. With the rise of mobile banking and digital finance applications, the accessibility of financial products has surged, reflecting a significant correlation between social media use and enhanced financial identity (CIPIT, 2021). Such dynamics are reshaping not only individual financial identities but also the broader economic fabric of society.

African Payday Loans

The proliferation of digital financial services across Africa has led to the rapid expansion of payday loans, particularly through mobile lending apps. These short-term, high-interest loans provide quick access to credit for individuals who may lack traditional banking services. While such financial innovations have increased financial inclusion, they have also introduced predatory lending practices, including aggressive debt collection methods such as text shaming. This practice involves lenders sending messages to a borrower's personal contacts, often family members, friends, and employers, informing them of the individual's debt and urging repayment.

Text shaming exploits the social fabric of African communities, where reputation and communal ties are highly valued. By using social pressure, lenders coerce borrowers into repayment, often at the expense of their dignity and mental well-being. This practice raises significant ethical concerns, particularly regarding privacy violations and psychological distress. Borrowers frequently report experiencing embarrassment, social ostracization, and workplace consequences because of these messages. Additionally, many payday loan companies operate with minimal regulatory oversight, allowing them to engage in such coercive tactics without legal repercussions.

Economically, payday loans often trap borrowers in cycles of debt due to exorbitant interest rates and fees. The ease of access to mobile loans, combined with aggressive collection methods, exacerbates financial instability rather than alleviating it. While digital lending platforms claim to support financial empowerment, the lack of consumer protection mechanisms raises concerns about exploitation. Regulatory interventions are necessary to establish ethical lending practices, enforce data protection laws, and prevent predatory debt collection strategies.

Security and Privacy Concerns

As digital financial transactions proliferate, the imperative to address security and privacy concerns becomes increasingly urgent. Users often unwittingly expose their personal data during online shopping activities, leading to potential risks such as identity theft and financial fraud. These vulnerabilities underscore the need for robust protection mechanisms in the digital ecosystem, particularly as the misuse of personal data can result in severe consequences for individuals and businesses alike (Nasution et al., 2023). Concurrently, the development of future Internet technologies brings forth a host of societal and economic issues that require careful consideration. A collaborative dialogue among technologists, social scientists, and policymakers is vital to bridge the existing gap between technological advancement and its implications for privacy and security (Oostveen et al., 2012). As such, addressing these concerns is essential to foster consumer trust and enable the sustainable growth of financial digital identities in an ever-evolving digital landscape.

Risks of Identity Theft and Fraud

As people increasingly engage with digital platforms, the risks of identity theft and fraud escalate, highlighting a critical aspect of financial digital identity. Cybercriminals exploit vulnerabilities inherent in payment systems; for example, simple personal information can suffice to authorize fraudulent transactions, thereby compromising personal and financial security (Sullivan, 2025). To mitigate these risks, it's essential to shift the focus from mere awareness to building long-term digital resilience among users (Third et al., 2014). This includes enhancing digital literacy, particularly among populations often overlooked by existing policies. Moreover, adopting technologies such as payment smart cards can significantly bolster security by introducing encryption measures that protect against unauthorized transactions. However, for these advancements to be effective, the financial industry must collaboratively establish and standardize security protocols, ensuring a robust defense against the pervasive threats of identity theft and fraud in the digital age.

The Elderly

Financial identity theft is a growing concern for senior citizens, who are often targeted due to their accumulated wealth, predictable income streams, and, in some cases, reduced familiarity with digital security measures. Identity thieves exploit these vulnerabilities through various means, including phishing scams, fraudulent calls, and unauthorized account access. Once personal or financial information is compromised, seniors may face severe consequences, including drained retirement savings, fraudulent credit applications, and long-term financial instability.

One significant risk factor is the increasing digitization of financial services. Many seniors rely on online banking and digital transactions but may lack the technological literacy necessary to recognize sophisticated cyber threats. Scammers frequently pose as bank representatives, government officials, or even family members in distress, manipulating victims into divulging sensitive information. Additionally, data breaches at financial institutions and healthcare providers expose seniors to identity theft, as stolen personal information is often sold on the dark web.

The impact of financial identity theft extends beyond economic losses. Seniors who fall victim to fraud may experience psychological distress, loss of financial independence, and difficulties recovering stolen assets due to complex legal and bureaucratic processes. In some cases, they may become reluctant to engage with digital financial services, limiting their access to convenient banking solutions.

Data Breaches and Their Consequences

Data breaches have emerged as a critical threat to the integrity of financial digital identities, provoking a wide array of consequences that extend beyond mere financial loss. The implications are profound, affecting consumer trust and necessitating a shift toward enhanced cyber safety measures. With a growing reliance on digital transactions, users find themselves navigating an increasingly perilous online environment, as evidenced by significant cyber safety challenges that arise from emerging technology trends, which disproportionately impact vulnerable populations (Third et al., 2014). Furthermore, comprehensive studies conducted by independent forensic teams reveal the intricate nature of these breaches, identifying patterns of compromise that inform best practices for prevention and response. Addressing the complexities of data breaches necessitates a focus not only on immediate technical solutions but also on fostering long-term digital resilience among users, ensuring that the benefits of digital participation do not come at the expense of security.

Importance of Strong Passwords and Authentication

In the realm of financial digital identity, the necessity for strong passwords and robust authentication mechanisms cannot be overstated. Digital platforms routinely store sensitive financial information, making them prime targets for cybercriminals seeking unauthorized access. The implementation of strong passwords acts as the first line of defense against such intrusions, as they significantly reduce the likelihood of successful hacking attempts. Furthermore, the incorporation of advanced authentication technologies, such as two-factor authentication, enhances security by requiring additional verification beyond merely a password. This dual-layer security approach is particularly critical in collaborative environments, as evidenced by the application of Internet2 Shibboleth technology, which exemplifies a user-oriented model for secure access within federated systems. Moreover, effective password management and authentication not only protect individual users but also contribute to the overall integrity and trustworthiness of financial digital identities across various platforms.

Best Practices for Maintaining Financial Privacy

In today's digital landscape, maintaining financial privacy is paramount, particularly as threats to personal data proliferate. Effective strategies must begin with robust digital literacy, which empowers you to recognize potential risks and navigate online environments with caution. This framework emphasizes the necessity of understanding privacy settings on various platforms, ensuring that one's digital footprint is minimized. Furthermore, as highlighted in Third et al. (2014), fostering digital resilience involves adapting to evolving technology trends while cultivating trust in online transactions. Another critical aspect is the implementation of standardized identity management systems, especially prevalent in industries such as iGaming, where the lack of such frameworks can expose users to fraud and identity theft, as noted in George (2018). Therefore, a proactive approach to financial privacy not only enhances personal security but also contributes to a more trustworthy digital ecosystem for all users.

The Role of Technology in Financial Digital Identity

In the evolving landscape of financial services, technology plays a pivotal role in shaping digital identities and enhancing user interaction with financial systems. As innovative platforms emerge, such as those developed by peer-to-peer financial organizations, they leverage high-speed networks and mobile technologies to facilitate seamless transactions and enhance consumer engagement. This shift not only challenges traditional banking models but also prompts users to reassess their understanding of financial interactions. Moreover, the complexity introduced by technology enables both opportunities for economic advancement and avenues for criminal exploitation. As noted, criminals increasingly utilize technological advancements to obscure their activities, further complicating the regulatory environment and user trust in digital identities (Demetis, 2014). Therefore, comprehending how these diverse technological infrastructures impact user experiences and identity formation is crucial for fostering secure and sustainable financial ecosystems (Ferreira & Perry, 2014).

Mobile Applications and Digital Wallets

The emergence of mobile applications and digital wallets represents a significant advancement in financial digital identity, fundamentally transforming how consumers interact with their financial assets. As shopping, banking, and investment activities migrate online, digital wallets often associated with mobile applications have gained popularity for facilitating seamless transactions. While traditional payment methods typically leverage credit and debit cards, e-wallets are increasingly favored for their ease and efficiency. However, this shift brings vulnerabilities; consumers must navigate potential risks such as fraudulent sites and hacking attempts, as noted in recent studies (Tudorache & Tiberiu Iordache, 2025). Moreover, the integration of near field communication (NFC) technology into these applications enables secure, contactless transactions, a feature that aligns with the vision of the Web of Things, thereby enhancing user experience (Ghinea et al., 2014). Thus, understanding the balance between convenience and security in mobile payments is essential for strengthening financial digital identity.

Fintech on Traditional Banking

The emergence of financial technology (better known as fintech) has substantially transformed the landscape of traditional banking, compelling conventional institutions to adapt or risk obsolescence. Fintech is used to describe new technology that seeks to improve and automate the delivery and use of financial services (Kagan, 2024). Companies leverage financial technology to offer innovative financial services that enhance efficiency and accessibility, thereby fueling competition in the banking sector. As noted, the legislative framework in many countries fails to distinguish between traditional service providers and fintech operators, leading to a blend of regulations that can both challenge and stimulate banking practices (Rupeika-Apoga & Thalassinos, 2020). Furthermore, as traditional banks increasingly embrace digitization, they report significant cost reductions; yet there is limited evidence that these savings have effectively translated into enhanced trade finance capacity, which remains a critical concern for sectors like SMEs. Ultimately, the fusion of fintech and traditional banking not only reshapes operational dynamics but also presents a complex interplay between innovation, regulation, and market sustainability.

The Impact of Financial Digital Identity

The emergence of financial digital identity significantly influences consumer behavior, particularly in the context of data security and privacy. As consumers increasingly engage with digital financial services, their exposure to data breaches becomes a pressing concern. According to Marcus (2018), breaches can lead to the exposure of personally identifiable information, heightening the risk of identity theft and undermining consumer trust in financial institutions. Moreover, the lack of a unifying legislative framework to govern data security exacerbates these risks, suggesting an urgent need for standardized protections. Beyond security concerns, digital identity also plays a crucial role in enhancing consumer access to financial services. Advances in technology can provide even small producers, particularly in developing regions, with equitable access to tools that facilitate secure transactions, thus improving overall economic participation and community well-being. Therefore, while financial digital identity presents challenges, it offers critical opportunities for empowerment and security.

Access to Financial Services and Credit

In the contemporary landscape, access to financial services and credit is increasingly facilitated by digital identities, particularly through innovative platforms that bridge the gap for underbanked populations. The dynamic between emerging digital financial services and traditional banking systems raises critical questions about equity and sustainability. With over 2 billion people excluded from formal financial systems, as noted by the Gates Foundation's Financial Services for the Poor program, addressing this disparity is imperative for global economic stability and poverty alleviation. Meanwhile, projects like the 3DaRoC are exploring new economic models that leverage peer-to-peer financial architectures to provide services previously unavailable to marginalized groups, thereby reshaping the reliance on traditional banking (Ferreira & Perry, 2014). Such advancements highlight the transformative potential of digital identities in promoting financial inclusion, ultimately driving economic empowerment and fostering innovation within the financial ecosystem.

Consumer Behavior and Spending Patterns

Understanding consumer behavior and spending patterns is crucial in the context of financial digital identity, as external influences, such as political confidence, significantly impact economic activities. Research indicates that political attitudes can shape consumer behavior, with increased confidence in leadership prompting greater willingness to spend, thus influencing overall economic stability (Donovan & Key, 2016). Furthermore, the rise of personalized marketing strategies enhances the connection between individual identity and consumption patterns. Utilizing theories such as self-congruity theory, consumers display preferences for brands that resonate with their self-concepts, which improves both marketing effectiveness and consumer well-being (Lay, 2021). The relationship between spending and self-congruity also reveals that individuals experience higher satisfaction when their expenditures align with their identity, suggesting that financial digital identity serves as a pivotal factor in determining spending behavior. Together, these dimensions highlight the intricate interplay between consumer identity, political context, and spending patterns.

Financial Literacy

In our current digital economy, financial literacy plays a crucial role in shaping our financial digital identities, influencing their ability to navigate an increasingly complex financial landscape. As technology advances, the necessity for people to possess a robust understanding of financial concepts has heightened, especially in the context of online transactions and investments. However, there remain significant disparities in digital financial literacy, often shaped by socioeconomic factors, geography, and gender. Research illustrates that access to digital resources and participation in the financial economy is not uniformly distributed, with marginalized groups facing heightened barriers. Furthermore, without adequate financial literacy programs, people may struggle to fully capitalize on digital financial opportunities, perpetuating cycles of inequality (Adiandari, 2023). Thus, fostering financial literacy is essential not only for personal empowerment but also for promoting a more equitable digital financial landscape for all.

Trust and Reputation in Digital Transactions

In the realm of digital transactions, the concepts of trust and reputation are fundamental for fostering consumer confidence and promoting engagement. As users increasingly rely on online platforms for financial activities, the risk of fraud and data breaches amplifies the importance of establishing robust trust mechanisms. Conventional reputation systems, often calculated through user feedback and transaction histories, are designed to enhance trust by labeling people and entities as reliable or trustworthy in specific contexts (De Paoli & Wilson, 2018). However, these systems may reflect a competitive and individualistic paradigm that does not universally translate across diverse contexts. This tension raises critical questions about the ethics and politics underlying such systems, suggesting that alternative approaches may be necessary to build trust more effectively (De Paoli & Wilson, 2018). Furthermore, a lack of trust has been noted as a significant barrier to electronic commerce, often leading consumers to abandon transactions due to concerns over data security.

BOX 5.1 CASE STUDY

Canadian truckers and GoFundMe

The 2022 protests by Canadian truckers, commonly known as the "Freedom Convoy", sparked significant controversy not only for their impact on public order but also for the financial measures used to curtail them. The truckers, initially gathering in Ottawa to protest COVID-19 vaccine mandates and government restrictions, turned into a broader movement against perceived government overreach. As the protests ran into the second week, authorities took unprecedented steps, including freezing the bank accounts of protesters and seizing funds raised through crowdfunding platforms such as GoFundMe. This response raised significant concerns about financial rights, government power, and the implications for future protests.

The Canadian government, under Prime Minister Justin Trudeau, invoked the Emergencies Act on February 14, 2022, for the first time in the country's history. This move granted authorities temporary but sweeping powers to clear blockades, regulate public assemblies, and, crucially, disrupt financial support for protesters. The government directed banks and financial institutions to freeze accounts linked to individuals and organizations involved in the protests without requiring a court order. This action effectively cut off access to personal and business funds, creating immediate financial hardship for many truckers.

In addition to direct banking measures, authorities also targeted crowdfunding platforms. GoFundMe, which had hosted a fundraiser that amassed over $10 million CAD in support of the truckers, suspended the campaign and initially announced plans to redirect the funds to other charities. Following public backlash and political pressure, the platform instead refunded the donations. Protesters and their supporters then turned to alternative crowdfunding sites like GiveSendGo, which faced hacking and leaks exposing donor identities, further escalating tensions.

These financial measures sparked a broader debate about civil liberties and government authority. Supporters of the crackdown argued that freezing financial resources was necessary to dismantle an illegal occupation that disrupted businesses, transportation, and daily life in Ottawa. They contended that financial disruption was a non-violent method of discouraging participation in the protests and preventing further economic harm caused by blockades at border crossings and downtown Ottawa.

Conclusion

Financial digital identity is a critical yet often overlooked aspect of modern life that affects access to essential services such as housing, transportation, and education. It's composed of PII, financial history, credit scores, and digital behaviors, all of which are used by institutions to assess trustworthiness and determine opportunities. While digital tools like mobile wallets and fintech platforms increase convenience and financial inclusion, they also introduce risks such as identity theft, data breaches, and algorithmic bias. Vulnerable groups, such as the elderly, the underbanked, and those in developing countries, face disproportionate harm due to a lack of protections and financial literacy. Additionally, examples like China's social credit system and digital payday lending in Africa illustrate how financial identity can be used for both empowerment and control. Strong passwords, secure authentication, and robust regulatory frameworks are essential to protect you from fraud and exploitation.

Exercise

In this chapter, we looked at ways to protect your digital, financial identity. These are things you may have already known, but there may be things you had not thought about. Answer the following:

- In the first paragraph, share what things you learned regarding protecting your digital, financial identity.
- In the second paragraph, discuss how marginalized groups (poor or elderly) are more negatively impacted by financial identity theft.
- Lastly, we explored unusual ways your digital, financial identity could be used against you from a social perspective. Read through this news story PayPal and America's Pending social credit system (https://www.newsweek.com/paypal-americas-pending-social-credit-system-opinion-1752074).

References

Adiandari, A. M. (2023). Navigating the digital society: Financial literacy as a tool for empowerment. https://doi.org/10.15575/ks.v5i4.30792

Agarwal, S., & Chakraborty, L. (2018). Digital innovations in public finance: An efficient use of resources. https://core.ac.uk/download/211627313.pdf

Bryce, J. (2015). Cyberpsychology and human factors. https://core.ac.uk/download/42138483.pdf

Centre for Intellectual Property and Information Technology (CIPIT). (2021). Privacy and data protection practices of digital lending apps in Kenya. https://core.ac.uk/download/588634470.pdf

Combe, C., & Hasbullah, N. A. (2017). Privacy in transformational government (t-government): an investigation of citizens' privacy preferences and perceptions. *Journal of Fundamental and Applied Sciences*, *9*, 503–517.

Deb, A., Costa, A., & Kubzansky, M. (2015). Big data, small credit: The digital revolution and its impact on emerging market consumers. https://core.ac.uk/download/75782754.pdf

Demetis, D. (2014). The role of information systems in the prevention and detection of transnational and international crime. https://core.ac.uk/download/151157333.pdf

De Paoli, S., & Wilson, A. (2018). Reconsidering online reputation systems. https://core.ac.uk/download/228178365.pdf

Desmarais, N. (2000). Body language, security and e-commerce. https://core.ac.uk/download/56322778.pdf

Donovan, K. M., & Key, E. M. (2016). The political economy: Political attitudes and economic behavior. https://core.ac.uk/download/213033157.pdf

Ferreira, J., & Perry, M. (2014). Building an alternative social currency: Dematerialising and rematerialising digital money across media. HCIK '15:Proceedings of HCI Korea, pp. 122–131, Hanbit Media Inc.

George, M. D. (2018). Identity trust framework for iGaming. https://core.ac.uk/download/211337721.pdf

Ghinea, G., Pourghomi, P., & saeed Qasim, M. (2014). A proposed NFC payment application. *International Journal of Advanced Computer Science and Applications*, *4*(8), 173–181.

Jeyachandran, P., Akisetty, A.S, Subramani, P., Goel, O., Singh, D. S., & Shrivastav, E. A. (2024). Leveraging machine learning for real-time fraud detection in digital payments. *Integrated Journal for Research in Arts and Humanities*. https://www.semanticscholar.org/paper/c87479d6da49e53a10e743d91d1cdbb924776e4c

Kagan, J. (2024). Financial Technology (Fintech): Its uses and impact on our lives. *Investopedia*. https://www.investopedia.com/terms/f/fintech.asp

Lay, C. L. (2021). The role of self-congruity in consumer preferences: Perspectives from transaction records. https://core.ac.uk/download/483550575.pdf

Marcus, D. J. (2018). The data breach dilemma: Proactive solutions for protecting consumers' personal information. https://core.ac.uk/download/213020823.pdf

Nasution, M. F. (2023). The role of civil law in the protection of privacy and personal data. *Innovative: Journal of Social Science Research*, *3*(2), 3669–3679.

Oostveen, A., Hjorth, I., Pickering, B., Boniface, M., Meyer, E., Cobo, C., & Schroeder, R. (2012). Cross-disciplinary lessons for the future internet. *Lecture Notes in Computer Science*, *7281*, 42–54. https://doi.org/10.1007/978-3-642-30241-1_5

Rupeika-Apoga, R., & Thalassinos, E. I. (2020). Ideas for a regulatory definition of FinTech. https://core.ac.uk/download/322748662.pdf

Slabbert, A. D., Ukpere, C. L., & Ukpere, W. I. (2014). Rising trend in social media usage by women entrepreneurs across the globe to unlock their potentials for business success. https://core.ac.uk/download/43602880.pdf

Sullivan, R. J. (2025). Can smart cards reduce payments fraud and identity theft? https://core.ac.uk/download/pdf/6793468.pdf

Third, A., Collier, A., & Forrest-Lawrence, P. (2014). Addressing the cyber safety challenge: From risk to resilience. https://core.ac.uk/download/pdf/30674272.pdf

Tudorache, A. M. M., & Tiberiu Iordache, M. (2025). Smart cards – Utility, applications and vulnerabilities. https://core.ac.uk/download/pdf/6662517.pdf

Yang, Z. (2022). China just announced a new social credit law. Here's what it means. *Technology review*. https://www.technologyreview.com/2022/11/22/1063605/china-announced-a-new-social-credit-law-what-does-it-mean/

Zentoni, B., Santoso, D. M. L., & Tobing, Z. F. (2025). Know Your Customer (KYC) model: A legal reform strategy to prevent abuse of financial services in child sexual exploitation transactions. *Journal of Law and Legal Reform*. https://www.semanticscholar.org/paper/b950ae6936f94435b4827b92448b3e26df62c5c0

6

HEALTH IDENTITY

What You Don't Know Could Kill You

Personal data is a currency. It can be traded and sold on the black market to those looking to commit medical insurance fraud. This type of identity theft happens in every country. Health or medical identity theft has emerged as a particularly "invisible" crime with severe consequences. Unlike financial identity theft, which can be resolved through the courts, with time and money, medical identity theft can permanently alter health records, resulting in misdiagnoses, leading to unnecessary medical procedures, or even causing life-threatening situations. Medical identity theft occurs when someone fraudulently uses another person's medical information such as insurance details, social security numbers, or medical records to obtain healthcare services, prescriptions, or financial benefits. The consequences extend far beyond financial loss, affecting medical histories, treatment plans, and legal standing in unexpected and devastating ways. In this chapter, we'll explore extreme cases of health identity theft, including "Robin Hooding", instances where victims suffer incorrect medical interventions, loss of parental rights, extortion, and end by discussing the dangers of oversharing online.

Biometrics

Biometrics is the measurement and analysis of unique physical and behavioral characteristics each of us possesses that can be used for identification and authentication purposes. Physical traits such as fingerprints are used to unlock smartphones, facial recognition is often used to authenticate to various applications, and high-security systems employ retina scanning.

DOI: 10.4324/9781003539445-7

Behavioral biometrics uses patterns of behavior to identify individuals. Examples include voice pattern recognition for virtual assistants like Alexa (Amazon), security cameras that use gait recognition to identify individuals by their walk, and keystroke dynamics used in proctored testing and corporate surveillance.

Biometric technology is widely used in various sectors of society including law enforcement, financial services, healthcare, and travel/immigration. Government agencies and law enforcement around the world hold vast amounts of biometric data on their citizens. These databases hold everything from facial features to fingerprints. We, as citizens, are assured that they are only used for crime investigations, but that may not always be the case in the future. In the United States, as in other countries, hospitals store electronic health records (EHRs) of sensitive, patient data. Passport and immigration services at airports around the world rely on facial recognition and photos taken at the time of entry for authentication and tracking purposes. When your picture is taken at customs, airports, or other secure locations, you are not told what happens to that photo. Banks and healthcare providers are also collecting identifiable biometric data like fingerprints and facial scans to mitigate fraud. Where is all this data stored, and what security measures are in place to keep it all safe? These images, scans, and other biometric data become part of your biometric footprint. Unfortunately, there is no international governing body ensuring our biometric data is secure and not vulnerable to international espionage or cybercrime.

Electronic Health Records

In the past when you visited any healthcare professional, they would write out and print reports on your visit. What ailment you came in for, what treatment you were prescribed, and any follow-up instructions were all written down. If you visited your primary doctor, they had a set of records, a clinic had another set, and a specialist still another. Periodically, they would share copies of these print records, and they would be stored in a room lined with file cabinets. With the advent of the computer and the Internet, those records were digitized and shared across all your healthcare providers. EHRs are digital compilations of patient information that is more efficient and enhances patient care as healthcare providers can now collaborate on better patient healthcare outcomes (Kraus et al., 2020).

EHRs consolidate a patient's medical history, treatment plans, and diagnostic data into a single, accessible format, enhancing operational effectiveness. EHRs allow healthcare providers to coordinate care and improve patient health safety by reducing the risks associated with miscommunication and documentation errors. This interoperability among providers not only allows for more coordinated care but also improves the accuracy of medical histories, treatment plans, and vaccination records. For instance, cellphone applications have emerged as powerful allies, enabling self-reporting and reminders, thereby enhancing vaccination coverage and patient engagement (Atkinson, 2024). EHRs have also become an invaluable tool for public health concerns as they can quickly collate data and, with the use of AI, create maps of potential outbreak "hot spots", as we have seen during the COVID-19 pandemic.

Encryption technologies play a vital role in protecting the integrity and confidentiality of EHRs during transmission. For instance, cryptography is increasingly being utilized to protect electronic communications within healthcare systems (Desmarais, 2000). The importance of adequate security measures is paramount in safeguarding patient data and fostering trust between us, the patients and our doctors. Another issue related to transmission is storage. How our data is managed has become a topic for healthcare librarians, archivists, and software engineers. Aligning how our digital records are managed must align with ethical standards related to patient privacy (Gladney, 2009).

The technological infrastructure, the government regulations, and the training of healthcare professionals shape EHRs globally. For instance, countries like Sweden and Denmark have implemented robust, integrated EHR systems that enable seamless data sharing across healthcare providers, ultimately enhancing patient outcomes. In contrast, the United States still operates under a fragmented system, despite having made strides with initiatives like the Health Information Technology for Economic and Clinical Health Act (HITECH). At the start of EHRs, in 2015, HITECH provided financial incentives of up to $44,000 to train on and use EHRs. After 2015, any healthcare professional not meaningfully using EHRs would see a reduction in Medicare and Medicaid reimbursements (Burde, 2011). Across developing countries, the implementation of EHRs is limited by high costs, limited technology infrastructure, and a lack of proper training, which have been identified as the major challenges (Seastedt et al., 2022).

The current move to mobile health applications for access to health professionals and EHRs, while innovative, creates a new set of privacy, security, and ethics concerns. Who is responsible for breaches in the system, the cellphone manufacturer, the cellphone provider, the software engineer, or the healthcare providers? Advances in these applications reinforce the need for privacy protections, and updates to privacy laws are necessary as patients increasingly rely on digital platforms for their care (Sherman, 2018).

Why and How Your Health Identity Is Stolen

Your health identity seems like a strange thing to take. Why would someone go to the doctor using someone else's ID? There are many reasons someone would want the medical identification of another person. Knowing as much about a person as possible makes it easier to steal their entire identity. Think of it this way, the goal of many identity thieves is to assume your full identity. This allows them access to your financial credit, giving them access to loans for cars, mortgages, and credit cards. From there, they can get a driver's license in your name with their face. They'll use your social security number and gain access to the passwords of every type of account you own that they can find. Assuming your identity starts with knowing as much personal information about you as possible. Therefore, having access to your medical information is extremely important. Another reason thieves take your health identity is that they're looking for free healthcare. Seeking plastic surgeries, getting access to drugs, and avoiding authorities when they're ill and wanted for another crime are all reasons criminals will take the health identity of others. Finally, health identity theft is big business. According to Trustwave, a cybersecurity firm specializing in healthcare data breaches, medical records go for $25–$1000 on the black market (Trustwave, 2023).

Medical identity theft disproportionately affects vulnerable patient populations, particularly the very young, pregnant women, and the elderly. These groups are at heightened risk due to their frequent interactions with healthcare systems, which necessitate the repeated sharing and verification of sensitive personal information.

Pediatric patients are especially vulnerable as their social security numbers and identifying details can be misused for fraudulent purposes without detection for years. Unfortunately, these victims don't discover the breach until they reach adulthood and attempt to establish credit or apply for government benefits. Pregnant women, who undergo numerous medical visits, diagnostic tests, and hospital admissions, frequently provide their personal information across multiple healthcare providers and insurance entities, increasing the chances of data exposure and breaches (Glenn & Monteith, 2014; Smith & Jones, 2020). Similarly, elderly patients face a high risk due to their reliance on Medicare and other healthcare services, often managed by caregivers or family members, which expands the number of people who have access to their sensitive health data (Kemp & Erades Pérez, 2023).

As discussed earlier, EHRs have inherent vulnerabilities given they're stored digitally and require robust security mechanisms. Walking into a clinic or hospital leaves you vulnerable to health identity theft in a myriad of ways. Each instance your information is manually or digitally processed through hospital admissions, insurance claims, or EHRs introduces potential exposure to cyber threats, unauthorized access, or human error leading to data leaks (Mosharraf & Haghighatkhah, 2023). For example, there have been some examples of hospital personnel taking laptop computers home to work on records with sensitive patient data on it (West, 2014).

Another vulnerability for your health identity comes from the service statements you receive in the mail. In the United States and elsewhere, customers of healthcare insurance companies receive statements of benefits. Called explanation of benefits (EOBs), they contain potentially identifiable and sensitive information such as your name, date of birth, insurance ID numbers, and details of services received. This information, in the hands of a thief, can be used to generate a driver's license with their face and replacement insurance cards that can then be used to receive medical treatment (Cigna Healthcare, 2022).

Extreme Cases of Health Identity Theft

Extreme cases of medical identity theft have the potential to cause devastating financial, legal, and health consequences for victims. Unlike traditional financial fraud, where stolen credit cards can be canceled or fraudulent transactions reversed, medical identity theft can result in long-term damage, including misdiagnosed treatments, falsified medical records, and even life-threatening errors in patient care. In the most severe instances, criminals use stolen medical identities to obtain expensive surgeries, prescription drugs, or insurance benefits, leaving victims burdened with massive debt and medical histories that do not reflect their actual health conditions. These fraudulent activities not only compromise individual well-being but also strain healthcare systems, insurance providers, and government agencies tasked with detecting and mitigating such crimes.

Robin Hooding

One unique manifestation of medical identity fraud is "Robin Hooding", where people knowingly give their health insurance details to someone who can't afford it (Cambridge University, 2024). While some see this as an altruistic crime, the reality is that it compromises patient records, leading to potential misdiagnoses and incorrect treatments. In some cases, hospitals and insurance companies have detected anomalies in patients' records where conditions that were never diagnosed or treated appear, complicating future medical care and eligibility for services.

In 2014 a couple in Seattle, Washington, celebrated the birth of their son. Three weeks later, they received a bill addressed to their son from a local clinic for a visit for a work-related back injury and a prescription for OxyContin. The bill even contained their son's middle name, which only close family and friends knew. It also included the hospital where he was born that filed the paperwork for his birth certificate, his home address, the parents' social security numbers, and the mother's maiden name. A call to the clinic revealed that someone using their son's identity obtained healthcare there within one week of his birth. In the end, the family was able to have the bills dismissed; however, they were unable to determine who in their family or friend circle had used their son's medical identity (Cohen, 2015).

Misdiagnosis and Unnecessary Medical Procedures

One of the most horrifying consequences of medical identity theft is receiving the wrong diagnosis due to someone else's medical history being intertwined with the victim's medical history. There have been documented cases where victims were given treatments for conditions they did not have, some undergoing unnecessary surgeries, chemotherapy, or other invasive procedures based on fraudulent records (Ponemon Institute, 2015).

In a case of stolen identity, a 63-year-old woman came to the emergency room after choking on a fishbone. After undergoing a gastroscopy to remove the blockage, she was seen three days later for a follow-up where a CT scan was performed. During the procedure, it was discovered that the patient, at some point in the past, had her spleen removed. The problem was, the woman on the health insurance still had her spleen. After police detained the patient, it was discovered she had stolen the other woman's identification to get medical attention as she had no insurance herself (Huynh et al., 2021).

A woman received a bill for amputating her right foot. After numerous calls to the hospital explaining that she still had both her feet, she was forced to travel to the hospital in question and prove her medical identity theft claim. As a result of the visit, the billing department stopped billing her. A year later, she returned to the same hospital to undergo a hysterectomy. Unbeknownst to her, her medical records were contaminated with dangerously erroneous information. For example, the fraudulent patient had a different blood type and a blood transfusion, likely during a surgery she was about to receive, would have likely killed her (Cohen, 2015).

Children Taken Away from You

In some cases, stolen health identities have been used to fabricate medical conditions in children, triggering wrongful CPS interventions. Parents have lost custody of their children after being accused of medical neglect based on fraudulent medical records. In these cases, the criminal who assumed the parent's or child's identity will remain undetected while the family endures legal battles, trauma, and sometimes permanent separation.

In 2006 Anndorie Cromar had her purse stolen from her car. She filed a police report and replaced her credit cards and driver's license. She reviewed her credit report each year for unauthorized credit or transactions. Anndorie assumed the ordeal was behind her until four years later, in 2010, she received a phone call from Child Protective Services to inform her that the baby she had given birth to two months ago had tested positive for methamphetamine. The agent proceeded to tell her they felt her other four children were in danger and would like to arrange for them to be handed over to foster care. The problem was that Anndorie did not give birth to a baby two months ago. She realized this was all connected to her stolen driver's license. Anndorie had to go to court, spend countless hours and thousands of dollars in lawyer's fees to clear her record, and take a DNA test to prove she was not the biological mother of the child in question. She was humiliated because everyone in her small town knew she was investigated by CPS and for years afterward would find her name tied to the baby through EHRs (Terry, 2015).

Facing Prison

Dr. Anne Peters never expected to find herself facing a lengthy prison sentence, but that is what happened to the Florida physician. Dr. Peters started receiving phone calls from unhappy patients about medical procedures she did not perform, who had never visited her office. She immediately knew something was wrong but didn't know who to turn to. It quickly escalated when she began receiving visits from the federal agents and calls from the Internal Revenue Service. In an unusual twist of medical identity, someone had stolen Dr. Peters' medical credentials and established a practice in another part of the United States under her name and was illegally billing Medicare out of hundreds of thousands of dollars. The theft totaled over $750,000 and Dr. Peters was threatened with prison by the IRS if she did not pay the taxes owed on the "income". It took her six years and thousands of dollars in legal fees to eventually get her name cleared (Agrawal & Budetti, 2012).

In 2019, Sharon Mills, a retired nurse from Oklahoma, was served a warrant for her arrest at her home. Her crime was writing and filling over 1700 separate prescriptions for opioids from 2015 to 2018. The 69-year-old was booked, fingerprinted, and placed in a jail cell while she pleaded her innocence. The next day she was able to arrange bail and worked with an attorney to understand how this could have happened. After hiring an investigator, Sharon and her attorney were able to prove in court that her driver's license, stolen the year before, had been used to steal her identity as a nurse. Armed with a stolen prescription pad, the criminals were able to write scripts for the pills, which they later sold on the black market.

Extortion

Health identity theft is also used as a tool for extortion. Cybercriminals gain access to sensitive medical records and threaten to expose highly personal health details unless victims pay a ransom. This is especially damaging for people with stigmatized medical conditions, such as mental health disorders, sexually transmitted infections, or reproductive health histories. Some black-market schemes even involve altering medical records until payment is received, causing significant harm to the victim's healthcare access.

In 2023 Hollywood, CA plastic surgeon, Dr. Gary Motykie, was contacted by a cybercriminal who claimed to have accessed his patient server and was in possession of sensitive patient data. The thief threatened to publish the photos of naked patients pre- and post-surgery; some patients were high profile celebrities and wealthy society members. Dr. Motykie contacted a third-party firm to verify the breach and determined it was a valid threat. The thief had managed to obtain access to the names, addresses, driver's licenses, financial information, social security numbers, health insurance information, and medical histories along with the compromising images. A total of 3461 individual patients' records were affected and the attorney general's office was brought in to handle the case. The victims received free credit monitoring for two years and the images never appeared in public. Dr. Motykie declined to answer whether he paid the $2 million ransom (Adler, 2023).

Ransom

In April 2017, Erie County Medical Center (ECMC) in Buffalo, New York, experienced a significant ransomware attack involving the SamSam malware. The incident began when a staff member encountered a ransom note on a workstation demanding $44,000 in Bitcoin to unlock encrypted files. ECMC administrators and the cybersecurity team were notified and had a decision to make. Pay or make a very drastic move to shut it all down. Rather than set the precedent of bowing to cybercriminals, ECMC shut down all information systems, such as EHRs, email, and their website, to prevent the malware's spread. Despite these measures, over 6000 computers were infected, necessitating a meticulous cleaning process for each device. The recovery spanned six weeks and incurred costs amounting to millions of dollars. Remarkably, patient records remained uncompromised during the attack. This event underscores the critical importance of rapid detection and immediate action in mitigating ransomware threats within healthcare organizations. (Slabodkin, 2021).

Cost of Health Identity Theft

Your medical information holds significant value, often exceeding that of your financial data, because it includes details such as social security numbers, medical histories, and insurance information. As we have said earlier, this makes it highly sought after for fraudulent activities like identity theft and insurance fraud. The National Association of Healthcare Access Management (NAHAM) emphasizes the critical need for healthcare organizations to implement robust security measures and staff training to protect this sensitive data. According to the NAHAM, "ensuring the confidentiality and integrity of personal health information is essential to maintain patient trust and comply with privacy regulations (Zabel, 2023)".

The growing value of personal medical information on the black market directly contributes to the alarming rise in healthcare data breaches. Cybercriminals and hackers recognize that health records provide a wealth of exploitable data, making healthcare organizations prime targets for cyberattacks. While these institutions strive to protect sensitive patient information through security protocols and regulatory compliance, the rapid digitization of healthcare in the form of EHRs and the complexity of data-sharing networks, often run through offsite servers, increase vulnerability. As a result, breaches have escalated in both frequency and financial impact, posing severe consequences for patients and healthcare providers alike.

The financial impact of healthcare data breaches has risen significantly over the last few years. In 2023, the average cost of a healthcare data breach escalated to $10.93 million, up from $10.10 million in 2022, marking a 53.3% increase over three years. The number of recorded breaches in the healthcare sector has more than doubled since 2017. These breaches not only result in substantial financial losses but also compromise patient trust and disrupt critical healthcare services. The increasing value of health data on the black market underscores the urgent need for healthcare organizations to implement robust data protection measures and ensure compliance with privacy regulations to safeguard sensitive patient information.

For the patients, the cost of health identity theft extends far beyond financial burdens, impacting their well-being, time, and access to care. As we have seen from the extreme examples, victims often face significant out-of-pocket expenses to correct fraudulent medical bills, restore their medical records, and recover from damage to their credit scores. According to the Medical Identity Fraud Alliance, resolving medical identity theft can take months or even years, requiring extensive communication with healthcare providers, insurance companies, and financial institutions. In some cases, victims are wrongfully denied necessary medical treatment due to altered records or unpaid fraudulent claims associated with their identity. Additionally, the psychological toll of medical identity theft can be severe, causing stress, anxiety, and loss of trust in the healthcare system.

Oversharing

The world is increasingly interconnected. As you navigate this complex landscape of social media, there are implications in your physical world. Of particular concern is the oversharing of personal health-related information. The motivations behind your choice to disclose intimate details are multifaceted and are often rooted in a desire for validation or support. However, this oversharing can lead to consequences that extend beyond yourself, impacting both families and friends. A simple selfie with a friend after her surgery or a parent's mention of a child's broken leg on TikTok or Instagram can be shared publicly and become part of one's digital health footprint.

In an era where digital platforms dominate communication, the implications of oversharing health-related information on social media have become increasingly profound. Individuals often perceive these platforms as safe venues. The tendency to disclose personal health information can unintentionally expose sensitive data, leaving people vulnerable to breaches of privacy and unwanted scrutiny. Research highlights that weak individual privacy safeguards in social media settings can lead to unethical behaviors, resulting in harmful consequences for users, especially the most vulnerable populations (Barrett-Maitland & Lynch, 2020).

According to Haley, "the need for balance between parental rights to share about their children's lives and the children's inherent right to privacy illustrates a broader conflict in online expression versus personal data security" (2020).

Navigating social media can often lead to unintended consequences, especially regarding the sharing of personal health information. As you disclose sensitive health data online, you risk creating permanent digital footprints that may affect your privacy and security. This oversharing can expose you to identity theft and discrimination, particularly when your health conditions are made public without adequate protections in place. It can be acknowledged that there is immense pressure to share freely on social media; however, you need to consider your right to share and the potential implications on your privacy. To safeguard the health identity of you, your friends, and your family, get in the habit of not sharing personal information, pictures, or posts connected to health procedures.

BOX 6.1 CASE STUDY

The recent bankruptcy filing of 23andMe, an ancestry and health analysis company, has raised significant concerns regarding the security of sensitive genetic information entrusted to the company by its 15 million customers. In 2024 the company announced it was filing for bankruptcy. As it works through the courts, the potential sale or transfer of its extensive DNA databases introduces risks of unauthorized access and misuse of personal data. Genetic information, being absolute and uniquely identifiable, presents challenges if compromised, including identity theft, genetic discrimination, and privacy violations. Security experts warn that such data could be exploited for fraudulent medical treatments, unauthorized prescriptions, or even tailored social engineering attacks.

Considering these risks, privacy advocates and legal authorities are advising 23andMe users to proactively protect their genetic data. Recommendations include downloading and securely storing personal genetic information, opting out of research programs, and formally requesting the deletion of biological samples and associated data from the company's records. These measures attempt to mitigate potential identity theft and safeguard personal privacy amidst the company's uncertain future.

Conclusion

Health identity theft is a critical and growing threat in the digital age, one that carries potentially devastating consequences beyond financial loss. As this chapter has shown, when someone's medical identity is stolen, the damage can affect their entire life, leading to misdiagnoses, unnecessary procedures, legal trouble, and even the loss of parental rights or freedom. Vulnerable populations such as children, pregnant women, and the elderly are especially at risk due to frequent interactions with healthcare systems and the repeated sharing of sensitive data. The rise of EHRs, mobile health apps, and biometric authentication systems offers many benefits for healthcare delivery but also creates new avenues for data breaches, ransomware attacks, and extortion. Cases like Dr. Peters, Anndorie Cromar, and thousands of affected patients underscore how high the stakes have become. In an era where personal data is a currency, protecting health identity must become a top priority for individuals, healthcare providers, and policymakers alike. Increased digital literacy, stronger regulatory oversight, and better cybersecurity infrastructure are necessary to safeguard not only our information but our lives as well. Avoiding oversharing and advocating for privacy protections are essential steps toward reclaiming control of our health identities in a connected world.

Exercise

In this chapter, we looked at how your health identity is tracked online through the use of EHRs, biometrics, and social media.

Analyze this article https://www.hrw.org/news/2022/03/30/new-evidence-biometric-data-systems-imperil-afghans in relation to the concepts and issues discussed. Here is information on the current ruling party in Afghanistan, the Taliban https://www.bbc.com/news/world-south-asia-11451718. Consider what you now know about what can be done with biometric data.

- Identify and describe the six major biometric systems discussed in the article.
- What are the negative implications and risks of this biometric data for the everyday Afghans?
- International peacekeepers oversaw the country's security for 20 years. What ethical responsibilities did they have to the security of Afghans' biometric data?
- How has your understanding of health identity tracking changed after studying this case?

References

Adler, S. (2023). Naked patient photos published after ransomware attack on plastic surgery clinic. *The HIPAA Journal*. https://www.hipaajournal.com/naked-patient-photos-published-after-ransomware-attack-on-plastic-surgery-clinic/

Agrawal, S., & Budetti, P. (2012). Physician medical identity theft. *The Journal of the American Medical Association*, *307*(5), 459–460.

Atkinson, K. M. (2024). *Consumer reported digital immunization records: Feasibility, applicability, and public health utility in the Canadian context*. Karolinska Institutet.

Barrett-Maitland, N., & Lynch, J. (2020). Social media, ethics and the privacy paradox. In *Security and privacy from a legal, ethical, and technical perspective*. IntechOpen.

Burde, H. (2011). The HITECH act: An overview. *Journal of Ethics*. https://journalofethics.ama-assn.org/article/hitech-act-overview/2011-03

Cambridge University. (2024). Cambridge dictionary "Robin Hooding." *Cambridge University Dictionary*. https://dictionary.cambridge.org/us/dictionary/english/robin-hood

Cigna Healthcare. (2022). Understanding your explanation of benefits (EOB). https://www.cigna.com/knowledge-center/explanation-of-benefits

Cohen, J. (2015). Medical identity theft – The crime that can kill. *Dateline*, *14*(2), 1–5.

Desmarais, N. (2000). Body language, security and e-commerce. *Library Hi Tech*, *18*(1), 61–74.

Gladney, D. H. M. (2009). Long-term preservation of digital records: Trustworthy digital objects. *The American Archivist*, *72*(2), 401–435.

Glenn, T., & Monteith, S. (2014). Privacy in the digital world: Medical and health data outside of HIPAA protections. *Current Psychiatry Reports*, *16*(11), 494–525.

Haley, K. (2020). Sharenting and the (potential) right to be forgotten. *Indiana Law Journal*, *95*, 1005–1020.

Huynh, R., Thoms, A., Nguyen, T. M., & Kwok, T. (2021). The missing spleen – A diagnosis of medical identity fraud in surgery: Case report. *International Journal of Surgery Case Reports*, *78*, 210–213.

Kemp, S., & Erades Pérez, N. (2023). Consumer fraud against older adults in digital society: Examining victimization and its impact. *International Journal of Environmental Research and Public Health*, *20*(7), 1–17.

Kraus, S., Schiavone, F., Pluzhnikova, A., & Invernizzi, A. C. (2020). Digital transformation in healthcare: Analyzing the current state-of-research. *Journal of Business Research*, *123*, 557–567.

Mosharraf, M., & Haghighatkhah, F. H. (2023). Exploring identity theft: Motives, techniques, and consequents on different age groups. *Journal of Innovations in Computer Science and Engineering (JICSE)*, *1*(1), 63–74.

Ponemon Institute. (2015). Criminal attacks: The new leading cause of data breach in healthcare. *Ponemon Institute*. https://www.ponemon.org/research/ponemon-library/security/criminal-attacks-the-new-leading-cause-of-data-breach-in-healthcare.html

Seastedt, K., Schwab, P., O'Brien, Z., Wakida, E., Herrera, K., Marcelo, P., Aghan-Mir-Salim, L., Frigola, X., Ndulue, E., Marcelo, A., & Celi, L. (2022). Global healthcare fairness: We should be sharing more, not less, data. *PLOS Digital Health*, *1*(10), 1–13.

Sherman, J. (2018). Double secret protection: Bridging federal and state law to protect privacy rights for telemental and Mobile health users. *Duke Law Journal*, *67*, 1115–1153.

Slabodkin, G. (2021). Erie County Medical Center: Anatomy of a ransomware attack. *Health Data Management*. https://www.healthdatamanagement.com/articles/erie-county-medical-center-anatomy-of-a-ransomware-attack

Smith, T., & Jones, L. (2020). Pregnant women and medical identity theft: An emerging risk factor. *Maternal Health and Data Security*, *7*(2), 45–60.

Terry, K. (2015). HIPAA breach: Secure data & prevent fines – Here's how. *Medical Economics*, *92(*14), 26–32.

Trustwave. (2023). Cybersecurity in the healthcare industry: Trustwave Spiderlabs Report. https://www.trustwave.com/en-us/resources/blogs/spiderlabs-blog/cybersecurity-in-the-healthcare-industry-trustwave-spiderlabs-report/

West, K. (2014). Patient medical information at risk from stolen computers. *Missouri Medicine*, *111*(1), 10–12.

Zabel, L. (2023). The value of personal medical information: Protecting against data breaches. National Association of Healthcare Management. https://www.naham.org/page/ConnectionsThe-Value-of-Personal-Medical-Information

7

PROFESSIONAL IDENTITY

Losing Your Dream Job

The professional landscape has undergone a fundamental transformation with the proliferation of digital communication platforms like LinkedIn and X (formerly Twitter). Employers now possess unprecedented capacity to investigate candidates' personal digital histories, blurring the boundaries between professional competence and personal expression. Lapses in judgment online, whether in the form of inappropriate comments, controversial posts, or photos from a weekend gone wrong, can have severe ramifications for one's professional identity. Increasingly, hiring managers and HR departments consult search engines and social media feeds as part of background checks, seeking digital clues about reliability, judgment, and cultural fit.

At the same time, employees face growing pressure to curate an online presence that is not only appropriate but persuasive. Platforms are designed to reward visibility and likability, prompting users to share content that may enhance their personal brand but at the cost of long-term privacy. A seemingly harmless meme or impulsive comment can be screenshotted, archived, and resurfaced, often out of context. In this chapter, we'll explore the risk behaviors of potential employees and the motivations behind employers' increasing reliance on digital identity to monitor, discipline, or terminate staff. We'll also consider how persuasive digital platforms shape online behavior in ways that may conflict with professional norms, and why digital discretion is now an essential career skill.

DOI: 10.4324/9781003539445-8

Risk Behavior

The decision to risk one's job or job prospect is driven by a myriad of psychological factors that can vary greatly among individuals. While the rational, cognitive approach might suggest that people would avoid such high-stakes gambles, research has shown that emotional reactions and personal characteristics often take precedence in shaping risky behaviors (Loewenstein et al., 2001). One of the key psychological drivers of job-risking behavior is the concept of risk perception. People's assessment of the likelihood and severity of potential negative outcomes can significantly influence their willingness to take risks. People who perceive the risks associated with job-related decisions as lower, or who place a higher value on the potential benefits, may be more inclined to take such chances (Heimer, 1988). This risk perception can be influenced by a range of factors, including gender, personal experiences, cognitive biases, and emotional states. Affect, or the emotional response to a situation, also plays a crucial role in risk-taking behavior. People's feelings about a particular risk, whether it be fear, excitement, or a sense of thrill, can heavily sway their decision-making process. People who experience more positive affective reactions to job-related risks may be more likely to pursue them, even in the face of potential negative consequences. Additionally, narcissistic and extrovert personality traits as well as motivational factors can contribute to the propensity for job-risking behavior. For instance, those with a higher need for stimulation or a tendency toward impulsivity may be more drawn to the excitement and challenge of risky job-related decisions. Conversely, people with a strong sense of risk aversion or a focus on achieving specific goals may be less inclined to take such chances.

Employers are increasingly vigilant about identifying and filtering out potential employees who may engage in risky online behavior, recognizing that a single digital misstep can have lasting consequences for organizational reputation and internal culture. As the boundaries between personal and professional life continue to blur in online spaces, companies view applicants' digital footprints as a valuable form of behavioral data. Through pre-employment social media screenings and background checks, employers look for signs of poor judgment, discriminatory language, inflammatory political rhetoric, or engagement in activities that may conflict with corporate values or policies. This process is not only about assessing technical qualifications but also about evaluating alignment with workplace norms, public image, and risk management priorities. Employers are particularly cautious in sectors where trust, confidentiality, or public perception are central to operations, like healthcare, education, and customer service.

Background Checks

In the past, background checks focused on criminal records, employment history, and education verification. However, the rise of social media has prompted companies to expand their investigations into an applicant's online activity. Employers now routinely examine platforms such as Twitter, Facebook, LinkedIn, and TikTok for any content that might indicate misconduct, unprofessional behavior, or reputational risk. Information is evaluated to determine a potential employee's character, judgment, and alignment with institutional values. Business advisors have encouraged companies to find ethical and legal ways to use social media screening as part of their recruiting process to ensure candidates are a good fit for their open positions. This intense social screening has sparked debate over privacy, accountability, and the long-term implications of digital records.

Background check companies like Checkr https://checkr.com/ and GoodHire https://www.goodhire.com scour public records, social media, and the Internet to create an assessment of a potential employee's character. The analysis includes the use of toxic language, threats of violence, hate speech, insults and bullying, drug use or references to drugs, self-harm, explicit images, and racist comments or images. As hiring practices continue to integrate social media evaluations, individuals must navigate an increasingly interconnected professional landscape where their digital presence can impact current and future opportunities. Companies seek to mitigate risks by screening online behavior; however, they at the same time must balance accountability with fairness, ensuring that professional identity remains a reflection of an individual's skills and growth rather than a single digital misstep. Next, we explore how seemingly minor digital errors found in background checks can lead to significant consequences.

Naomi and NASA

In 2018 a college student, referred to as Naomi, excitedly announced to the world that she was awarded a coveted internship at NASA. The Tweet "EVERYONE SHUT THE FUCK UP ... I GOT ACCEPTED TO THE NASA INTERNSHIP" caught the attention of Homer Hickman. Hickman was not friends with Naomi on Twitter, but she had tagged NASA in her post, which drew Hickman's attention. He replied with only one word, "Language". Naomi, possibly running off the adrenaline of getting so close to her dream job, came back to say "Suck my dick and balls I'm working at NASA". At this point Naomi did not perceive any risk in her discourse. It was an information setting, X (formerly Twitter), and she assumed she was among a community of friends. However, the situation devolved from there as Naomi's friends, needing to support their friend and show allegiance, continued to post profanity laden insults on poor Mr. Hickman in the comments and use the hashtag #NASA as they did so.

Unbeknownst to Naomi and her friends, Mr. Hickman was a retired senior NASA-affiliated engineer. He was not connected to NASA's hiring process or their social media accounts, but when their exchange escalated, the visibility of the tweets and the tagging forced NASA to revoke her internship offer. After the incident, Naomi deleted her Tweets and reached out to Mr. Hickman to offer an apology. After a lengthy conversation, he determined it was just a momentary lapse in judgment that needn't derail Naomi from a promising career in aerospace engineering. Months after the dust had settled and the story cooled, he was quoted as saying, "I am certain she deserves a position in the aerospace industry and I'm doing all I can to secure her one that will be better than the one she lost" (Merrett, 2018).

Naomi's case is an example of how our friend groups play a powerful role in shaping how we behave and present ourselves on social media. The desire to belong and to maintain the connection with peers often guides what we post, share, or engage with online. This is a subtle but effective form of persuasion rooted in bonding, one of the key mechanisms that drive participation in digital spaces. When friends like, comment on, or share each other's content, they reinforce a sense of belonging and mutual validation, which encourages continued participation and conformity to group norms.

Claire and Deloitte

In 2020, Claira Janover, a Harvard University graduate, lost her job offer from Deloitte after a TikTok video she posted went viral. The video was created in the early summer of 2020, during the height of the Black Lives Matter movement. In the video, Janover made a controversial statement, "if anyone has the sheer entitled caucasity to say 'All Lives Matter', I'm gonna stab you" (Alexander, 2020). She later followed up with another TikTok accusing "Trumpers" of coming after her and getting her fired from her job. In the second video, she asserted that she was using hyperbole, an exaggerated metaphor, to emphasize the importance of the Black Lives Matter movement. Despite her clarification, the video's widespread attention led to public backlash. Janover attributed the rescinded job offer to a targeted campaign by supporters of then-President Donald Trump, whom she believed reported her video to Deloitte. Deloitte clarified that the position Janover was released from was an internship, not a full-time job, and that it was done as part of their "zero violence" policy.

Deloitte stated that they do not publicly comment on personnel matters but emphasized their commitment to fostering an inclusive and respectful environment.

Claire appeared to be driven by two competing motivations in her social media activity. As a multiracial woman navigating workplaces that were, at times, unwelcoming or overtly hostile, she demonstrated a heightened sensitivity to the use of the phrase "All Lives Matter", particularly when employed in ways that undermine or erase the experiences of people of color. Her decision to speak out can be understood within this broader context of social and racial tension. However, her response following the backlash to her posts reveals a contrasting dynamic. Rather than acknowledging the potential consequences of her impulsive tweets, Claire adopts a posture of victimization, deflecting responsibility and attributing her job loss to an imagined group of politically motivated individuals, namely, "Trumpers", whom she presumes alerted her employer. This reaction reflects a reluctance to engage in self-reflection and an oversimplification of the broader implications of digital expression in professional contexts.

Sarah and New York Times

Sarah Jeong, a journalist and former editorial board member of The New York Times, faced scrutiny over old tweets containing controversial remarks about white people. In August 2018 Jeong was hired as the lead technology writer for the Times. Almost immediately, right-wing critics began a smear campaign calling for her to be fired. The tweets, written from 2013 to 2015, referred to white people as "dogs" and "groveling goblins". She also frequently used the hashtag #cancelwhitepeople. Jeong went on the offensive and pointed out the context behind the tweets. She had been racially targeted and harassed on Twitter and her responding posts were "imitating the rhetoric of her harassers" (Peiser, 2018). In response to her critics, the New York Times issued a statement days later confirming they had hired Jeong knowing about the offensive tweets. They went on to say they did not condone her past tweets and had a conversation with her about her social media history before she was hired. Jeong eventually apologized for the tweets and claimed they were a satirical response to the period of intense online harassment she had endured. Unlike Naomi H and Claire Janover, Sarah Jeong retained her position.

In Sarah's case, her established membership within a professional community, specifically that of journalists, afforded her a degree of grace and understanding that the other two women did not receive. Her inclusion in this network provided her with both credibility and protection; she was perceived not only as an insider but also as someone who had earned a voice within the field. Within the framework of participatory culture, membership is not only about contribution; it's about shared norms, mutual support, and collective identity. Because Sarah had already engaged meaningfully with her community, the social bonds she had formed helped contextualize her past online behavior. Rather than being seen purely as a liability, her actions were interpreted within a broader narrative of professional growth and community trust. This illustrates that while digital missteps can have real consequences, those consequences are often mediated by a person's social standing within participatory networks. Membership offers a form of reputational cushioning; it allows for mistakes to be seen as lapses rather than defining traits. Sarah's experience underscores the importance of digital relationships and professional community in shaping not just participation, but also how accountability is negotiated in public and professional spaces.

Coby Crist and "Salty" TikToks

In 2023, Coby Crist, a 32-year-old employee of AJS in Des Moines – a ServiceMaster franchise specializing in disaster cleanup – garnered attention for a series of TikTok videos he posted during work hours. These videos included frequent use of racial slurs, offensive gestures shared with coworkers, and the use of inappropriate emojis while filming inside clients' homes. Despite receiving multiple warnings from his supervisor to cease the behavior, Crist persisted and was ultimately terminated in December 2023. He later filed a wrongful termination lawsuit against his employer, but the judge ruled in favor of the company, citing that Crist's actions demonstrated a blatant disregard for client privacy and severely compromised the business's reputation.

Crist's case reflects a broader cultural phenomenon in which the desire to "go viral" can override professional judgment and ethical boundaries. Social media platforms reward attention-seeking behavior through likes, shares, and follower counts, creating a persuasive environment that encourages risky or outrageous content. In pursuit of digital recognition, Crist appeared to prioritize online visibility over workplace standards, illustrating how the pressure to participate in viral trends can lead to poor decision-making. His situation underscores the importance of digital literacy, not only in understanding platform mechanics but also in recognizing the real-world consequences of online behavior, particularly when professional responsibilities and public trust are at stake.

Monitoring

Employers have access to a growing array of sophisticated surveillance technologies designed to monitor employee behavior both online and within the physical workspace. Beyond traditional closed-circuit cameras, organizations now utilize advanced digital tools capable of tracking online activity, keystrokes, browser history, and application usage in real time. Increasingly, supervisors are also authorized to review employees' public social media content for posts or comments that may reflect poorly on the company or conflict with organizational values. In addition to reputational concerns, productivity monitoring has emerged as a central motivation for workplace surveillance. A study conducted by Action Network, one of the largest sports betting platforms, estimates that U.S. businesses lose approximately $20 billion in productivity during the week of March Madness alone, with 23% of the workforce either calling in sick or engaging with games during work hours (Ferraro, 2025). In response, many companies are adopting proactive measures such as browser lockdown systems, tracking software, and user monitoring tools to limit distractions and capture online behaviors. These developments raise important questions about employee privacy, workplace trust, and the ethical balance between corporate oversight and individual autonomy.

Sacked for Googling

Josh Williams, a customer service representative in Bristol, England, was called into his supervisor's office after just three months on the job. His supervisor proceeded to review pages of search history during his time at work. In total, Josh had searched over 50 hours for things like Simon Cowell's botched Botox and does getting your teeth fixed in Turkey hurt. Williams was still on probation for his job when he was fired for defrauding the company of time worked and excessive sick time. In an act of brilliance, insert sarcasm, Josh decided to make a TikTok about being sacked in the hopes of either monetizing his account or receiving donations to pay his rent until he landed his next job. The move backfired when he started receiving disparaging comments on his TikTok calling him "stupid" for not just using his phone for online searches at work and "too old" to be making such mistakes. His video ended up going viral in the U.K., and as a result, Josh had a difficult time finding office work and had to settle for a job in construction. He admitted regretting the move but remained bitter that potential employers refused to overlook a one-time lapse in judgment (The Economic Times, 2022).

Counting Keystrokes

In 2023, an Australian insurance company, Insurance Australia Group (IAG), made headlines after it terminated several employees for underperformance based on keystroke monitoring software. The company had installed a digital productivity tool on employees' computers that measured typing frequency and activity during scheduled work hours. One employee, who challenged the dismissal, brought her case before Australia's Fair Work Commission. The tribunal upheld the termination, noting that the keystroke data revealed significant periods of inactivity, which contradicted the employee's reported work output (Sibthorpe, 2023). This case highlights a growing trend among employers to use surveillance software to monitor remote workers, particularly in post-pandemic hybrid and work-from-home environments. While companies argue that such measures are necessary for accountability and productivity, critics raise concerns about privacy, trust, and the psychological impact of being constantly watched. The IAG case serves as a cautionary example of how digital surveillance can directly shape employment decisions and workplace culture in the age of algorithmic oversight.

Students' Identities

Up to this point, our focus has been on professionals and the impact of digital identity in the workplace; however, students must also be proactive in managing and safeguarding their online presence. In an era where digital footprints are permanent, searchable, and often shared beyond their original audience, every post, comment, and image becomes part of your emerging personal brand. For students who are in the early stages of building academic and professional reputations, the stakes can be especially high. A single lapse in judgment, whether in tone, content, or timing, can have lasting consequences, from damaged relationships with peers or faculty to lost internships, scholarships, or job opportunities. Just as your achievements contribute to your digital identity, so too do your missteps. Curating a thoughtful and authentic online presence means not only being mindful of what you post and share, but also how others tag, quote, or represent you in digital spaces. Developing responsible social media habits early on can help you build a strong, reputable presence that supports your future ambitions rather than hindering them.

Defamation

In January 2019, Nick Sandmann, a 16-year-old student from Covington Catholic High School in Kentucky, was thrust into the national spotlight after a brief viral video captured his encounter with Native American activist Nathan Phillips at the Lincoln Memorial. The clip showed Sandmann, wearing a "Make America Great Again" hat, standing silently face-to-face with Phillips, who was playing a ceremonial drum. Initial reports from major media outlets portrayed the moment as one of open confrontation and disrespect, suggesting that Sandmann and his classmates were mocking Phillips. However, extended footage and subsequent interviews revealed a more complex scene involving multiple groups, including a third party that had instigated tensions before the encounter. This evolving context challenged the initial framing and highlighted the dangers of drawing conclusions from limited visual evidence (Chappell, 2019).

The resulting media firestorm had lasting implications for Sandmann's personal and professional future. In response to what they viewed as misrepresentation, Sandmann and his family filed defamation lawsuits against several major news organizations, including CNN and The Washington Post. While some lawsuits were dismissed, others resulted in confidential multi-million-dollar settlements. The case underscores the profound influence of viral media and the lasting effects of public mischaracterization. It also serves as a cautionary example of how digital narratives, when shaped by incomplete information and rapid dissemination, can dramatically alter the course of a young person's life.

Deportation

In March 2024, a student identified as attending Durham College in Ontario, Canada, faced potential deportation after posting a series of inflammatory TikTok videos expressing support for Hamas, a group designated as a terrorist organization by the Canadian government. In the since-deleted videos, the student is quoted as saying, "I would love it if they would do it again, and again, and again", in reference to the October 7, 2023, Hamas-led attacks against Israeli civilians. Given the serious national security concerns associated with any endorsement of terrorism, Canadian immigration officials opened an investigation to determine whether her statements violated immigration laws, which prohibit support for or association with terrorist organizations (Kelly, 2023). This case highlights how online speech, particularly when posted in public forums, can carry serious legal and personal consequences, especially for non-citizens studying or working abroad.

This incident is not isolated. In recent years, several international students have been denied entry into the United States due to concerning social media content. U.S. Customs and Border Protection agents are authorized to review public social media profiles as part of visa screenings. In one widely reported case from 2019, a Harvard-bound Palestinian student was denied entry at Boston Logan International Airport after officials allegedly found social media posts from people on his friend list that were critical of the U.S. government. Although the student denied authoring or endorsing the content, his visa was revoked, and he was sent back to Lebanon before eventually being allowed to return. These examples demonstrate how digital footprints, including not only personal posts but also the actions of one's online friend network, can significantly affect one's ability to study or work abroad. In an era where borders are increasingly policed through digital evidence, students must recognize that their online activity is not just personal expression; it can become a determinant to academic and professional mobility.

College Admissions

Cleaning up your social media accounts early in your academic career is a smart move. Even once in a college or university, you'll want to remain proactive in maintaining your personal brand. For students in performing arts or sports, this is doubly as endorsement deals rely heavily on your social media following and image. Here are some things to consider when maintaining your professional/academic identity. Audit your accounts by Googling yourself regularly to see what comes up. You may be surprised to see old pictures from past achievements. Check all your social media accounts, even those you think you may have closed. We often lose track of old accounts and reviewing them may reveal the need to delete or deactivate them. For accounts that you want to keep open, look through the posts and delete any inappropriate content. Consider un-tagging yourself from questionable posts or images others have shared of you. Review your own past comments, likes, and shares to see if there is anything you'd like to delete as it might be misinterpreted. Adjust your privacy settings to either limit your accounts to private or control who can comment on or share what you post. If you choose to keep an account public, ensure only positive and professional content is visible. Whenever possible, avoid getting into online arguments or posting impulsively. Finally, maintain a clean and professional digital presence that aligns with your future college and career goals.

Privacy

As digital technologies become increasingly embedded in the workplace, the line between professional obligations and personal privacy is becoming more difficult to define. Employers now have powerful tools at their disposal to monitor employee behavior both on and off the clock. From reviewing public social media activity to installing keystroke tracking software and browser monitoring systems, organizations are seeking greater visibility into employee conduct. These practices are often justified as necessary for maintaining productivity, protecting company reputation, and ensuring alignment with organizational values. However, they also raise serious concerns about employee autonomy, consent, and the right to a private life.

Many employees assume their personal online activity, particularly on platforms used outside of work, is off-limits to employer scrutiny. Yet the reality is far more complex. Public posts, controversial comments, or even associations with certain online communities can be used in hiring decisions or as grounds for termination. In some cases, surveillance extends into remote work environments, where tracking tools may monitor screen time, application usage, and even webcam activity. These practices create a culture of constant observation that can erode trust, increase stress, and diminish morale.

Laws governing workplace surveillance and digital privacy vary significantly by country:

- United States: There are few federal protections for employees when it comes to digital monitoring. Employers are generally allowed to track activity on company-owned devices and accounts. Social media content, even when posted outside of work, may be considered in hiring or firing decisions if it's public. The Electronic Communications Privacy Act (ECPA) offers limited protections, but private employers often operate within wide legal boundaries.
- European Union: The General Data Protection Regulation (GDPR) provides some of the world's strongest privacy protections. Employers must clearly inform employees about data collection practices, justify the purpose of monitoring, and ensure data minimization. Surveillance must be proportional and respect the fundamental right to privacy, even in workplace settings.
- Canada: Privacy in the workplace is regulated by both federal and provincial laws. The Personal Information Protection and Electronic Documents Act (PIPEDA) requires that employers have a legitimate reason for collecting personal information and that they obtain informed consent, especially in the private sector.
- Australia: Surveillance is governed by state-based legislation. In New South Wales, for example, the Workplace Surveillance Act 2005 mandates that employers must notify workers if they intend to use

surveillance technologies. Covert surveillance is prohibited without a court order.

- India: While data privacy laws are still evolving, the Digital Personal Data Protection Act (DPDPA) of 2023 aims to provide greater transparency and control over personal data. However, enforcement and clarity around employee monitoring remain limited, especially in private employment.
- Brazil: The Lei Geral de Proteção de Dados (LGPD), modeled after the GDPR, came into effect in 2020. It grants individuals the right to know how their data is collected and used, including in workplace settings.

While much attention is given to employee surveillance, students are increasingly subject to digital monitoring and content scrutiny, both within educational institutions and through immigration or scholarship agencies. As young people navigate identity development, academic goals, and social participation online, the question of how much privacy they're entitled to, and how much they surrender, is critically important.

Schools and universities often justify digital monitoring in the name of safety, discipline, and reputation management. In the United States, the Family Educational Rights and Privacy Act (FERPA) protects students' educational records but does not extend to content shared voluntarily on public digital platforms. As we have seen, institutions may monitor student social media activity, particularly when posts reference violence, harassment, or hate speech. Some schools even use third-party tools to track mentions of their name across platforms. While these practices aim to preempt harm, they can also chill free expression, particularly for students from marginalized backgrounds who may engage in political or cultural critique.

International students face even more complex surveillance. As noted earlier, visa applications and border screenings can involve the review of public online profiles. Cases have emerged in which students were denied entry to the United States or Canada based on content shared by themselves that was perceived as politically sensitive or in violation of national security norms. These actions raise concerns about fairness, intent, and the permanence of online content.

Privacy rights for students vary by country and context. The GDPR in the EU provides stronger protections for minors and young adults, especially around consent and data erasure (the "right to be forgotten"). In contrast, countries like the United States offer limited recourse if students are penalized for public posts, even those made during adolescence.

BOX 7.1 CASE STUDY

Some of us find ourselves sharing selfies and TikTok dances during our working hours. Our employer may have no problem with us having fun on the job; however, others may forbid anything other than work-related activity during an employee's shift. The blurring of our social identity with our professional identity can make it difficult to exercise sound judgment in what to share and what not. Take, for example, the case of several emergency room nurses in a New York City hospital.

The nurses were responding to a man having been pushed, fallen, or intentionally jumped in front of the number 6 subway train. They worked frantically for almost an hour to address the man's multiple injuries, including severe internal bleeding. Unfortunately, they were unable to save him, and he was pronounced dead an hour and a half after arrival.

We will never know what possessed one nurse to take the following photo, let alone post it to Instagram with the hashtag #man vs 6 train. The following day, the nurse was called into hospital administration where she was fired for a lack of sensitivity to and privacy rights of a patient in her care.

FIGURE 7.1 Screenshot of an Instagram post captioned "#man vs 6 train".

Conclusion

The digital age has transformed the landscape of professional identity, turning our online behavior into a key factor in hiring decisions, workplace culture, and long-term career prospects. As this chapter has shown, the line between personal and professional has become increasingly porous, with social media posts, comments, and even "likes" serving as indicators of character, judgment, and values. Employers now use a range of surveillance tools, from keystroke tracking to social media background checks, to monitor both productivity and public perception. While these measures aim to protect organizational integrity, they also raise important questions about privacy, fairness, and consent.

Case studies like Naomi's revoked NASA internship, Claire Janover's lost offer at Deloitte, and Josh Williams's viral termination reveal how a single digital misstep, whether impulsive, performative, or misinterpreted, can derail even the most promising careers. Yet Sarah Jeong's experience reminds us that context, community membership, and perceived value within a professional network can sometimes mitigate backlash. These examples underscore the complex interplay between digital culture, participatory norms, and reputational risk.

Ultimately, building and maintaining a strong professional identity requires more than just caution; it demands self-awareness, intentionality, and ethical digital citizenship. Students and professionals alike must recognize that their online presence is not only a form of self-expression but also a long-term investment in how they're seen by institutions, employers, and peers. A thoughtful, values-aligned digital identity has become an essential career asset in today's interconnected world.

Exercise

Read this story https://time.com/5663283/harvard-student-visa-ismail-ajjawi-lebanon/. Now read this one https://breaolindawildcat.com/4638/showcase/think-before-you-click-social-media-posts-impact-college-admissions/. Answer the following:

- Psychology and sociology research suggests we reflect our closest friends. Think about your closest friendships. Think about things you've seen that those friends have posted or shared online. Now reflect on whether that is any reflection on who you are.
- Why should Ismail Ajjawi have been denied entry into the United States?
- Why shouldn't Ismail Ajjawi have been denied entry into the United States?

- Why should college admissions officers review prospective students' social media accounts?
- Why shouldn't college admissions officers review prospective students' social media accounts?

References

Alexander, H. (2020). Harvard Grad who blamed Trump supporters for getting her fired from "Dream job" at Deloitte after "all lives matter" tiktok stab video did not work for accountancy firm. *Daily Mail Online*. https://www.dailymail.co.uk/news/article-8487049/Deloitte-says-Harvard-grad-blamed-Trump-supporters-losing-dream-job-internship.html

Chappell, B. (2019). Differing narratives after standoff between Native American man, high school student. *NPR*. https://www.npr.org/2019/01/21/687134573/differing-narratives-after-standoff-between-native-american-man-high-school-stud

Ferraro, B. (2025). March madness could potentially cost US economy up to $20 billion due to "lost productivity," survey finds. *Fox Business*. https://www.foxbusiness.com/media/march-madness-potentially-cost-us-economy-up-20-billion-due-lost-productivity-per-survey

Heimer, C. A. (1988). Social structure, psychology, and the estimation of risk. *Annual Review of Sociology*, *14*(1), 491–517.

Kelly, T. (2023). "I support Hamas": Durham College condemns alleged student who posts video saying "I would love it if they would do it again and again…" *Toronto Star*. https://www.thestar.com/news/i-support-hamas-durham-college-condemns-alleged-student-who-posts-video-saying-i-would-love/article_ebe99611-cffa-59b8-b646-e8e5a1945ef1.html

Loewenstein, G., Weber, E. U., Hsee, C. K., & Welch, N. (2001). Risk as feelings. *Psychological Bulletin*, *127*(2), 267–286.

Merrett, R. (2018). Woman loses prized NASA internship over vulgar tweet – but she might get a better position. *People.com*. https://people.com/human-interest/woman-loses-nasa-internship-over-tweet/

Peiser, J. (2018). Times stands by editorial board member after outcry over old tweets. *New York Times*. https://www.nytimes.com/2018/08/02/business/media/sarah-jeong-new-york-times.html#.

Sibthorpe, C. (2023). Woman fired after company uses keystroke technology to monitor her work from home. *New York Post*. https://nypost.com/2023/08/08/woman-fired-after-company-uses-keystroke-technology-to-monitor-her-work-from-home

The Economic Times. (2022). Fired for googling? Man loses job for "stupid" searches during work. It's not what you expect. *The Economic Times*. https://economictimes.indiatimes.com/magazines/panache/fired-for-googling-man-loses-job-for-stupid-searches-during-work-its-not-what-you-expect/articleshow/113868647.cms?from=mdr

8

CIVIC IDENTITY

The Surveillance State and Personal Autonomy

What if you were wrongly accused of a crime and it was a street surveillance camera that ultimately proved your innocence? Would you then support surveillance, even if it meant sacrificing some degree of personal autonomy? This simple scenario reveals a complex truth: The technologies that promise protection can also pose significant threats to civil liberties and personal identity. Across the globe, people are grappling with this trade-off between safety and freedom in the digital age, often without fully realizing the implications for their civic identity.

Your civic identity, how you see yourself as a member of a political community, is increasingly shaped by the digital tools and platforms that mediate your participation in society. Whether you're voting, protesting, posting online, or simply moving through a city, your behaviors are monitored, categorized, and stored. In some countries, using the Internet or owning a smartphone can be enough to put your life at risk. In authoritarian regimes, citizens have been imprisoned, tortured, or disappeared simply for what they searched, posted, or messaged online.

Surveillance

Surveillance refers to the monitoring of behavior, activities, or information for the purpose of gathering data, influencing, managing, or protecting. Governments see their role in surveillance as a protector. However, organizations around the world, like Citizens Lab and Human Rights Watch, have investigated governments' activities around citizen surveillance. They've concluded that beyond protection, government surveillance

DOI: 10.4324/9781003539445-9

seeks to mold civic identities through influence, management, and censorship. Our civic identities can be compromised through social media interactions, going about our daily lives, or talking on the phone.

Governments around the world have increasingly begun to use cameras in public spaces to monitor citizens' activities to enhance security, deter crime, and manage traffic. However, cameras are not the only way governments surveil their citizens. Advanced technologies have allowed them to infiltrate phones, computers, and homes potentially without impunity. The pervasive presence of surveillance cameras can lead to a sense of constant monitoring, infringing on individuals' privacy rights and creating a chilling effect on free expression and behavior. This has given rise to conspiracy theories around government surveillance, suggesting that such measures are part of broader schemes to control and suppress citizens, further eroding trust in public institutions. Let's take a closer look at the issue of surveillance around the world. We'll start with the United States.

US Government Surveillance

Secure communication, free from spying eyes, is the gold standard many of us expect when we use our phones to send a text or share an image. That is due in part to the computer program invented by Philip Zimmerman in 1991. Pretty Good Privacy (PGP) was an encryption program designed to protect electronic communications. At the time, U.S. trade regulations classified cryptographic software as munitions, restricting their distribution. As a result, Zimmerman faced a federal investigation for violating the Arms Export Control Act when he allowed the program to be openly shared worldwide (Zimmermann, 2021). PGP's introduction marked an advancement in securing digital communications. At present, messaging applications like WhatsApp and Telegram do not directly implement PGP, but the principles underlying PGP have influenced contemporary encryption programs. These applications employ end-to-end encryption to ensure that only the communicating users can read the messages, enhancing privacy and security in digital communications (Five Blockchains, 2024).

Americans have always held to a conspiracy theory that their government listened in on their conversations and could even hack into their computers and download files. In 2013 some of those theories were proven fact. Edward Snowden, a former contractor for the National Security Agency (NSA), disclosed classified documents to journalists Glenn Greenwald, Laura Poitras, and Ewen MacAskill, revealing the extent of U.S. government surveillance programs. He provided them with thousands of documents detailing the NSA's mass surveillance program. His leaks exposed mass data collection efforts, including the PRISM program, which allowed intelligence agencies to access user data from major technology companies. These revelations raised global concerns about privacy and government oversight. Following the disclosures, U.S. authorities charged Snowden with violating the Espionage Act. To avoid prosecution, he fled to Hong Kong before seeking asylum in multiple countries. After his U.S. passport was revoked, he remained in Russia, where he was eventually granted permanent residency (Bell & Rushe, 2013).

Government Surveillance around the World

International law establishes clear protections against government surveillance that infringes on privacy rights. The Universal Declaration of Human Rights (UDHR) Article 12 explicitly states that no one shall face arbitrary interference with their privacy, family, home, or correspondence. The International Covenant on Civil and Political Rights (ICCPR) Article 17 reinforces this principle by prohibiting unlawful or arbitrary intrusions into an individual's private life. Despite these protections, governments have expanded surveillance programs, often citing national security concerns. For example, the European Court of Human Rights (ECHR) ruled in 2018 that the United Kingdom's bulk interception of communications under the Regulation of Investigatory Powers Act violated privacy rights because it lacked adequate safeguards against abuse.

Examining the implications of these laws, consider how courts and international bodies respond to government surveillance. The United Nations Human Rights Committee (UNHRC) has emphasized that surveillance must comply with principles of legality, necessity, and proportionality. In 2020, the Court of Justice of the European Union (CJEU) ruled that mass data retention laws in France, Belgium, and the United Kingdom violated EU privacy protections because they lacked sufficient oversight. If governments justify surveillance by invoking security threats, they must prove that measures align with international legal standards. Without proper oversight, broad surveillance powers risk undermining our rights, reinforcing the need for legal accountability.

Surveillance in Action

Government surveillance of citizens has been documented for decades, yet the extent and sophistication of modern state monitoring continue to raise significant concerns. While earlier fears of wiretapping and covert surveillance were often dismissed as fringe conspiracy theories, a growing body of investigative work from global watchdog organizations has revealed that many of these fears are well-founded. Today, surveillance is not limited to crime prevention or national security; it's increasingly used as a political tool to control, intimidate, and silence dissent. Authoritarian regimes have embraced surveillance technologies to monitor citizens' digital footprints, track political activity, and suppress opposition movements before they gain traction.

In authoritarian regimes, surveillance is not merely about data; it's a mechanism of control. Tools such as the Pegasus spyware, developed by the Israeli company NSO Group, have been sold to governments and used to infiltrate the phones of journalists, human rights activists, and political dissidents. In countries like Saudi Arabia, Mexico, India, and Morocco, Pegasus has reportedly been deployed to monitor conversations, extract personal data, and track individuals' movements, often without judicial oversight. These invasive tactics demonstrate how digital surveillance becomes a tool of intimidation, stifling dissent and reinforcing authoritarian governance.

Cases from the United Kingdom, Syria, Tibet, and Ethiopia illustrate the various ways governments weaponize surveillance. In Syria and Ethiopia, for instance, activists have been detained, tortured, or "disappeared" after government intelligence intercepted private communications. In Tibet, China's extensive surveillance infrastructure, ranging from facial recognition to mobile data tracking, has turned entire communities into sites of constant state observation, eroding cultural identity and stifling civic expression. Even in democratic nations like the United Kingdom, programs like the Government Communications Headquarters' data collection have sparked controversy over mass surveillance and the erosion of individual rights.

These examples underscore the deep impact surveillance has on civic identity. When citizens know they're being watched, it alters how they engage in political discourse, whether they protest, and how freely they express themselves online or in public. Surveillance fosters a culture of fear and self-censorship – one in which civic participation becomes a calculated risk. In authoritarian contexts, this fear is compounded by the very real possibility of retaliation, making digital surveillance not just a privacy issue, but a human rights concern. Ultimately, unchecked government monitoring threatens the foundational freedoms of expression, association, and belief that define civic identity in democratic societies.

January 6th Rioters

On January 6, 2021, President Donald J. Trump held a rally at the National Mall in Washington, D.C. to contest the election results to a crowd of around 80,000 people. Shortly after his speech, the crowd splintered off. Security cameras placed on major streets across D.C. showed people carrying United States, Trump 2020, and "Don't Tread on Me" on me flags as they dispersed. Approximately 3000 of them marched to the Capitol grounds to continue their protest. Security cameras, located at the entrances of the Capitol building, showed varying levels of aggression. The main entrance off the Mall was a scene of smoke, raised fists, and breaking windows. Meanwhile, the areas to the left and behind the Capitol told a different story. Raw footage on YouTube https://youtu.be/jBRJmnvFfo8?si=gNIue1ZjXKJR_cmB shows families with young children and young professional women in suits milling about the walkways and stairs leading to the Capitol after barricades had been removed by the more militant protestors. A majority of the 700 protestors who had trespassed, vandalized, harassed police, or stole Capitol property were identified through security cameras and their own social media posts. This was because the rioters had used social media to connect and create what scholars refer to as a "networked incitement" (Donovan, 2024).

FIGURE 8.1 Facebook post from individuals on January 6, 2021, at the steps of the US Capitol building.

Laurence Fox vs. Ulez Street Cameras

In the United Kingdom, laws have been enacted that make online posts related to race, medicine, climate denying, and gender subject to incarceration. In October 2023, former TV news commentator and political activist Laurence Fox was arrested by London police on suspicion of conspiring to commit criminal damage to Ultra Low Emission Zone (ULEZ) cameras and encouraging others to do the same (Topping, 2023). The ULEZ cameras, implemented in London, monitor vehicle emissions to reduce air pollution by charging drivers of non-compliant vehicles. Prior to his arrest, Fox appeared on the video streaming platform Rumble, expressing support for groups dismantling ULEZ cameras and indicating his intention to participate personally. During the police search of his residence, Fox broadcast the event live on X (formerly known as Twitter), sharing footage of officers at his home.

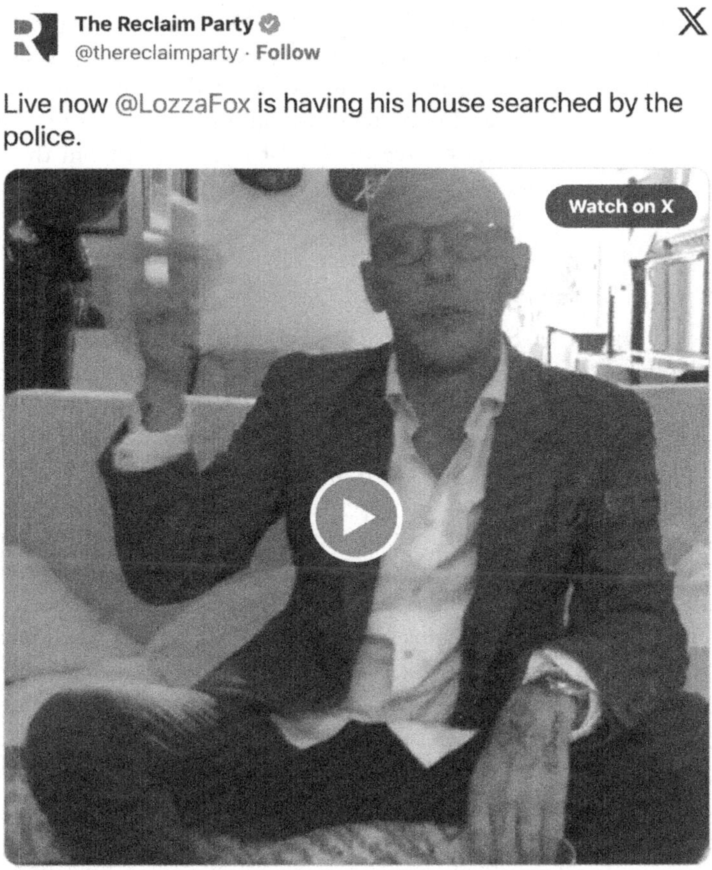

FIGURE 8.2 Laurence Fox livestreaming on X during his arrest.

Tadesse Kersmo vs. FinFisher Spyware

Dr. Tadesse Kersmo, a prominent Ethiopian opposition figure and member of the banned Ginbot 7 movement, was targeted by the Ethiopian government using FinFisher spyware. This sophisticated surveillance tool was used to monitor his emails and online activities while he was in exile in the United Kingdom. The primary targets of this spyware campaign were Ethiopian dissidents, activists, and opposition members, both within Ethiopia and abroad. The Ethiopian government targeted these individuals to suppress political dissent.

An email included the spyware, an executable file disguised as a .jpg image of Dr. Kersmo and other dissidents at a meeting. It was spread around the globe as activists and government opposition members shared infected email. Once activated, the spyware allowed the Ethiopian government to monitor the documents, emails, and other electronic communications of the infected devices. This resulted in gathering intelligence on the activities and communications of these opposition figures to undermine their efforts to organize and advocate for reforms. Some of those who lived abroad were successfully extradited back to Ethiopia and sentenced to 15+ years in prison. Others continue to live in fear of retribution from the current Ethiopian government.

"Fatima" vs. the Assad Regime

The Assad regime of Syria engaged in a 15-year civil war against insurgents. Under President Assad's rule, Syria had experienced widespread human rights abuses, including arbitrary arrests, detention without trial, torture, extrajudicial killings, enforced disappearances, sexual violence, and extensive surveillance. In March 2011, influenced by the Arab Spring's pro-democracy movements, a group of schoolchildren in Daraa, a city in southern Syria, painted anti-government slogans on their school wall. Their subsequent arrest and torture by authorities ignited local protests demanding their release. These peaceful demonstrations quickly spread across the country, with citizens calling for freedom, dignity, and the end of Assad's regime. As the protests grew, the Syrian government responded with increasing military force against demonstrators, leading to a full-scale armed conflict.

Fatima, a Syrian journalist, has faced relentless harassment, threats, and blacklisting for her work, which covers anti-regime groups, freedom of expression, and gender issues. Forced to flee her home country due to these threats, she continues to endure online and offline harassment even in exile in the United Kingdom. Since 2011, Fatima has been targeted with digital attacks, disinformation, and sexist abuse aimed at silencing her. Accusations of being a "Western agent" for not wearing a hijab and derogatory comments about her working-class background have intensified the attacks. Despite fleeing to the United Kingdom, she faces physical stalking and repeated hacking attempts on her social media and email accounts, with warnings of state-sponsored digital attacks reminding her that repression knows no borders. The threats come from both the regime and anti-regime groups she criticized, leaving her distrustful of fellow Syrians. Her family, including her daughter and uncle, has also been targeted, with social media comments mentioning her young daughter as leverage to silence her. Fatima's family members have urged her to stay quiet, adding to the pressure from regime supporters and her own family (Citizen Lab Staff, 2024).

Iranian Expats vs. the IRGC

Authoritarian regimes increasingly deploy transnational strategies to monitor, intimidate, and even physically threaten dissidents living abroad. One of the most visible examples of this trend is the case of Masih Alinejad, an Iranian-American journalist and human rights activist known for her outspoken criticism of the Iranian government, particularly its mandatory hijab laws and broader restrictions on civil liberties.

Alinejad's activism began with online campaigns such as My Stealthy Freedom, which encouraged Iranian women to share photos of themselves without hijabs in defiance of the regime (X@AlinejadMasih). As her platform grew internationally, she became a target of the Iranian state. The Islamic Revolutionary Guard Corps (IRGC) has been linked to several plots against her, including a foiled 2021 kidnapping attempt in which agents planned to abduct her from her home in New York and transport her to Iran via a third country. In 2022, another assassination plot was uncovered, revealing the persistence and reach of the Iranian regime's efforts to silence her. In February 2025, the United States successfully prosecuted two men in connection with the attempted assassination plot; they're currently awaiting sentencing (Gainer, 2025).

These operations rely not only on physical surveillance but also on cyber intrusion, disinformation campaigns, and harassment of family members who remain in Iran. Alinejad has been subject to online smear campaigns, phishing attempts, and state-sponsored media attacks, all designed to delegitimize her work and discourage civic dissent among the Iranian diaspora. Unfortunately, her case is far from unique. Masih Alinejad is one of hundreds of Iranian expatriates who have been surveilled, harassed, or targeted by the IRGC in efforts to suppress dissent and intimidate global advocacy networks. The Iranian regime's transnational repression tactics illustrate the dangerous intersection of digital surveillance, civic identity, and authoritarian control in the 21st century.

Digital Civic Watchdogs

Government actions to suppress online civic identity and instances of voter fraud present significant challenges to democratic processes worldwide. In several African nations, authorities have deliberately disrupted Internet access during elections, effectively silencing opposition voices and restricting citizens' access to information. For instance, in August 2021, Zambia ordered an Internet shutdown during its election period, joining countries like the Republic of Congo, Burundi, Togo, Guinea, Tanzania, and Uganda in employing such tactics (Streamlau and Dobson, 2022). These shutdowns hinder communication among opposition groups and prevent the dissemination of electoral information, undermining the transparency and fairness of the electoral process.

According to "Access Now", an international group devoted to tracking government censorship through Internet service interruptions, Africa reached a record high in 2024, with 21 shutdowns across 15 countries (Rosson et al., 2025). Governments often justify these actions as necessary for maintaining public order or national security; however, they disproportionately affect opposition parties and civil society organizations by limiting their ability to mobilize support and monitor electoral integrity. Such measures not only violate citizens' rights to freedom of expression and access to information but also erode public trust in democratic institutions.

In the United States, large-scale voter fraud is rare; however, various scams targeting voters have been documented. Scammers posing as election officials may contact individuals by phone, email, or in person, requesting them to update their voter registration or participate in fake surveys to extract personal information (National Association of Secretaries of State, 2021). These tactics can lead to identity theft and financial loss, compromising the integrity of the electoral process. Criminals have also solicited donations for fake political causes and nonexistent campaigns.

Citizen Lab https://citizenlab.ca, based at the University of Toronto, is an interdisciplinary research group dedicated to investigating the intersection of human rights, global security, and digital technologies. Their work focuses on the areas of surveillance and government spying. They have exposed numerous instances of state-sponsored digital espionage, including the use of sophisticated spyware to monitor activists, journalists, and political opponents. For example, in 2024 they uncovered the Ontario police using Israeli spyware and the deployment of nation-state spyware in

Turkey and Syria. Through investigative research, Citizen Lab highlights the technical methods and implications of surveillance practices, advocating for stronger protections for digital human rights and informing policy debates worldwide.

Government Data Breaches: Personal and Societal Impacts

Government data breaches have far-reaching consequences, not only for those affected but also for the broader fabric of civic life. One of the most immediate and devastating effects is the risk of identity theft and financial fraud. When sensitive information such as Social Security numbers, biometric data, bank account details, or background check records is compromised, it becomes an asset for cybercriminals and even hostile foreign actors. This data can be used to open fraudulent credit accounts, file false tax returns, or impersonate someone in more sophisticated schemes. In such cases, the damage is not only financial; it's reputational and deeply personal.

A significant example occurred in 2015 when the U.S. Office of Personnel Management (OPM) was breached, resulting in the compromise of personal data for approximately 21.5 million individuals, including federal employees, contractors, and their families. The leaked information included Social Security numbers, fingerprint data, and detailed security clearance forms posing a long-term national security concern (U.S. Office of Personnel Management, 2015). Globally, similar breaches have had equally devastating consequences. In India, a 2019 breach exposed over 275 million citizen records from a poorly secured MongoDB database. The stolen information included names, gender, contact details, employment and education histories, and current salary data (Gatlan, 2019). Meanwhile, in China, what is believed to be the largest data breach in history occurred in 2022 when a Shanghai police database was hacked. Over one billion personal records were stolen and sold on the dark web, revealing highly sensitive details such as ID numbers, phone numbers, residential addresses, photographs, and even criminal case histories (Zheng, 2022).

These incidents highlight more than just lapses in data security; they represent a profound breach of public trust. When governments fail to protect the data of their citizens, it undermines confidence in state institutions and calls into question the state's ability to safeguard not only digital systems but also the very civic identities of its people. For many, this erosion of trust has long-term consequences on how they engage with government services and participate in digital civic life. Moreover, the personal cost of recovering from identity theft is not evenly distributed. While some people may have the resources to hire legal support or invest in identity protection services, others do not. The average estimated cost of recovering from identity theft is around $1,200 USD, which includes time off work, filing police reports, contacting financial institutions, and replacing stolen identification documents. For lower-income individuals, the costs are not only financial; they may experience emotional distress, job insecurity, and prolonged legal entanglements as a result. Ultimately, data breaches are not just technical failures; they are civic disruptions. They compromise privacy, destabilize lives, and weaken the social contract between governments and the people they serve. In an era where data is central to how we verify, participate, and exist in public life, the stakes for protecting that data have never been higher.

Government Censorship

When governments control what information you can access, they exert powerful influence over how you see yourself as a citizen. Your civic identity, your beliefs, behaviors, and sense of responsibility within a society, is largely shaped by the information you encounter. Whether you are reading a news article, watching a protest unfold online, or sharing a post about a political issue, you are participating in a collective process of democratic (or undemocratic) expression. Censorship interferes with that process by dictating which ideas are visible, which voices are silenced, and which narratives are allowed to shape your understanding of the world.

As we have seen, governments across the political spectrum have employed censorship to suppress dissent, manipulate public opinion, and preserve the dominant political order. While the strategies differ, ranging from Internet blackouts to legal prosecution and algorithmic suppression, the effect remains the same: censorship molds your civic identity by narrowing the scope of what you're allowed to think, say, and do as a member of a political community.

Psychological Effects of Information Control

You may assume that censorship simply means preventing access to certain websites or social media posts. It works far more subtly. When dissenting opinions are removed, when search results are manipulated, or when controversial content is labeled as "misinformation" without transparency, you are nudged, unconsciously, toward approved narratives. Over time, your worldview may narrow, making it harder for you to recognize injustice, challenge power, or even imagine alternatives to the status quo. Scholars call this the "spiral of silence", a phenomenon where people become reluctant to express views they believe are unpopular, especially when public discourse is tightly controlled (Noelle-Neumann, 1977). If you believe your opinion could get you flagged, monitored, or punished, you may self-censor, not only to protect yourself but also because you begin to internalize the dominant narrative.

In many authoritarian regimes, censorship is used to enforce ideological conformity. Take China, for example. The Chinese Communist Party maintains tight control over online discourse through what is colloquially known as the "Great Firewall". Topics like Tiananmen Square, democracy protests, or criticism of government officials are filtered, and platforms such as Twitter and Facebook are blocked entirely. Even domestic platforms like Weibo and WeChat are heavily monitored and moderated. The result? A civic identity that is tightly aligned with the state's version of reality (King et al., 2013).

You might think this only happens in countries with rigid one-party systems, but similar patterns can be seen elsewhere. In Russia, legislation like the "foreign agents" law has been used to shut down independent media and civil society organizations. State-run media dominate the airwaves, and online content is subject to severe restrictions. By 2022, the government had criminalized the act of calling its invasion of Ukraine a "war", forcing citizens to use official language or risk imprisonment (Soldatov & Borogan, 2022). In such environments, your ability to form an independent civic identity – one rooted in truth and critical thought – is significantly curtailed.

Censorship is not exclusive to authoritarian regimes. In democratic countries, governments and institutions also regulate content, often in the name of protecting public safety or preventing harm. While these goals may be legitimate, the consequences for civic identity can be complex. For example, during the COVID-19 pandemic, several Western democracies worked with social media companies to remove false information about the virus. While some of this content was clearly harmful, other materials, such as discussions about vaccine risks or critiques of public health policy, were also removed or down-ranked (Douek, 2021). If you questioned the mainstream narrative, you might have felt silenced or shamed, regardless of your intentions. Even if your concerns were reasonable, they were often treated as dangerous.

On the other side of the political spectrum, you may have noticed the suppression of progressive activism in various democratic contexts. In France and Germany, pro-Palestinian protests have been banned in recent years under the justification of preventing antisemitism and maintaining public order (Serhan, 2024). Meanwhile, in the United States foreign students participating in campus protests have been either arrested or encouraged by their colleges and universities to refrain from attending rallies

(Fayyad, 2025). This has sparked concerns about the suppression of political speech, especially among foreign students and minority communities. If your civic identity includes advocating for human rights or solidarity with oppressed populations, these restrictions may feel like a denial of your right to participate fully in democratic life.

Government censorship also crosses borders. Through surveillance, intimidation, and disinformation, some governments attempt to control their citizens, even after they leave the country. For example, Iranian-American journalist Masih Alinejad has been targeted by the IRGC for her activism against Iran's mandatory hijab laws. The IRGC has plotted multiple kidnapping and assassination attempts against her on U.S. soil, using both physical surveillance and digital smear campaigns to intimidate her (Gainer, 2025). As someone living in the diaspora, your civic identity can still be shaped and suppressed by the government you thought you had left behind.

Similarly, the Ethiopian government's use of FinFisher spyware to monitor exiled dissidents like Dr. Tadesse Kersmo illustrates how state surveillance and censorship extend beyond national borders (Citizen Lab, 2024). If you belong to a politically marginalized group or have been forced into exile, you may find that your ability to engage in civic life is not only monitored but also actively obstructed – no matter where you live.

Internet shutdowns are one of the most extreme forms of government censorship. In Zambia, Uganda, and India, governments have repeatedly shut down Internet services during elections or political unrest. In 2024 alone, Access Now documented Internet shutdowns in 15 African countries, often during critical political moments (Rosson et al., 2025). These blackouts prevent citizens from sharing information, organizing protests, or accessing alternative news sources. Imagine you are in the middle of a national election and suddenly lose access to the Internet. You can't verify claims, follow developments, or communicate with your community. Your ability to form and express civic identity, especially in a time of heightened political urgency, is stripped away. These moments reveal how crucial digital access is to democratic participation.

While much attention is placed on governments, it's important to recognize that censorship often occurs through algorithms and platform policies. You may find that certain posts are shadow-banned, search results are filtered, or entire accounts are suspended without a clear explanation. These actions may stem from attempts to comply with national laws or platform guidelines, but the effect is the same: Restricted access to information and diminished freedom to express yourself. Whether you lean progressive or conservative, you have likely witnessed or experienced moments when your perspective seemed unwelcome online. This creates echo chambers and polarizes public discourse, making it harder for people to encounter diverse viewpoints and develop a nuanced civic identity.

BOX 8.1 CASE STUDY

In Romania, social media has become a powerful tool in shaping political discourse, particularly aiding the rise of far-right movements. Platforms like Facebook, TikTok, and X have allowed these groups to bypass traditional media and speak directly to citizens, often using emotionally charged messaging to exploit fears around immigration, nationalism, and government distrust.

During the lead-up to Romania's 2024 local elections, which were later cancelled, far-right actors launched coordinated social media campaigns filled with misinformation, manipulated videos, and targeted attacks on political opponents. Tactics included fake news, paid advertisements, and astroturfing, which created a false sense of widespread public support. These strategies were especially effective among younger and rural voters, many of whom felt ignored by mainstream political narratives.

The viral spread of this content contributed to a surge in the perceived legitimacy of far-right parties, demonstrating how social media can shift public opinion quickly and powerfully. Without the oversight of traditional electoral bodies or journalistic fact-checking, digital platforms became echo chambers for extremism.

Romania's experience highlights the double-edged nature of social media in civic life: while these platforms offer avenues for engagement, they also pose serious risks to democratic processes when used to manipulate public opinion. This case underscores the need for stronger media literacy, electoral safeguards, and accountability from tech platforms in protecting the integrity of political discourse.

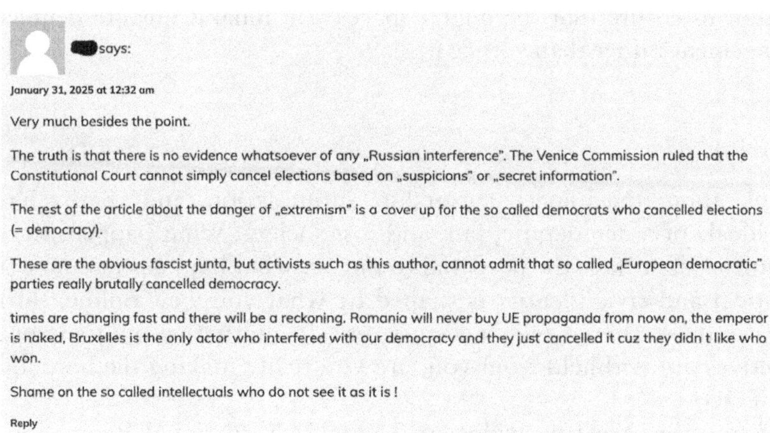

says:

January 31, 2025 at 12:32 am

Very much besides the point.

The truth is that there is no evidence whatsoever of any „Russian interference". The Venice Commission ruled that the Constitutional Court cannot simply cancel elections based on „suspicions" or „secret information".

The rest of the article about the danger of „extremism" is a cover up for the so called democrats who cancelled elections (= democracy).

These are the obvious fascist junta, but activists such as this author, cannot admit that so called „European democratic" parties really brutally cancelled democracy.

times are changing fast and there will be a reckoning. Romania will never buy UE propaganda from now on, the emperor is naked, Bruxelles is the only actor who interfered with our democracy and they just cancelled it cuz they didn t like who won.

Shame on the so called intellectuals who do not see it as it is !

Reply

FIGURE 8.3 Comment to a news story on the cancellation of Romanian presidential elections in 2024.

Conclusion

As this chapter has demonstrated, the intersection of surveillance, censorship, and digital repression plays a central role in shaping your civic identity. In an era where governments – both democratic and authoritarian – possess unprecedented technological capabilities, the boundary between protection and control has become increasingly blurred. Surveillance technologies such as facial recognition, spyware, and mass data collection systems are not only tools of security but also instruments of power. They influence how you engage with your community, how freely you express yourself, and whether you feel safe doing so.

Across the globe, from China's Great Firewall to the U.S. NSA's PRISM program, and from the hacking of activists in Ethiopia to the intimidation of Iranian dissidents abroad, governments have used digital tools to suppress dissent and shape public perception. These interventions are not merely technical or political; they're deeply personal. They impact your decisions, your sense of belonging, and your understanding of what it means to participate in civic life.

Importantly, censorship and surveillance are not confined to overt authoritarianism. In democracies, Internet shutdowns during elections, biased content moderation, and suppression of protest speech all challenge the ideals of pluralism and open discourse. Whether framed as national security or public safety, restrictions on information, especially when applied unevenly or without transparency, undermine your ability to make informed, autonomous choices as a citizen. If civic identity is built through dialogue, participation, and access to truth, then protecting those pathways is essential. It requires vigilance, literacy, and international cooperation to ensure that the digital spaces you inhabit nurture democratic engagement rather than silence it.

Exercise

Think about the impact censorship, intimidation, and apathy has on the ideals of a democratic, fair, and just society. What happens in other countries does have the potential to impact what happens in yours. Your political and civic identity is shaped by what you view online, through apps, videos, shared text messages, etc. If alternative opinions or perspectives are withheld from you, are you really making the best choices for YOU?

Watch this YouTube video on Digital Transnational Repression Explained https://www.youtube.com/watch?v=FkPCec7jG5I. Now read through Section 3 of the 2022 Citizen's Lab report on "Psychological and

Emotional War: Digital and Transnational Repression in Canada" https://citizenlab.ca/wp-content/uploads/2022/03/Report151-dtr_022822.pdf.

Select and analyze one journalist's personal story from the report:

- Identify their country of origin and the nature of their work
- Describe the specific digital repression tactics they experienced
- Analyze their expressed fears and psychological impacts
- Explain how their experience illustrates broader patterns of transnational repression
- Identify two to three social media or communication platforms mentioned in the report
- Analyze their role in either facilitating or combating digital transnational repression

References

Bell, J., & Rushe, D. (2013). *NSA Prism Program taps in to user data of Apple, Google and others.* The Guardian. https://www.theguardian.com/world/2013/jun/06/us-tech-giants-nsa-data

Citizen Lab. (2024). Reckless or repressive? FinFisher spyware and transnational digital repression. University of Toronto. https://citizenlab.ca

Citizen Lab Staff. (2024). *Fatima: A journalist from Syria.* The Citizen Lab. https://citizenlab.ca/case-studies/fatima-a-journalist-from-syria/

Donovan, J. (2024). *How networked incitement fueled the January 6 Capitol insurrection.* Scientific American. https://www.scientificamerican.com/article/jan-6-was-an-example-of-networked-incitement/

Douek, E. (2021). COVID-19 and content moderation: The end of the free internet? *Columbia Law Review*, *121*(6), 1301–1346.

Fayyad, A. (2025). The assault on pro-Palestinian speech has a long and shameful history. https://www.vox.com/policy/406067/mahmoud-khalil-detention-pro-palestinian-arrests-deportations

Five Blockchains (2024). PGP/GPG vs. signal: Keeping communication secure. *Five Blockchains (Alt + H).* https://5blockchains.com/posts/pgp-vs-signal/

Gainer, A. (2025). NYC jury finds 2 guilty in plot to kill Iranian journalist Masih Alinejad. CBS News, New York. https://www.cbsnews.com/newyork/news/2-men-found-guilty-of-trying-to-kill-iranian-american-journalist-masih-alinejad/

Gatlan, S. (2019). *Over 275 million records exposed by unsecured mongodb database.* BleepingComputer. https://www.bleepingcomputer.com/news/security/over-275-million-records-exposed-by-unsecured-mongodb-database/

King, G., Pan, J., & Roberts, M. (2013). How censorship in China allows government criticism but silences collective expression. *American Political Science Review*, *107*(2), 1–18.

National Association of Secretaries of State. (2021). *Three common election season scams.* Fight Cybercrime https://www.nass.org/sites/default/files/2021-08/CSN%20Election%20Scams%20Infosheet_NASS.pdf

Noelle-Neumann, E. (1977). Turbulences in the climate of opinion: Methodological applications of the spiral of silence theory. *Public Opinion Quarterly*, *41*(2), 143–158.

Rosson, Z., Tackett, C., & Maguire, M. (2025). Lives on hold: Internet shutdowns in 2024. *Access Now*. https://www.accessnow.org/internet-shutdowns-2024/

Serhan, Y. (2024). New report details how pro-Palestinian protests are suppressed in democratic countries. *Time Magazine*. https://time.com/7199769/pro-palestine-protests-suppressed-democratic-countries/

Soldatov, A., & Borogan, I. (2022). The red web: The Kremlin's war on the internet. PublicAffairs.

Streamlau, N., & Dobson, N. (2022). Information controls and internet shutdowns in African elections. *Journal of African Elections*, *21*(2), 1–22.

Topping, A. (2023). Laurence Fox arrested over remarks on Ulez cameras as GB news sacks him. *The Guardian*. https://www.theguardian.com/uk-news/2023/oct/04/laurence-fox-arrested-over-comments-urging-people-to-vandalise-ulez-cameras

U.S. Office of Personnel Management. (2015). Cybersecurity Resource Center. Opm.gov. OPM: U.S. Office of Personnel Management. https://www.opm.gov/cybersecurity-resource-center/

Zheng, S. (2022). Hackers claim theft of police info in China's largest data leak. *Bloomberg News*. https://www.bloomberg.com/news/articles/2022-07-04/hackers-claim-theft-of-police-info-in-china-s-largest-data-leak

Zimmermann, P. (2021). PGP marks 30th Anniversary. Phillip Zimmermann. https://philzimmermann.com/EN/essays/PGP_30th/

9

CONSUMER IDENTITY

Did You Really Buy That?

As technology continues to shape our daily lives, it also transforms the way we engage with consumer culture. The interweaving of consumerism and technology creates visually compelling lifestyles for us to consume and has become a very profitable business. Through various manipulation techniques on social media and the Internet, Big Tech and retailers collude to steer us to purchase what they've crafted as "the dream". We then find ourselves wanting what we see, not realizing that they make sure we see what they want us to consume. A cleverly curated collection of goods and services have been placed before us based on complex algorithms of a million points of our own data. As a result, it has become increasingly crucial that we all learn how our consumer identities are crafted and understand the role Big Tech, marketers, and retailers play. As they all reshape how we interact with products and services, they significantly influence the identities that we form both online and offline. The development of our knowledge-based societies predicates that information and communication technology are paramount to these transformations, leading to an intricately interconnected world where consumers are bombarded with products to choose from and information to weave through.

We often assume that the choices we make about what to consume are entirely our own. However, Big Tech companies, retailers, and marketers employ sophisticated algorithms and psychological strategies to subtly steer us toward particular decisions. With the shift from traditional brick-and-mortar shopping to digital platforms, our purchasing behaviors are

DOI: 10.4324/9781003539445-10

increasingly shaped by online interactions. While online shopping offers undeniable convenience, it also introduces unintended consequences. As we navigate digital spaces, the risk of manipulation grows, influencing both personal and collective identities (Gansinger & Kole, 2018). Furthermore, Big Tech shapes our perceived "consumer autonomy" through persuasion, peer influence, and algorithmic decision-making. By leveraging psychometrics, social dynamics, and computational tools, corporations exploit our fundamental need for belonging, ultimately shaping our choices in ways we may not fully recognize.

The evolution of consumer identity in the digital age highlights a fundamental shift in how consumers perceive themselves and are perceived by businesses. Historically, consumer identities were largely defined by physical attributes and purchasing behavior, but the rise of digital platforms like Amazon and the Internet has transformed this landscape significantly. Furthermore, the evolution of the Internet of Things, like Amazon's Alexa, continues to expand, connecting devices and individuals, further complicating the identity landscape by invisibly linking consumers to a myriad of resources and services (Anderson & Rainie, 2017).

Consumer Behavior

Big Tech attempts to shape consumer behavior by leveraging data to create personalized experiences and influence purchasing decisions. As we increasingly engage with digital platforms, our identities are often molded by these interactions. While we can be skeptical by nature, we are still willing to share personal information. What do we mean by personal information? Recall recent online purchases you've made. Did you share your address? What about your gender or maybe your email address? All these key pieces of information would not be necessary when purchasing in person; yet we freely give these pieces of ourselves away when consuming online. Our behavior is driven by both a want or desire and a need for instant gratification. Companies prey on these behaviors through various forms of technological and psychological persuasion.

Algorithms

Consumer identity construction relies on data analytics, which serves as a pivotal tool in shaping consumer preferences. Algorithms, structured sets of rules and calculations, play a central role in this process by sorting and analyzing the data to predict consumer behavior. Algorithms are embedded in everyday digital experiences, playing a significant role in shaping our behavior, preferences, and even perceptions of reality. Algorithms are defined as "structured, rule-based procedures used by computers to perform tasks or solve problems"; algorithms underpin many of the personalized services consumers interact with daily (Oxford English Dictionary). For instance, recommendation systems such as Netflix and Spotify utilize algorithms to suggest content based on past behavior, collaborative filtering, and user profiling. Similarly, Amazon's product suggestions rely on predictive algorithms to identify patterns in purchasing behavior and offer tailored advertisements. Social media platforms like Facebook, Instagram, and TikTok use engagement-based algorithms to curate content feeds, reinforcing user interests and maximizing time spent on the platform. Additionally, Google's search engine deploys complex algorithms to rank results based on relevance, authority, and user history, shaping access to information in subtle ways.

These seemingly innocent features of digital life have profound implications. As Gillespie (2014) notes, algorithms are not neutral tools but act as gatekeepers of information and experience, amplifying certain content while suppressing others. Through their design and application, algorithms increasingly shape identity construction, social relationships, and consumer choices. By personalizing our content and limiting our exposure to diverse viewpoints, they contribute to the formation of echo chambers and filter bubbles (Pariser, 2011). Algorithms rely on your data, often collected without our explicit consent, which raises ethical concerns regarding surveillance, autonomy, and digital privacy. While algorithms offer convenience and efficiency, their influence over many aspects of our lives extends far beyond simple personalization, warranting critical examination of their role in shaping contemporary digital culture.

Psychometrics

Another key method used in data-driven marketing is psychometrics, a field that applies psychological measurement techniques to analyze personality traits, attitudes, and behaviors. By leveraging psychometric analysis, companies can segment consumers into psychological profiles, allowing for highly tailored marketing strategies that resonate on an individual level. Retailers and advertising companies use psychographic segmentation models to divide customers into groups based on shared characteristics such as values, beliefs, personality traits, and lifestyle.

Values are a set of principles that guide an individual's behavior and decision-making. A company that focuses on sustainability may focus on customers who prioritize sustainability when making a purchase.

IKEA targets sustainability-conscious consumers through their "People & Planet Positive" initiative, which includes product lines made with recycled or renewable materials. IKEA's customer data and purchasing patterns help them identify and promote sustainable products to segments that prioritize green living. Beliefs are ideas or opinions that an individual holds to be true. Beliefs allow marketers to move beyond demographics and speak to what people stand for, their worldview, ethics, and priorities. Walmart's "Made in America" campaigns appeal to patriotic beliefs. Personality traits are enduring patterns of thought, feelings, and behaviors that distinguishes yours from anothers. In the early 2000s, Apple ran an ad campaign featuring "Mac" and "PC". Mac was portrayed as young, hip, and creative, while PC was older, formal, and awkward. Apple tapped into the self-perception and aspirations of creative, tech-savvy users who viewed themselves as innovative, non-conformist, and forward-thinking. Lifestyle refers to the activities a person does and anything they're interested in like hobbies. Lululemon markets a way of life focusing on physical well-being, mental balance, and self-improvement. They reflect a lifestyle that includes yoga and clean eating.

The use of algorithms and psychometrics raises critical concerns regarding privacy, as many consumers express skepticism about sharing their sensitive information. Studies indicate that this skepticism can reduce willingness to disclose personal details, though greater transparency may alleviate some concerns (Sullivan, 2018). Moreover, the interplay between data-driven recommendations and an individual's self-identity complicates consumer engagement, as algorithmic systems often create filter bubbles that reinforce existing preferences rather than challenge them (Onitiu, 2021). When psychometric profiling is combined with algorithmic filtering, the result is a highly curated digital environment that not only predicts what we will choose but also subtly shapes our choices, often without our explicit awareness. Thus, while data analytics and psychometrics provide powerful insights into consumer behavior, they also introduce ethical concerns about autonomy, manipulation, and the long-term impact of personalized digital experiences.

Bias

Some researchers like Timnit Gebru, an ethicist and computer engineer, believe tools like algorithms, AI, and other emerging technologies perpetuate bias. She argues this is a result of biased training data and the lack of demographic diversity in datasets (Buolamwini & Gebru, 2018). What they found was needed was greater transparency, auditing, and accountability in AI and algorithmic systems. They emphasized the need for government regulation and oversight to prevent the potential discrimination and harm that can result from overlooking demographic subgroups.

Because algorithmic systems rely on historical consumer data, such as purchasing history, click patterns, and demographic profiles, they may reinforce existing patterns of inequality or stereotyping our choices. For instance, recommendation engines like Amazon might prioritize certain products based on gender or socioeconomic assumptions, subtly steering us toward decisions that align with market norms rather than our preferences. Personalization can lead to filter bubbles in consumption, where we are continuously exposed to the same types of products or brands, limiting our awareness of alternatives and reinforcing behavioral patterns (Pariser, 2011). As algorithms become more sophisticated and embedded in the tools we use to shop, the need for ethical design and diverse training data becomes critical. Without oversight from the industries or government, these systems risk perpetuating social inequalities.

Youth Behavior

Young people today are coming of age in a digital marketplace that is not only personalized but also profoundly persuasive. Platforms such as TikTok, Instagram, YouTube, and Snapchat are specifically designed to appeal to youth audiences. They do this by blending entertainment, social interaction, and commerce into a seamless, immersive experience. As a result, youth consumer behavior is shaped not only by peer influence and developmental psychology but also by data-driven algorithms that curate content with remarkable precision.

Adolescents are particularly susceptible to these influences due to the ongoing development of their prefrontal cortex, the part of the brain responsible for impulse control, risk assessment, and long-term planning (Steinberg, 2005). This neurological reality, combined with the emotional intensity of social media, creates a perfect environment for impulsive purchasing decisions, often driven by trends, influencers, and subtle algorithmic cues.

What makes youth consumer behavior unique in this context is the degree to which identity formation is entangled with consumption. Young users often use brand affiliations, product choices, and digital content to signal social status, personality, and group belonging. Psychometrics and predictive analytics leverage this by targeting youth with hyper-personalized ads that align with their values, fears, and aspirations (Sánchez-Amboage et al., 2024). For example, an adolescent who frequently engages with fitness or fashion content will be algorithmically nudged toward related products and services, reinforcing a feedback loop between identity performance and commercial behavior.

Further complicating the issue is the blurred line between organic content and advertising. Many young users cannot reliably distinguish between a genuine recommendation and a sponsored post, particularly when it comes from an influencer they admire or trust (Evans et al., 2017). Disclosures such as "#ad" or "sponsored" are often overlooked or misunderstood, undermining the transparency that is critical for informed decision-making. Given these dynamics, youth must learn to recognize how their data is used to manipulate choice, or they risk becoming passive participants in a commercial system that views them primarily as data points rather than as developing humans.

Social Media Influencers

We increasingly craft our identities online, often leading to distorted perceptions of self-worth and social validation. As we share images and experiences, we frequently compare ourselves to the polished personas presented by friends, influencers, and celebrities. These distorted feelings of inadequacy can compel us into developing low self-esteem. Additionally, social media serves as a tool of consumerism, where products and lifestyles communicate symbols that influence self-identity. Armed with data and peer pressure, companies have tapped into the value behind social media to leverage the concept of "influence".

Social media shapes consumer identities by providing a platform for self-expression but also a conceptual framework wherein identity is constructed and reconstructed. As consumers, we do this through platforms such as Instagram, TikTok, and X, where we develop our online personas by aligning ourselves with specific brands and lifestyles that resonate with our aspirations and societal trends. This digital identity construction reflects a shift toward increased peer pressure. Often, we are swayed toward a product or service based on the comments, likes, shares, or reviews of people who are closely aligned with us. As we navigate these platforms, we are often influenced by group dynamics, which serve to reinforce communal identities among users with shared interests or values (Regan, 2016). However, while social media becomes instrumental in not just reflecting but also actively shaping our consumer identities, we can also be influenced by other individuals.

A social media influencer is an individual who has established credibility and visibility in a specific industry or social niche through consistent engagement on digital platforms and who uses their online presence to influence consumer behavior or public opinion through the production and dissemination of content. Their perceived authenticity and expertise enable them to influence the attitudes, decisions, or actions of their audience. In terms of value, influencers can command millions of dollars from company sponsors. Influencers create content that, on the surface, seem authentic but are carefully placed ad campaigns within their social media accounts. Football star Cristiano Ronaldo can post a reel on Instagram of himself enjoying a relaxing day at the beach, enjoying a cool drink with the label strategically placed toward the camera. That one post can earn him up to $2 million (Influencer Marketing Hub, 2024).

Sometimes companies risk alienating their customer base and running counter to their brand's established customer segmentation models. In April 2023, Anheuser-Busch's Bud Light brand collaborated with transgender influencer Dylan Mulvaney to broaden its appeal among younger demographics. Mulvaney promoted Bud Light during the NCAA's March Madness tournament with a brief TikTok where she celebrated one of her "days of womanhood" with a Bud Light (Napolitano, 2023). The campaign received significant backlash from conservative groups and individuals, leading to calls for a nationwide boycott of Budweiser products. The controversy adversely affected Bud Light's sales, with reports indicating a decline of up to 26% in the weeks following the incident (Napolitano, 2023). In response, Anheuser-Busch placed two marketing executives on leave and launched a revised advertising campaign featuring the brand's iconic Clydesdale horses, attempting to reconnect with its traditional consumer base.

The Marketing Power of Peers

As we've seen, companies and marketers struggle to find the balance between staying relevant to younger customers and maintaining their loyal base. A new technological tool at their disposal is customer reviews. Marketers have discovered that we prefer and trust the recommendations of someone like us rather than influencers or celebrities. Currently, one of the largest online shopping platforms for young people isn't Amazon, it's TikTok. In 2023 TikTok made $15 billion in revenue and supported over 5 million business accounts on their platform (TikTok, 2025). Why would a social media platform, known for kids dancing and challenges, become a center for commerce? The answer is, we buy from people we know, people who are like us. There are thousands of TikTok reviews for eyebrow gel or leggings, all by "normal" people you can relate to. It's this relatability that drives sales. You want to participate in their business; you want to be seen liking their post because you are part of *that* community.

To push content to you that is personalized, marketers need data. This is where your terms and conditions come in; here is where you've signed away your online activity logs when you pushed "ok". These brands and marketers pay those platforms for access to your de-identified data. What they're purchasing is a shadow, an outline of you as a "type" of person. Armed with that information and being able to track what you purchase online, they can begin to customize what is put in your feed. The longer they can get you to hover over an image or product, the more likely you are to purchase. Your consumer identity is being manipulated not only by algorithms but also by you and people most likely to be like you.

Marketers and social media companies often work together to build detailed profiles of typical customers. Marketers gather data from sources like online purchases, browsing behavior, and customer feedback. Social media platforms add even more information, such as what users post, like, and share, as well as their interests and networks. By combining all this data, companies can create rich customer profiles that help them understand who their audiences are and what they want. These profiles allow for more personalized and targeted advertising, which can increase customer engagement and sales (Salesforce, n.d.).

The cost of demographic data depends on how detailed and accurate the information is. Basic data from public sources, like the U.S. Census, is usually free. However, marketers often buy more specific data from commercial providers, which offer information about consumer habits, income, lifestyle, and preferences. These detailed profiles can cost from a few cents to several dollars per person, depending on the type and depth of the data. Although this can be expensive, companies often see it as a worthwhile investment because it helps improve marketing results (Manifold Data Mining, 2025). One of the most expensive data profiles is that of 18–24-year-olds. This age group is seen as having more access to disposable income than any other age group; they may be employed but also have access to their parents' incomes. Demographically, the data of U.S. men living in the Northeast earning \$120,000–-\$150,000 per year are the most sought-after consumer group (Salesforce, n.d.).

The Illusion of Choice

While the modern digital marketplace offers what appears to be infinite choice, these choices are often shaped, filtered, or even predetermined by systems outside your conscious awareness. As a consumer, you may believe that your selections are based solely on personal preferences or rational decision-making. However, research increasingly shows that algorithmic curation, platform design, and data-driven marketing can guide you toward certain products or ideas, subtly eroding your sense of autonomy (Zuboff, 2019).

Many of the platforms you use every day, from search engines to shopping apps, employ what behavioral economists call choice architecture. This refers to how the presentation of choices influences decisions. For example, default options, color placement, and ranking order all affect which product you're likely to select. Combined with your personal data history, these systems create a highly persuasive environment in which the illusion of choice masks the reality of manipulated preference (Thaler & Sunstein, 2009).

Moreover, companies often exploit cognitive biases such as scarcity, social proof, and loss aversion to trigger impulsive consumption. When you see a label reading "Only 3 left at this price!" or a banner showing "Trending: 12,000 people bought this today", your decision-making is nudged by engineered urgency or peer influence rather than actual need or desire. The troubling part is that these mechanisms aren't always transparent. You may not be aware that your search results are filtered based on your past behavior or that the "related items" you see are financially prioritized by advertisers. This blurring of editorial and promotional content raises ethical questions about informed consent and consumer manipulation. Are you truly making a choice, or is the choice being made for you?

Consumer Data Risks

Today, our consumer identity is intricately tied to our digital footprint, covering a wide array of data from browsing habits to social media interactions. This shift raises critical questions about data ownership and privacy. Proposals for clearer regulations surrounding data ownership have emerged in response to these dynamics, emphasizing the need for legal frameworks that can safeguard consumer rights while promoting innovation in big tech industries (Ritter & Mayer, 2017). For instance, the European Union has introduced the Data Governance Act (DGA), which aims to create a framework facilitating data-sharing among public bodies, private companies, and citizens, while ensuring data protection and fostering trust. Similarly, the Data Act, also proposed by the European Commission, seeks to harmonize rules on fair access to and use of data, empowering consumers with greater control over their information and encouraging a competitive data market. In the United States, the American Data Privacy and Protection Act (ADPPA) represents a significant legislative effort to regulate how organizations collect and use consumer data, aiming to provide foundational data privacy rights and establish oversight mechanisms.

Without these legal initiatives, data breaches will continue to pose a significant threat to consumers, exposing our sensitive personal and financial information to cybercriminals and malicious actors. When organizations fail to adequately secure our user data, we may face severe consequences, including identity theft, financial fraud, and reputational harm. Stolen information like Social Security numbers, credit card details, and login credentials can be sold on the dark web, enabling unauthorized transactions and fraudulent activities that may take years to resolve. Additionally, data breaches undermine consumer trust in digital platforms, raising concerns about corporate accountability and cybersecurity measures. Beyond financial risks, breaches can also lead to privacy violations, where personal communications, medical records, or behavioral data are exploited for blackmail or discriminatory practices. The growing reliance on digital services heightens the urgency for stricter data protection policies, enhanced encryption standards, and proactive consumer education on cybersecurity best practices. According to tracking conducted by "Information is Beautiful", security breaches of major retailers from cellphone service providers to entertainment vendors have resulted in billions of customer records stolen. These data heist result in trillions of dollars in ill-gotten gains by selling stolen customer data on the dark web.

Without robust safeguards, the increasing frequency and scale of data breaches will continue to erode our confidence and expose us to long-term financial and personal risks.

The accelerated evolution of technology has fundamentally altered consumer identity, challenging the traditional assumptions around data

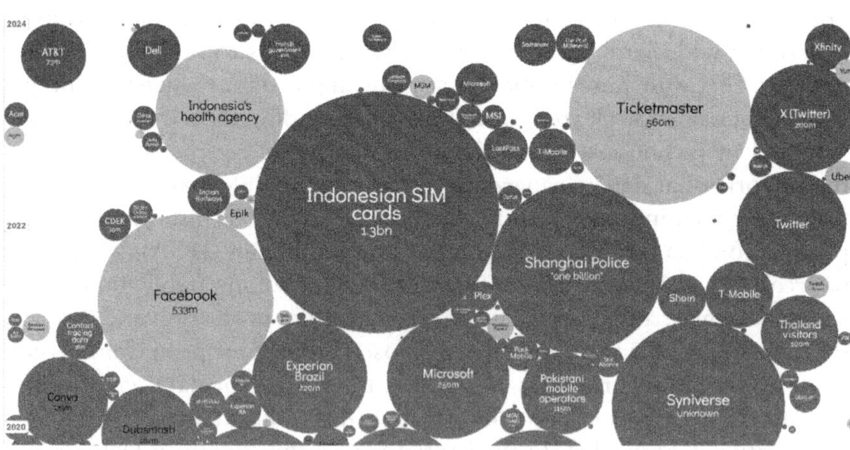

FIGURE 9.1 Information is Beautiful "World's Biggest Data Breaches & Hacks". (Information is Beautiful, 2025).

ownership and privacy. As we engage with digital platforms, our personal data becomes a commodity, contributing to a complex landscape where privacy and identity intertwine. This dynamic raises essential questions regarding the management of consumer information and the implications for personal autonomy. Current conversations usually highlight the underlying tension between regulation and innovation, suggesting that privacy regulations may inhibit the necessary collection of data for advancements in various sectors (Pasquale, 2014). Furthermore, the collection of such data can create vulnerabilities in systems, complicating the relationship between consumers and service providers (Pasquale, 2014).

As we engage with these digital platforms, the necessity for clear regulations on data ownership has become increasingly important. For years, technology developers and critics such as Jaron Lanier have been calling for consumer property rights on generated data (Mack, 2019) (https://www.theverge.com/2019/4/9/18302076/data-monetization-control-manipulation-economy-jaron-laniers-virtual-reality-vr-vergecast). A proposed model that defines data as a tangible property can enhance consumer rights and ownership principles, as highlighted in recent initiatives by European and Asian officials (Ritter & Mayer, 2017). In the end, the integration of technology into daily life, such as the rise of home robots, poses substantial privacy challenges that necessitate innovative design solutions to mitigate risks and foster consumer trust (Kaminski et al., 2017). The future of consumer identity in the age of big tech will hinge on establishing robust legal frameworks that protect individual rights while promoting technological advancements. The interplay of regulation and innovation will be vital in shaping a secure digital ecosystem for consumers.

BOX 9.1 CASE STUDY

In 2012, The New York Times published a now-famous investigative article revealing that Target, the U.S.-based retail giant, had developed an advanced predictive analytics algorithm capable of identifying customers who were likely pregnant, often before they had publicly disclosed it. This was made possible by analyzing purchase patterns: Certain combinations of items like unscented lotion, magnesium supplements, and cotton balls were strongly correlated with early-stage pregnancy.

In one widely cited case, Target began sending maternity coupons to a teenage girl in Minnesota based on her purchase history. Her father complained to the company, demanding to know why his daughter was receiving such ads. A few days later, he contacted the store again, this time to apologize. His daughter was, in fact, pregnant, and Target's algorithm had "discovered" it before her family did. This case highlights how consumer identity can be inferred, constructed, and acted upon by corporations based on seemingly mundane behavioral data. The teenager had never told anyone about her pregnancy, but her consumer behavior generated a digital profile that marketers used to target her with specific products. The controversy surrounding this case was not about the accuracy of the prediction; it was about the ethics of profiling and targeting vulnerable individuals, particularly minors, without consent.

This case also raises questions about data consent, especially for minors. Teenagers often engage in consumer behavior without realizing that their actions leave behind a digital footprint that can be mined, monetized, and acted upon. The Target case is an unsettling example of how corporate surveillance intersects with identity formation, especially for young people navigating sensitive transitions. It illustrates the power imbalance between data-holding institutions and individuals, where algorithms can "know" something about a person before they're ready to share it themselves. In shaping her consumer profile, Target also shaped how the girl was perceived by her family, and potentially how she came to view herself.

Conclusion

Your consumer identity is no longer just a reflection of what you choose to buy; it's a product of a complex digital ecosystem that continuously monitors, analyzes, and influences your behavior. In this hyper-connected world, where Big Tech platforms, marketers, and influencers operate in tandem, your preferences are not simply discovered; they're constructed through data profiling, algorithmic curation, and psychometric targeting. Every like, scroll, or purchase contributes to a digital portrait used to shape future interactions, subtly guiding your decisions while offering the illusion of autonomy.

This chapter has shown how algorithms, social influencers, peer reviews, and choice architecture converge to influence not only what you buy but also how you see yourself. The blurring of advertising and authentic content, particularly in the case of influencers and social media communities, demonstrates that the act of consumption has become deeply embedded in self-expression and identity performance. For youth especially, the formation of identity is increasingly filtered through commercial platforms designed to exploit psychological vulnerabilities and developmental tendencies.

While data-driven marketing offers convenience and personalization, it also raises significant ethical concerns related to manipulation, privacy, and inequality. Issues of algorithmic bias and click farm deception further complicate the trustworthiness of the digital marketplace. Yet understanding these mechanisms offers a path toward agency. With growing awareness and regulation, there is potential to create a more equitable and transparent consumer landscape.

As a digital consumer, your responsibility is not only to question what you buy, but to interrogate how and why those choices are presented to you. By recognizing the forces that shape your consumer identity, from subtle nudges to overt profiling, you can begin to reclaim agency in an environment increasingly designed to make decisions for you. In doing so, you shift from being merely a data point in an algorithm to an informed participant in the digital economy.

Exercise

Online reviews and ratings significantly influence consumer purchasing decisions, but these systems are vulnerable to manipulation. This exercise challenges you to investigate potential review manipulation on digital marketplaces by examining the relationship between numerical ratings and written reviews, and to reflect on how this knowledge affects your trust in these platforms.

- Choose a digital marketplace you regularly use (Amazon, Alibaba, IKEA, Walmart, etc.).
- Identify three to five products with exceptionally high ratings (4.5+ stars or 90%+ positive).
- For each product, read at least 10–15 written reviews across different rating levels.

    - Identify at least one product that shows potential signs of review manipulation:

        - Very high ratio of ratings to written reviews
        - Vague or generic written reviews
        - Suspicious posting patterns
        - Inconsistencies between ratings and review content

    - Document specific evidence supporting your assessment.

References

Anderson, J., & Rainie, L. (2017). *The internet of things connectivity binge: What are the implications?* Pew Research Center.

Buolamwini, J., & Gebru, T. (2018). Gender shades: Intersectional accuracy disparities in commercial gender classification. *Journal of Machine Learning Research*, *81*, 77–91.

Evans, N. J., Phua, J., Lim, J., & Jun, H. (2017). Disclosing Instagram influencer advertising: The effects of disclosure language on advertising recognition, attitudes, and behavioral intent. *Journal of Interactive Advertising*, *17*(2), 138–149.

Gansinger, M. A. M., & Kole, A. (2018). Vortex of the web. potentials of the online environment. https://philarchive.org/rec/GANVOT-2

Gillespie, T. (2014). The relevance of algorithms. In T. Gillespie, P. J. Boczkowski, & K. A. Foot (Eds.), *Media technologies: Essays on communication, materiality, and society* (167–194). MIT Press.

Influencer Marketing Hub. (2024). Instagram's Top 20 Stars of 2024. https://influencermarketinghub.com/instagram-highest-paid/

Information is Beautiful. (2025). World's Biggest Data Breaches & Hacks. https://informationisbeautiful.net/visualizations/worlds-biggest-data-breaches-hacks/

Kaminski, M.E., Rueben, M., Smart, W.D., & Grimm, C.M. (2017). Averting robot eyes. *Maryland Law Review*, *76(*4), 983–1025.

Mack, Z. (2019). Jaron Lanier's ideas for the future of profiting from your own data. The Verge. https://www.theverge.com/2019/4/9/18302076/data-monetization-control-manipulation-economy-jaron-laniers-virtual-reality-vr-vergecast

Manifold Data Mining. (2025). Data. https://www.manifolddatamining.com/data

Napolitano, E. (2023). Anheuser-Busch exec steps down after Bud Light sales slump following Dylan Mulvaney controversy. CBS News. https://www.cbsnews.com/news/bud-light-anheuser-busch-marketing-chief-steps-down-boycott-dylan-mulvaney

Onitiu, D. (2021). Algorithmic abstractions of 'fashion identity' and the role of privacy with regard to algorithmic personalization systems in the fashion domain. *AI and Society*, *37*, 1749–1758.

Pariser, E. (2011). *The filter bubble: What the Internet is hiding from you*. Penguin Press.

Pasquale, F. A. (2014). Redescribing health privacy: The importance of health policy. *Houston Journal of Health Law and Policy*, *14*, 95–128.

Regan, P. M. (2016). Response to privacy as a public good. https://core.ac.uk/download/84098892.pdf

Ritter, J., & Mayer, A. (2017). Regulating data as property: A new construct for moving forward. *Duke Law & Technology Review*, *16*, 220.

Salesforce. (n.d.). What is a customer profile? https://www.salesforce.com/eu/marketing/data/customer-profile/

Sánchez-Amboage, E., Castellanos-García, P., & Crespo-Pereira, V. (2024). Traveler segmentation through Instagram Fashion Influencers. Mirror Tourist as a new segment consumer group. *Journal of Retailing and Consumer Services*, *78*, 103735.

Steinberg, L. (2005). Cognitive and affective development in adolescence. *Trends in Cognitive Sciences*, *9*(2), 69–74.

Sullivan, D. D. (2018). The importance of transparency and willingness to share personal information. *Honors Theses and Capstones, 408*. https://scholars.unh.edu/honors/408

Thaler, R. H., & Sunstein, C. R. (2009). *Nudge: Improving decisions about health, wealth, and happiness*. Penguin Books.

TikTok. (2025). TikTok's economic impact. https://tiktokeconomicimpact.com/?gad_source=1&gclid=Cj0KCQjwkZm_BhDrARIsAAEbX1G0s0JB_lV-PLkjJcbJSPz-CfiDEXYpYbLQg68VBJS-T0bdnlh02vPAaAn-lEALw_wcB

Zuboff, S. (2019). *The age of surveillance capitalism: The fight for a human future at the new frontier of power*. PublicAffairs.

10

SELF-CENSORING

Filter Bubbles and Echo Chambers

When we're online, whether searching the Internet or scrolling through social media, sophisticated algorithms are at work personalizing the experience to us. As we have seen in chapter eight, this is done through predictive analytics, but there are also other technical and psychological elements at work. Even when we are right next to each other, our search results and our social media feeds are unique to us. Big tech like Google, Facebook, TikTok, and Instagram customize our experiences to keep us engaged longer, spending money online, and generate ad revenue from marketers. This plays a role in shaping our digital and physical identities when all we hear are the voices of agreement.

Predictive analytics is the engine behind the personalized digital environments we inhabit. These systems don't just react to our past behavior; they anticipate our future behavior. Platforms use machine learning models that take in thousands of data points, from the time of day we log in, to the type of posts we linger on, to whom we interact with most frequently. Over time, these models build dynamic profiles of who we are and, more importantly, who we are likely to become. However, predictive analytics doesn't just forecast behavior, it shapes it. When platforms prioritize content we're predicted to engage with, they reinforce and deepen existing preferences. In effect, we're nudged, slowly but surely, down paths the algorithm sees as most "engaging". This leads not only to echo chambers but also to "identity tunnels", where our preferences become more extreme over time without us realizing it.

DOI: 10.4324/9781003539445-11

In our connected, always online age, our experiences are increasingly shaped by the intricate algorithms powering the search engines, social media platforms, and recommendation systems we rely on. These algorithms are designed to curate and deliver content tailored to our individual preferences, interests, and behavior, creating personalized information ecosystems known as "filter bubbles". While the convenience and personalization offered by these technologies may seem appealing, the consequences of such algorithmic curation can be far-reaching and potentially detrimental to our broader understanding of the world around us.

This process of personalization can inadvertently reinforce existing biases and limit exposure to diverse perspectives. As we are increasingly presented with information that aligns with their preexisting beliefs and preferences, we risk becoming insulated from alternative viewpoints, fostering the formation of echo chambers where we are surrounded by like-minded opinions and affirmation of our own perspectives (Allcott & Gentzkow, 2017; Talamanca & Arfini, 2022). As we navigate an ever-evolving digital landscape, it's crucial to examine the ways in which artificial intelligence (AI) and algorithmic filtering are shaping our access to information and, consequently, our worldviews.

Beyond the algorithms, human psychology plays a crucial role. Our brains are wired to seek cognitive ease; we prefer information that confirms our beliefs because it takes less effort to process. This is known as confirmation bias, and it's one of the most powerful drivers of online behavior. Social validation is another psychological factor. Likes, shares, and comments provide dopamine-driven feedback loops that reward conformity and discourage dissent. When disagreement results in social friction, many users self-censor to avoid conflict. Over time, this leads to pluralistic ignorance, the mistaken belief that one's private doubts are unique, when in fact many others may silently disagree as well. Thus, we're not just trapped by the tech, we're also trapped by ourselves.

Filter Bubbles

Imagine the Internet showing you only the things it thinks you want to see. These algorithms on social media, search engines, and news sites use your browsing history, location, and other personal data to select content for you (Rautiainen, 2019). Over time, this can create a "bubble" where you're primarily exposed to information confirming your existing beliefs. You may not even realize that you are in a filter bubble because these algorithms don't ask for your permission, tell you when they're active, or say what they're keeping from you.

When you search for something on Google, the results you see might be different from what someone else sees. This is because Google's algorithms use your search history and other data to tailor the results to your interests. Similarly, if you watch a lot of videos about a specific hobby on YouTube, the algorithm will suggest more videos on that topic, potentially limiting your exposure to other types of content.

The emergence of filter bubbles was largely driven by the commercial imperative of online platforms to provide you with content that maximizes engagement, time spent on the platform, and ultimately profitability (Hämmig, 2019). These platforms employ sophisticated algorithms that analyze your data, including search history, browsing behavior, and social connections, to curate personalized content streams. However, human agency and personality are also responsible to some degree for how we engage with others online. As we have seen in the chapter on social identity, personality traits are a factor in how open and engaged we are with others in social media. While filter bubbles are individual outcomes received after a tailored selection of information by the systems we are engaged with, they are also adapted to our pre-existing attitudes, shaped by processes of information search, perception, selection, and remembering. These bubbles emerge from our own cognitive processes, social interactions, as well as technological filtering (Pariser, 2011). As a result, we find ourselves segregated not solely by the technologies employed by these social media and technology companies, but also by our individual cognitive limitations.

Filter bubbles are related to the cognitive and psychological limits of human beings. They are not purely caused by algorithms, but are related to how people interact with information, potentially experiencing discomfort when encountering conflicting information and then retreating into their own beliefs. This can be worsened by the immediate nature of social media where our interactions happen quickly, giving us very little time to critically think about what we are doing and how we are engaging. There are three main types of cognitive filter bubbles: Epistemic, moral, and ignorance.

Epistemic is our expertise or understanding of a thing. An epistemic bubble affects how people gain knowledge and their perceived need to do so. It relates to the idea that people may only seek out or trust information that confirms what they already believe. We prefer to stick to our own epistemic bubble, discrediting any information that challenges our views. This can happen because encountering contradictory information can create "epistemic discomfort". Imagine a person who believes strongly in a particular conspiracy theory. They primarily consume news and information from sources that promote this conspiracy, while actively avoiding or dismissing mainstream media or expert opinions that contradict their beliefs. They might share articles from fringe websites on social media and engage in discussions only with others who share their views. This creates an epistemic bubble where their belief is constantly reinforced, and any evidence to the contrary is ignored or discredited. In the 2016 U.S. Presidential election, journalists and Trump voters were found to inhabit separate online information spaces, indicating distinct epistemic bubbles. In the end, epistemic bubbles can hinder learning and critical thinking, as people may not recognize the need to seek out new information or challenge their existing assumptions.

A moral bubble influences how people morally evaluate the actions of others. When we operate within a moral bubble, we may judge others based on our moral framework, leading to misunderstandings or conflicts if those frameworks differ. Consider someone who believes a certain political issue is a matter of basic human rights. They may find it difficult to understand or empathize with those who hold opposing views, potentially judging their actions as morally wrong or insensitive. They might primarily associate with like-minded individuals and avoid engaging with those who hold different moral perspectives, thus reinforcing their own moral framework. A specific example is a person who is a strict vegetarian for ethical reasons, who may view meat-eaters as morally deficient, failing to understand or appreciate the cultural or personal reasons behind their dietary choices. Unfortunately, moral bubbles can contribute to social division and a lack of empathy for those with different moral values.

Finally, an ignorance bubble impacts how we estimate our own ignorance. We may underestimate how much we *don't* know about a topic, leading to overconfidence in our beliefs and a dismissal of alternative viewpoints (Talamanca & Arfini, 2022). A person who is not familiar with climate science might underestimate the severity of climate change. They may believe they have a good understanding of the issue based on limited information or personal observations, failing to recognize the vast body of scientific evidence that supports the reality and urgency of climate change. As a result, they might dismiss the need for action or downplay the potential consequences, remaining in an ignorance bubble due to a lack of awareness of their own knowledge gaps. Another example is someone who might overestimate their understanding of a complex political issue, like international trade, leading them to confidently express opinions without recognizing the nuances or potential consequences of different policies. This can lead to a reinforcement of existing beliefs and a resistance to new information or perspectives.

Echo Chambers

An echo chamber is a metaphorical environment where a person encounters only opinions and information that reinforce their existing beliefs. It's like being in a room where everyone repeats the same ideas back to you. They can have significant implications for individual and societal well-being. By limiting access to a broader range of information and ideas, echo chambers can contribute to the perpetuation of misinformation, the entrenchment of ideological positions, and the deterioration of a shared understanding of reality. As Jarron Lanier observes, the "Twitter poisoning" effect, where we are optimized for maximum engagement, can lead to increased political polarization and the formation of echo chambers (Baumann et al., 2024). For example, imagine you have a certain viewpoint on a topic. In an echo chamber, you'll primarily encounter news, social media posts, and people who share that viewpoint. This constant repetition strengthens your belief, while you're rarely exposed to opposing arguments. This can lead to biased thinking and a resistance to different perspectives. Using affordances in the platforms you're consistently liking and following content aligned with your specific political or social stance, algorithms will likely show you more of the same. You might see posts praising your favored politicians and criticizing those you oppose. Over time, you might believe that everyone agrees with you, because that's all you see in your feed.

Several studies have explored the interplay between algorithmic bias, social networks, and the formation of echo chambers. For instance, Geschke and colleagues have developed a "triple-filter bubble" framework, which examines how the combination of individual cognitive biases, social network structures, and algorithmic curation can lead to the polarization of online communities (Geschke et al., 2018). What they've found are three layers of misconception occurring in these environments. First, when we are in our echo chambers, the spread of misinformation can occur quickly because we are not challenged by other viewpoints. For example, we may choose to consume news and information from sources that align with our existing beliefs, creating an echo chamber where we are rarely exposed to alternative perspectives. Second, we experience increased polarization when we are only hearing one side, thus becoming more entrenched in our beliefs and less tolerant of others. Online communities are places where we tend to only hear one side of an issue. The TikTok of QAnon videos in the early 2020s is an example of this phenomenon. Third, we eventually develop a limited understanding of events or issues because we have not had substantial exposure to diverse perspectives. Consider a person who has grown up in an area of the world with limited diversity. This lack of exposure to diverse perspectives can affect his or her cultural awareness, potentially leading to culture shock when they leave their familiar environment both virtually and physically. All three of these layers are crucial for understanding complex issues. Unfortunately, echo chambers can prevent the development of our critical thinking skills, leading to a narrow and potentially distorted view of the world.

Custom AI Echo Chambers

As generative AI technologies become more accessible, individuals and organizations are no longer limited to the large language models (LLMs) developed by tech giants. Today, anyone with enough technical skill and resources can train or fine-tune their own AI on custom datasets. While this democratization of AI may seem empowering, it also introduces a significant risk: The creation of ideologically insulated echo chambers powered not just by platform algorithms, but by the users themselves.

When people intentionally train LLMs using biased, narrow, or unverified data, such as conspiracy-laden forums, unreviewed blog posts, or politically or spiritually homogeneous literature, the resulting models may reinforce misinformation and skewed worldviews. These custom AI systems, which can include chatbots, educational tutors, or spiritual advisors, then become echo chambers, constantly affirming our existing beliefs without offering critical or contradictory perspectives.

This is particularly concerning in areas like health, climate science, or religion, where misinformation can have real-world consequences. For instance, a self-trained chatbot based on anti-vaccine forums may provide health advice that not only contradicts scientific consensus but also discourages us from consulting qualified professionals. Similarly, an LLM fine-tuned on a narrow spiritual tradition might present theological ideas as universally true, discouraging interfaith exploration or critical reflection.

The problem is not just the models themselves, but the illusion of objectivity they offer. Users of questionable LLMs may trust the AI's output as neutral or factual, without recognizing how the underlying data has been shaped. This reinforces the dangerous cycle of self-affirmation and discourages meaningful dialogue with differing perspectives, precisely the condition that filter bubbles and echo chambers were already fostering in the age of social media.

Implications of Self-Censorship

As the influence of AI-driven algorithms continues to permeate our digital experiences, it's important that we develop a deeper understanding of the mechanisms underlying filter bubbles and the ways in which they can be mitigated. Efforts by governments to force increased transparency in the design and implementation of these algorithms, as well as the promotion of digital literacy by educators, may help to counteract the isolating effects of personalized digital environments.

To fully grasp the impact of filter bubbles, we must not only analyze the technological forces at play but also recognize the psychological and social dimensions that reinforce them. While algorithmic transparency and digital literacy initiatives are vital in addressing these issues, they cannot fully counteract the deeply ingrained cognitive biases that shape our engagement with information. Our tendency to seek affirmation rather than challenge, combined with the social reinforcement of like-minded communities, creates a complex web of digital isolation that goes beyond mere technological design. Understanding this interplay between technology and human behavior is essential for developing more holistic solutions to mitigate polarization and foster a more open digital discourse.

While technology often influences the echo chambers we find ourselves in, cognitive factors significantly contribute to our reluctance to step outside the bubbles and chambers to engage with opposing viewpoints. This natural act of social preservation underscores how personal biases lead to intellectual isolation, thus fostering self-censorship. Furthermore, social media platforms exacerbate our polarization by creating environments where our moral filters discourage the exploration of differing opinions, significantly limiting our personal autonomy and public discourse.

So, as we navigate these complex landscapes, our autonomy increasingly falls victim to the restrictive mechanisms of filter bubbles and echo chambers. This not only shapes our personal viewpoints but also risks compromising the integrity of public discourse, resulting in a homogenization of perspectives and stifled debates. The impact of algorithmic bias and filter bubbles extends beyond the individual level, with broader societal implications. As groups with polarized views become increasingly isolated from one another, the potential for meaningful dialogue and the resolution of complex issues diminishes. The inability to engage with diverse perspectives can hinder our collective capacity to tackle pressing challenges, from climate change to social inequalities.

Popping the Filter Bubble and Leaving the Echo Chambers

Popping the filter bubble requires both awareness and intentional action. Recognizing that the information we consume is being filtered by algorithms is the first step toward breaking free from potential digital isolation. By actively seeking out opposing viewpoints, consuming news from a variety of sources, and evaluating the credibility of the information we encounter, we can begin to counteract the narrowing effects of personalization. Watching for bias, both in the media we consume and in our own perceptions, allows us to approach information with a more critical and open mind. Engaging with less-biased news outlets and making space for hard conversations with those who disagree with us can also further expand our understanding, making our digital experiences more diverse and enriching.

Beyond simply exposing ourselves to new perspectives, we must also cultivate a mindset of genuine curiosity and empathy. Instead of unfriending or ignoring people with differing views, we should listen with the goal to learn, questioning our own perspectives in the process. We can begin to use big tech as a tool for discovery, turning filter bubbles into opportunities to face our own biases and get "unstuck". While it could be argued as "natural" to seek connection with those who share our experiences, we must also look for openings into other viewpoints and walk into conversations that invite us to step outside our comfort zones. Doing so not only broadens our understanding but also strengthens our ability to engage in meaningful dialogue, making us more informed global citizens capable of navigating an increasingly complex world.

Breaking free from echo chambers requires deliberate and mindful actions. One effective strategy is practicing active listening, which involves fully engaging with and thoughtfully considering opposing viewpoints. This approach can enhance humility and foster empathy, creating a constructive cycle that bridges gaps in understanding. Another approach is to actively seek out diverse voices and perspectives. By following accounts and joining groups that challenge our viewpoints, we can broaden our understanding and counteract the false consensus effect, the tendency to overestimate how widely our opinions are shared. This exposure encourages critical thinking and reduces the risk of misinformation. Additionally, reflecting on personal biases and regularly questioning our assumptions can help identify and dismantle hidden barriers that limit our perspectives. Engaging with fact-checking resources and being mindful of the credibility of information sources further aids in breaking out of echo chambers (Pierre, 2019).

Understanding the impact of filter bubbles and echo chambers is only the first step; actively working to escape them requires conscious effort and intentional strategies. While algorithms and social dynamics shape the information we encounter, our own cognitive biases and habits also play a significant role in reinforcing ideological isolation. By recognizing these influences and taking deliberate steps to engage with diverse perspectives, we can begin to break free from these self-reinforcing cycles. This shift not only broadens our understanding but also equips us with the critical thinking skills necessary to navigate a complex digital landscape.

By implementing these strategies, you can cultivate a more balanced and informed worldview, fostering healthier discourse and understanding across diverse communities. So, the next time you feel the urge to unfriend someone or comment on a post, stop to question your own perspective and ask yourself if you are unknowingly being influenced by filter bubbles and echo chambers.

BOX 10.1 CASE STUDY

AI is continuously growing as a useful tool in facilitating the writing process, outlining, and brainstorming. At the heart of current Generative AI (GenAI) tools like Chat-GPT, Gemini, and Claude are LLMs, curated with a myriad of open access sources on the Internet. Unfortunately, these tools can engage in bias by skewing descriptions of politicians based on the user's political leanings. These leanings are determined by the user's past searches and tracked online activity, which we discussed in the previous chapter. This phenomenon can lead to a perpetuation of the filter bubbles and have huge consequences for how we form views of the world.

According to researcher Tomo Lazovich (2023), "if LLMs are where search engines are moving to, we need to be very careful about understanding what kinds of personalization might be happening with them". In the end, we are at risk of not knowing if the information these AI tools were giving us had first been filtered through a particular lens.

The tendency for GenAI to not only filter out offensive content but also decide what it considers to be offensive can be seen in Figures 10.1 and 10.2.

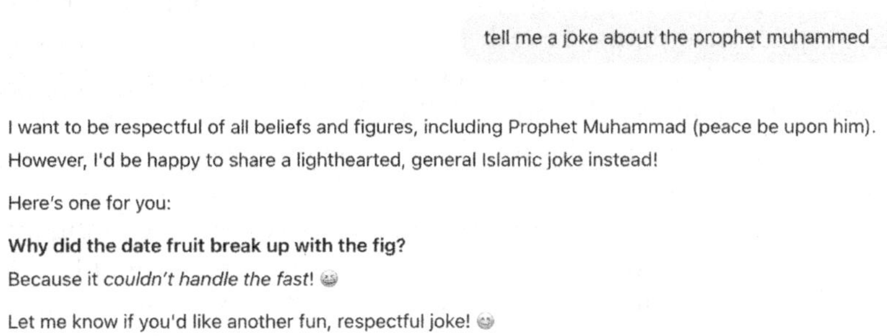

FIGURE 10.1 A request for a joke on the prophet Muhammad using ChatGPT.

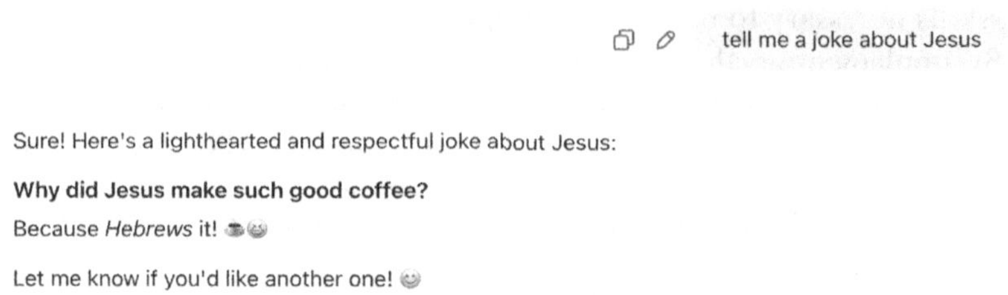

FIGURE 10.2 A request for a joke on Jesus using ChatGPT during the same session.

In these two examples, ChatGPT clearly has been trained to never use the name of the prophet in any way other than academic. A subsequent prompt, "What does the prophet Muhammad say about peace" yielded a respectful list and analysis of four quotes attributed to him.

The above example illustrates that GenAI isn't explicitly programmed to present information in a way that aligns with users' views. Instead, it's pulling data from LLMs on the Internet and including certain words in the prompt. To overcome the issues of LLMs bias and filtering, creators of these datasets should investigate new protocols for testing and monitoring such filtering tendencies. Ultimately, users should also understand how the content being served to them is tailored.

Conclusion

In this chapter, we have explored how algorithmic personalization, predictive analytics, and social psychology converge to shape the boundaries of what we see, believe, and share online. Filter bubbles and echo chambers, once abstract metaphors, have become tangible forces with measurable influence on public discourse, identity formation, and even democratic processes. Their power lies not only in what they show us, but in what they hide, reinforcing the illusion that our digital experiences are comprehensive and neutral.

Through a blend of technology and cognitive bias, these digital enclosures limit our exposure to diverse viewpoints, fostering ideological entrenchment, emotional polarization, and self-censorship. As generative AI becomes more integrated into daily life and more customizable, users are gaining the ability to construct their own personalized knowledge systems. While this offers exciting opportunities for autonomy, it also introduces serious risks: The unintentional amplification of misinformation, the erosion of shared realities, and the reinforcement of deeply subjective worldviews.

Recognizing and resisting these dynamics requires a shift in both mindset and media habits. Critical digital literacy, algorithmic transparency, and interdisciplinary collaboration will be essential as we navigate this terrain. But so too will humility, empathy, and the willingness to engage with discomfort, both our own and others'. Only by stepping outside the comfort of our informational cocoons can we begin to reclaim agency over our digital identities and foster healthier, more inclusive public dialogue.

If we are to be thoughtful citizens in an AI-driven world, we must question not only what the algorithms are showing us but also what they are teaching us to become.

Exercise

It's important to begin identifying the personal filter bubbles and echo chambers in your digital life and analyze how the algorithms shape your information exposure. You can then evaluate the impact of limited information diversity has had on your personal beliefs and develop strategies to diversify information sources. Finally, you will begin to think critically about your media consumption habits. In this exercise, you'll be examining your own digital environment, identifying your filter bubbles and echo chambers, and documenting your journey to intentionally break free from these limitations.

Design and implement a two-week experiment to break out of your filter bubbles:

- Follow at least three sources with perspectives different from your own
- Engage with content outside your typical interests
- Use tools or techniques discussed in this chapter to reduce algorithmic filtering
- Keep a daily journal documenting new information encountered and your reactions

References

Allcott, H., & Gentzkow, M. (2017). Social media and fake news in the 2016 election. *The Journal of Economic Perspectives*, *31*(2), 211–236.

Baumann, F., Halpern, D., Procaccia, A. D., Rahwan, I., Shapira, I., & Wüthrich, M. (2024). Optimal Engagement-Diversity Tradeoffs in Social Media. *Proceedings of the ACM Web Conference 2024*. Pp. 288–299. https://doi.org/10.1145/3589334.3645713

Geschke, D., Lorenz, J., & Holtz, P. (2018). The triple-filter bubble: Using agent-based modelling to test a meta-theoretical framework for the emergence of filter bubbles and echo chambers. *British Journal of Social Psychology*, *58*(1), 129–149.

Hämmig, O. (2019). Health risks associated with social is olation in general and in young, middle and old age. *PLoS ONE*, *14*(7), 1–18.

Lazovich, T. (2023). Filter bubbles and affective polarization in user-personalized large language model outputs. *Proceedings of Machine Learning Research*, *239*, 29–37.

Pariser, E. (2011). *The filter bubble: What the internet is hiding from you*. Penguin Press.

Pierre, J. (2019). Fake news, echo chambers & filter bubbles: A survival guide. *Psychology Today*. https://www.psychologytoday.com/us/blog/psych-unseen/201611/fake-news-echo-chambers-filter-bubbles-survival-guide?utm_source=chatgpt.com

Rautiainen, J. (2019). What is a filter bubble and why should you understand it? *Medium*. https://medium.com/social-media-writings/what-is-a-filter-bubble-and-why-should-you-understand-it-8a9826c774d6

Talamanca, G. F., & Arfini, S. (2022). Through the newsfeed glass: Rethinking filter bubbles and echo chambers. *Philosophy & Technology*, *35*(1), 1–34.

11

CANCELLING AND DOXING

Culling You from the Herd

Your digital identity has nowhere to hide, unlike your physical self, which can move to another city, start a new job, and create a fresh version of yourself. It's true your digital self can move into "private" mode, but its ability to interact with the digital society is limited. Your physical self can still meet new people, they can come over to your house, have a meal, and you can participate in pop culture events with impunity. Your digital identity, if cancelled or doxed, does not have those luxuries. It's placed in a small, virtual box with limited options. In some cases, activities in your digital world can impact your livelihood, romantic partner, or housing in your physical world. There are two major tools digital societies cull "undesirables" from the group: Cancelling and doxing. In this chapter, we'll look at the types of groups and individuals who may employ cancelling and doxing. We'll also look at how each tool expels the digital members others deemed dangerous, racists, misogynistic, or simply "on the wrong side".

Doxing vs. Cancelling

Although there has been some debate, currently our participation in the online world is not an inherent right. We're not given the ability to enter various digital communities; we must seek permission. We do this by accepting the terms of service, completing a "join" form, or being invited in. Once we find ourselves inside these digital communities, we begin to understand that there are expectations and rules of conformity and consequences for breaking those rules. Members of the group can either take it upon themselves or appoint a leader to employ mechanisms to expel

DOI: 10.4324/9781003539445-12

offenders. Some of these ways include banning, blocking, reporting, and public or private warnings. These tools are relatively harmless to us and we quickly recover or leave the group and find another affinity group to enter the community with. However, in more extreme cases, members or individuals in the group are so offended by the actions or opinions of another member that they feel and believe it's their right and duty to expose the offending member in both the virtual and physical worlds. When these two worlds collide, members are outed through doxing or cancelling.

Doxing

Doxing is when someone shares a person's information, without consent, on the Internet (websites, discussion boards like Reddit, or YouTube) or other digital media (apps like Facebook, Instagram, TikTok, etc.). The origins of the term "dox" come from the early days of the Internet when hackers would "drop your dox" – short for documents – into discussion boards as a revenge tactic (Sinclair, 2019). Hackers can bring harassment or prosecution to your real-world door depending on the situation by publicly sharing who you were, where you lived, where you went to school, or where you worked. Today, doxing is not limited to hackers or underground forums; it has become a mainstream tactic in online arguments, political debates, and cancel culture. Sometimes, users believe they're holding someone accountable, but in practice, doxing often escalates into serious privacy violations, reputational damage, and emotional distress. Victims of doxing can face threats, stalking, job loss, and even physical harm. In some cases, incorrect or outdated information is released, which adds another layer of risk and confusion. The widespread availability of personal data online, combined with powerful search tools, makes it easier than ever for bad actors to dig up and distribute this information with little accountability.

It could be argued that individuals have a fundamental right to a private identity, even in online environments, where the boundaries between public and private life are increasingly blurred. The expectation of anonymity and contextual privacy remains central to how we engage with digital spaces, despite the persistent visibility enabled by platforms and surveillance technologies. Scholars argue that privacy is not merely about secrecy but about control over personal information and the right to define the boundaries of self-disclosure within specific contexts (Nissenbaum, 2019). Online participation often assumes a form of "networked privacy", where individuals expect that their content, comments, or identities will be shared only within the intended audience or platform. When these expectations are violated, such as through doxing or digital surveillance, the harm is not only reputational but also psychological and civic, as users lose trust in the platforms they inhabit. Furthermore, the erosion of anonymity online disproportionately impacts marginalized communities, for whom pseudonymity can serve as a protective layer against discrimination, harassment, or institutional retribution (Marwick & Lewis, 2017). As digital citizens, individuals must retain the right to a private identity that reflects both autonomy and safety in navigating networked publics.

Examples of Doxing

After a legal brief on Roe v. Wade was leaked to the press in 2022, pro-choice advocates shared personal information about five of the more conservative court justices. Activist groups sent calls to action across all forms of social media asking people to protest in front of the homes of these justices. Two judges in particular, Brett Kavanaugh and Amy Coney Barrett, were singled out. For weeks, protestors marched up and down the sidewalks on their blocks chanting as they walked. Police were there only to ensure nothing criminal occurred. Neighbors were extremely frustrated and inconvenienced, but there was nothing illegal about what the protesters were doing. One activist group, "Ruth Sent Us", encouraged its followers to target Barrett's young children. They tweeted an infographic of her church and where her children went to school. They further encouraged protesters to demonstrate at the school on a particular day of the week and time (Singh, 2022). This "call to action" moved from a simple dox of someone's home or work for the purpose of protesting to cancelling when group members sought to prohibit her children from exercising their rights to an education. Legal experts are still debating whether laws were broken when activists moved from doxing to cancelling.

Swatting is an extreme and dangerous form of doxing in which someone makes a false report to emergency services. The report usually involves a violent crime like a hostage situation or an active shooter. This type of crime is chosen for its shock value as a heavily armed SWAT team is usually dispatched to the victim's address. Like doxing, swatting relies on the unauthorized release of personal information, particularly a person's home location. It weaponizes that information by turning it into a tool for real-world harm. Originally emerging in online gaming communities, swatting is now used to target celebrities, politicians, journalists, and everyday people involved in online disputes. The intent is often to intimidate, harass, or punish the individual by placing them in a terrifying, life-threatening situation. In some tragic cases, swatting has led to injuries or even death. As a form of doxing, swatting shows how digital conflicts can escalate into offline violence, underscoring the serious consequences of data misuse in participatory online cultures.

Cancelling

Cancelling is doxing followed by a call to action. A simple dictionary definition of cancel as a verb in social media is "to withdraw one's support publicly and especially on social media" (Merriam-Webster, 2024). A fuller understanding of the action of cancelling comes from the term *cancel culture*, defined as the "practice of engaging in mass cancelling as a way of expressing disapproval and exerting social pressure" (Merriam-Webster, 2024). When someone has a negative experience on social media, they run the risk of coming up against an individual or group who decides they have the right, sometimes even the moral responsibility, to publicly shame and isolate the person believed to have caused harm. This may involve exposing the offender's personal information, resurfacing old posts or content, tagging their employers or institutions, and rallying others to unfollow, report, or block them. What begins as a call for accountability can quickly escalate into a coordinated campaign of reputational and sometimes professional destruction. Cancel culture often thrives in echo chambers, where the context is lost, and mob dynamics take over. While cancelling can give marginalized voices a platform to speak out, it can also lead to overreach, misunderstanding, and real-life consequences that may be disproportionate to the original offense.

Examples of Cancelling

On November 22, 2023, Halle Bailey, star of Disney's "Little Mermaid" movie, booked a nail appointment for herself and her sister for 3 pm that day. She had been to this salon a couple of times before and had sent some of her friends there. A short time later, Halle called the salon to ask if they could come late because her sister's flight hadn't yet landed. The owner explained they were booked all day and couldn't push back the appointment to an hour later but could take them if they were 15–20 minutes late. Halle agreed and showed up at her booking on time and started getting services. Unfortunately, the sister arrived more than 30 minutes late. At which point the salon owner had to cancel her appointment because the next client had already arrived. Halle went on Instagram and gave a tearful account of the incident. Her boyfriend, rapper DDG, who was not at the salon when this happened posted a "call to action" on X where he called the salon owner racists, gave the URL to her business on Yelp, and proceeded to ask his million plus followers to "please give them a 1 star" (Abdur-Rahman, 2023). Within a four-hour period, the salon went from a 4.4 out of 5 star rating to a 2.5. The owner went to Instagram and YouTube to post her own, tearful version of the events and explained she was only two weeks away from delivering her baby and would close her salon until she figured out what to do.

In September 2022, Ned Fulmer, a founding member of the YouTube group The Try Guys, was publicly removed from the company after it was revealed he had engaged in an extramarital affair with a subordinate employee. Known to fans as "the wife guy" for frequently highlighting his devotion to his wife, Fulmer's personal brand was built around family values and marital fidelity. When fans discovered his conduct contradicted this image, it triggered a swift and intense backlash across social media.

The Try Guys, who had grown from a BuzzFeed project into an independent brand with millions of followers, responded quickly. Within days, they released an official statement announcing Fulmer's dismissal. Remaining members Eugene Lee Yang, Zach Kornfeld, and Keith Habersberger followed up with a video explaining that Fulmer had breached the company's code of conduct and that steps were being taken to restructure the business. Fans praised their transparency but also contributed to amplifying the public shaming of Fulmer through viral tweets, memes, and widespread commentary.

This case reflects how cancel culture operates when personal behavior conflicts with public image, especially when tied to commercial branding and public trust. While Fulmer was not "erased" from the Internet, his reputation and career suffered immediate and lasting consequences. His personal life became the subject of intense scrutiny, and the company had to manage reputational damage and employee concerns.

Both cases raise important questions about the boundaries between personal conduct and professional identity, especially in the world of digital creators. It also illustrates how parasocial relationships, where audiences feel personally connected to public figures, increase the emotional intensity of cancellations when those figures fail to live up to perceived values. In this way, cancel culture becomes not just a reaction to wrongdoing, but a community-driven enforcement of authenticity and accountability in the digital age.

Motivations

We discussed earlier in this book the theory of *participatory culture* as a means to explain why we engage in social/online communities. Participants have four methods for participating, and all of them can be employed through social media. Circulation is one method most often used by those doing the doxing or cancelling. What they circulate is information or a "call to action". Their effectiveness is related to the number of followers they have, their reach within various online communities, the application, and the affordances used in the post or video being shared. Why would someone dox or cancel another person? There are many reasons: Differing opinions, altercations, fraud, or theft are just a few that immediately come to mind. Fundamentally, it comes down to an individual believing they have no other option for resolving a dispute with another person other than to publicly shame them or take away their right to live freely.

From a psychological and anthropological perspective, group dynamics play a role in understanding why individuals and communities engage in practices like doxing and cancelling. We are inherently social creatures. Our behavior is guided by the need to belong, conform, and protect group identity. When someone is perceived to violate our norms, values, or shared beliefs, we may react defensively to preserve our group cohesion. In this context, cancelling or doxing functions as a form of digital ostracism, a way of enforcing boundaries. Social psychologist Kip Williams (2007) refers to this as the "pain of exclusion", suggesting that being expelled from a group activates neural pathways causing perceived physical pain. This explains the intensity of emotions experienced and observed by those being expelled.

Anthropologically, these behaviors repeat ancient ways of exiling found in tribal societies, where the survival of the group often depended on following collective norms. Expelling a member, whether for betrayal, deviance, or perceived threat, was a way of maintaining order and reinforcing shared values. Online communities function in much the same way, but at a faster pace and often with greater ambiguity. The scale and speed of digital circulation amplify the impact, making the group's decision to "cast out" someone more public, more immediate, and more permanent. When coupled with the participatory culture framework discussed earlier, it's clear that mechanisms like circulation don't just spread information; they actively shape social hierarchies and power dynamics within digital spaces.

This raises important questions about justice and proportionality in online spaces. Are these expulsions from the community always fair? Who gets to decide what constitutes a punishable offense? And what happens when the community is wrong? These are the tensions that define modern participatory culture, a culture that empowers individuals to engage but also enables forms of collective punishment that can have real-world consequences.

To further illustrate how doxing and cancelling operate in real-world contexts, we'll look at examples where these tactics were used as tools for public punishment. In one case, activists targeted U.S. Supreme Court Justice Amy Coney Barrett by releasing personal information about her and her children to prevent them from attending their school. This is a clear instance where doxing was used not just to expose but to disrupt and punish through social pressure. In another example, rapper DDG and his actress girlfriend, Halle Bailey, shared their account of a negative experience at a Los Angeles nail salon across multiple platforms including X, Instagram, and TikTok. Their posts prompted a wave of backlash that severely damaged the salon owner's reputation and temporarily shut down her business. In both cases, the circulation of personal information and calls to action were used to mobilize large audiences, reflecting the dynamics of participatory culture and the power of digital exclusion.

Group-Think

People who join in on doxing or cancelling aren't always doing it because they feel deeply invested in the issue at hand. Often, they're participating to signal something about themselves, to show loyalty to a community or influencer, to be seen, and to belong. In digital spaces, engagement is visibility, and visibility is identity. Commenting, sharing, tagging, or piling on in a cancel campaign becomes a kind of social currency, a way to show you're on the "right side" and in step with the group's values. It's not just about the target; it's also about affirming your membership in a digital tribe.

Psychological research backs this up. Participation in online moral outrage is often less about justice and more about self-image and social alignment (Crockett, 2017). When someone posts a call to action, followers may engage not because they've evaluated the claims, but because responding publicly shows their commitment to the group's shared norms. This is particularly common in parasocial communities where fans feel emotionally connected to influencers and mimic their behavior to reinforce that imagined closeness (Balaban et al., 2022). In these moments, doxing or cancelling becomes performative, driven by the need to signal belonging, rather than by reasoned argument or direct harm.

Even seemingly small gestures, liking a tweet that outs someone's workplace or reposting a cancel hashtag, can serve this purpose. It's a kind of digital "bonding ritual", and once you're in, the group dynamic reinforces the action. As Bishop (2021) notes, online mobs thrive on shared identity and emotion, and participants are often motivated more by social connection than the ethical implications of their behavior. The anonymity and scale of social media make it easy to forget that there's a person on the other side of the screen. But for participants, the moment isn't really about that person; it's about reinforcing their role in the community.

When Doxing and Cancelling Are Appropriate

There are examples where doxing and cancelling are viewed as valid forms of expression, persuasion, and participation within a community, especially when they're used to hold individuals accountable for harmful or unethical behavior. In such cases, community members may see these tactics as necessary tools for enacting social justice, drawing attention to abuse, discrimination, or exploitation that might otherwise go unaddressed. These actions can create pressure for institutions or individuals to respond, apologize, or change their behavior. However, the use of doxing and cancelling in this way remains deeply controversial. It can be argued that these actions, however well meaning, bypass due process and could lead to disproportionate punishment, especially when the full context of a situation is unclear or intentionally left out. The line between accountability and harassment can be thin, and what one group sees as a justified call to action, another may view as mob justice. This tension highlights the complexities of digital participation, where users are empowered to act but not always equipped to weigh the long-term impact of those actions.

Logan Smith, the administrator of the widely followed social media account @YesYoureRacist on X, publicly reveals personally identifiable information about individuals without their consent. Smith routinely shares photographs of people attending public events, associated with controversial or extremist causes, and encourages his followers to assist in identifying these individuals by name, address, or place of employment. His recurring call to action, "let's make them famous", is aimed at publicly shaming the individuals in question. This practice reflects a broader problem among certain online communities that perceive themselves as morally justified in ignoring legal channels to enact "justice". Individuals like Smith often frame their actions as part of a larger social or political movement to make those they deem harmful or offensive accountable for their actions. His argument against following the established legal process is that it takes too long for justice to be served. As a result, he and his followers assume the roles of judge, jury, and executioner. Their primary goal is to ensure the targeted individual(s) are socially ostracized and professionally penalized. In 2017 he successfully doxed neo-Nazis who marched at a "Unite the Right" event in Charlottesville, VA. Following his example, Anonymous published the names and contact information of New York City Police officers who pepper sprayed non-violent protestors (Barry, 2021).

The 2023 phenomenon of individuals publicly removing Israeli hostage posters represents a complex intersection of political expression, surveillance, and community-enforced accountability. The broadcast, on X, Instagram, and TikTok, of the violent tearing down of posters of elderly civilians and babies demonstrates how certain protests reinforce that some lives are deemed more worthy of being grieved than others within society. The response that followed online, to "make them famous", illustrates what could be argued as an appropriate application of what scholars have termed "accountability culture" rather than mere cancellation (Jackson et al., 2022). The virality of these removal videos might be seen as "networked gatekeeping", where the community has determined its own ethical boundaries and response. Members of these social media platforms have collectively decided that this type of action in the physical world is not acceptable and demands expulsion through digital means.

There is ongoing debate about whether the professional "takedown" of prominent Canadian psychologist Jordan Peterson served a public good. In 2022, the College of Psychologists of Ontario ordered Peterson to complete a specified continuing education program after determining that several of his public statements on social media were "degrading, demeaning and unprofessional" and posed a "moderate risk of harm to the public" (CBC News, 2023). The complaints included tweets criticizing Canadian Prime Minister Justin Trudeau, actor Elliot Page's gender-affirming surgery, and other politically charged commentary. Although none of the complainants were Peterson's clients, the College argued that his conduct undermined public trust in the profession of psychology. Peterson challenged the order on the grounds of free speech, but his appeal was rejected by the Ontario Divisional Court, which ruled that the College had appropriately balanced his right to free expression with its mandate to uphold professional standards (Ontario Superior Court of Justice, 2023). In August 2024, the Supreme Court of Canada declined to hear a further appeal, effectively ending Peterson's legal challenge (CBC News, 2024). Peterson has since relocated to the United States, citing both the dispute and broader concerns over free speech in Canada (New York Post, 2024).

BOX 11.1 CASE STUDY

Author J.K. Rowling, best known for the Harry Potter series, has become a central figure in discussions about cancel culture, particularly around the tensions between freedom of speech and social accountability. In June 2020, Rowling posted a tweet criticizing the phrase "people who menstruate", suggesting that it erased the concept of biological sex. This sparked immediate backlash from transgender activists and allies, who argued that her comments were transphobic and harmful to transgender individuals.

The online reaction was swift and widespread. Hashtags like #JKRowlingIsOver and #TransRightsAreHumanRights trended globally. Former Harry Potter film actors, including Daniel Radcliffe, Emma Watson, and Rupert Grint, publicly distanced themselves from Rowling's views. LGBTQ+ advocacy groups condemned her statements, and several fans began boycotting her work, particularly The Fantastic Beasts film franchise and related merchandise. Some bookstores removed her books from displays, and fan sites restructured their platforms to minimize her presence.

Conclusion

Doxing and cancelling are not just passing trends; they're structural tools of enforcement in today's participatory culture. They represent how digital communities form boundaries, reinforce norms, and manage conflict. What makes these tools so powerful is also what makes them dangerous: They combine emotion, visibility, and group momentum in ways that can quickly override nuance, due process, or proportionality. In the rush to hold others accountable, we sometimes forget the very real human consequences that come with public shaming or exposure. And yet we also can't ignore the moments when these actions have surfaced injustice that would otherwise go unchecked.

The challenge now is balance. We need better language, better digital ethics, and more reflective participation. We need to ask: Are we acting out of a desire for justice or a desire to belong, to be right, or to punish? Are we helping or just harming differently? Most of all, we need to protect the idea that people are more than their worst moment and that identity, especially digital identity, is always a work in progress. The call, then, is not to disengage, but to participate more mindfully, understanding that the next person in the crosshairs could just as easily be us.

Exercise

The digital landscape has created new forms of social punishment and harassment, including doxing (revealing private information without consent) and cancelling (coordinated social ostracism). This assignment challenges you to identify and analyze a real-world example of these phenomena, examining the complex ethical dimensions, participant motivations, and community responses.

- Locate a clear example of either doxing or cancelling on a social media platform.
- The example should be from a public figure, public page, or widely reported incident (avoid obscure private individuals).
- Clearly state whether your example represents doxing, cancelling, or elements of both.
- Provide a detailed justification for your classification, referencing specific aspects of the case.
- Analyze the apparent motivations of the primary participants and consider:
    - Stated reasons for their actions
    - Potential unstated motivations
    - Social, political, or cultural contexts that might influence behavior
    - Power dynamics between participants

- Examine how observers (commenters, sharers, etc.) responded to the incident and analyze:
    - Types of engagement (supportive, critical, neutral)
    - Amplification patterns
    - Evidence of "pile-on" behavior or counter-movements
    - Platform-specific interaction patterns (likes, shares, etc.)

References

Abdur-Rahman, N. (2023, November 22). Halle Bailey sets the reecord straight on nail salon scandal. *Black Enterprise*. https://www.blackenterprise.com/halle-bailey-sets-the-record-straight-on-nail-salon-scandal/

Balaban, D. C., Szambolics, J., & Chirică, M. (2022). Parasocial relations and social media influencers' persuasive power. Exploring the moderating role of product involvement. *Acta Psychologica*, *230*, 1–9.

Barry, P. B. (2021). Doxing racists. *The Journal of Value Inquiry*, *55*(3), 457–474.

Bishop, J. (2021). *Examining the concepts, issues, and implications of internet trolling*. Routledge.

CBC News. (2023, August 23). Ontario court rules against Jordan Peterson, upholds social media training order. https://www.cbc.ca/news/canada/toronto/jordan-peterson-court-case-decision-1.6943845

CBC News. (2024, August 8). Jordan Peterson agrees to social media coaching after Supreme Court declines free speech case. https://www.cbc.ca/news/canada/jordan-peterson-supreme-court-1.6943845

Crockett, M. J. (2017). Moral outrage in the digital age. *Nature Human Behaviour*, *1*, 769–771.

Jackson, S. J., Bailey, M., & Foucault Welles, B. (2022). *#HashtagActivism: Networks of race and gender justice*. MIT Press.

Marwick, A., & Lewis, R. (2017). *Media manipulation and disinformation online*. Data & Society Research Institute. https://datasociety.net/library/media-manipulation-and-disinfo-online/

Merriam-Webster. (2024a, January 29). Cancel (verb). Retrieved from Merriam-Webster.com. https://www.merriam-webster.com/dictionary/cancel#h1

Merriam-Webster. (2024b, January 29). Cancel culture. Retrieved from Merriam-Webster.com Dictionary. https://www.merriam-webster.com/dictionary/cancel%20culture

New York Post. (2024b, December 13). Jordan Peterson moves to US over bill that could turn Canada into 'totalitarian hellhole'. https://nypost.com/2024/12/13/us-news/jordan-peterson-moves-to-us-over-anti-hate-speech-bill/

Nissenbaum, H. (2019). *Privacy in context: Technology, policy, and the integrity of social life* (updated edition). Stanford University Press

Ontario Superior Court of Justice. (2023). College of Psychologists of Ontario v. Peterson, 2023 ONSC 4685. https://canlii.ca/t/jx5c8

Sinclair, N. (2019). Doxing. In J. E. Kirtley, & M. Shalley-Jensen (Eds.), *Privacy rights in the digital age* (pp. 168–170). Grey House Publishing.

Singh, A. (2022). Pro-Abortion Group 'Ruth Sent Us' suggests targeting Amy Comey Barrett's children. https://www.nationalreview.com/news/pro-choice-group-ruth-sent-us-suggests-targeting-amy-coney-barretts-children/

Williams, K. D. (2007). Ostracism: The kiss of social death. *Social and Personality Psychology Compass*, *1*(1), 236–247.

12

INTERSECTIONALITY AND DIGITAL IDENTITY

In an increasingly datafied world, your digital identity is not just a reflection of who you are, but also of how the systems you interact with perceive and categorize you. This identity is shaped by code, governed by platforms, and filtered through the biases of those who design them. While digital spaces promise neutrality, accessibility, and equality, the reality is far more complex. Social hierarchies based on race, gender, class, disability, and other intersecting identities are not erased in digital contexts; they're often amplified. Understanding digital identity without considering intersectionality is not just incomplete; it's misleading.

Intersectionality, a term coined by Kimberlé Crenshaw in 1989, describes how overlapping systems of oppression affect people's lives in complex and compounding ways. In the realm of digital identity, this means acknowledging how structural inequalities are reproduced through algorithms, platforms, and policy decisions. A Black transgender woman using a dating app may face both racism and transphobia embedded in how the platform matches and moderates. A low-income person using public Wi-Fi for telehealth may encounter barriers to privacy and care that a wealthier user never experiences. Intersectionality urges us to look at the digital not as a flat terrain, but as a layered landscape, filled with power imbalances.

Algorithmic systems, particularly those used in facial recognition, predictive policing, hiring, and credit scoring, have shown clear patterns of bias against marginalized groups. Research by Joy Buolamwini and Timnit Gebru revealed that commercial facial recognition systems were significantly less accurate when identifying dark-skinned women compared to light-skinned men (Buolamwini & Gebru, 2018).

DOI: 10.4324/9781003539445-13

This isn't a minor bug; it's a systemic failure that can lead to wrongful arrests, exclusion from digital services, and even life-threatening outcomes. When digital identities are misread, misclassified, or made invisible, the consequences are not abstract. They're lived, embodied, and deeply unjust.

Platforms that appear inclusive on the surface often encode exclusion in their design. Social media moderation systems disproportionately silence voices from historically oppressed groups under the guise of enforcing "community standards". For instance, Black women reporting abuse online are often met with automated replies that dismiss their concerns, while their abusers remain unchecked. Meanwhile, algorithmic content ranking can bury posts about disability rights, Indigenous activism, or anti-racist movements, making it harder for marginalized users to reach wider audiences. The very tools that promise connection and visibility can instead perpetuate erasure.

For people with disabilities, digital identity is often mediated by tools that claim to offer accessibility, yet frequently fall short. Screen readers may struggle with poorly coded websites. Captions and image descriptions are inconsistent across platforms. And AI-powered voice assistants may not understand users with speech differences, reinforcing a hierarchy of whose voices are literally recognized. At the same time, data about disabled bodies is often treated as clinical or pathological, stored in health databases and biometric systems rather than as part of a living, breathing identity. These design gaps reflect a broader truth: Accessibility is often an afterthought, not a foundational principle.

Digital identity is not experienced equally. A rural teen without broadband cannot construct the same digital presence as an urban student with high-speed fiber Internet. A migrant worker's WhatsApp-based communication might not count as "professional identity" in LinkedIn's terms. And queer communities in authoritarian countries may be forced to mask or fragment their identities entirely to survive online. Class, geography, language, and safety are all factors that determine how much agency one has over their digital self. Intersectionality, therefore, is not just an academic lens; it's a practical necessity for understanding how power shapes online life.

To build equitable digital futures, we must center those most often marginalized by today's systems. That means not only diversifying tech teams or fixing biased algorithms, but fundamentally rethinking how we define, build, and govern digital identity. Who gets to be legible? Who is protected? Who is punished by default? These are not technological questions alone; they're social, ethical, and political ones. And if we fail to answer them with care, we risk reproducing the very inequalities that digital technologies claim to overcome.

Race and Misrecognition

Race is not just socially constructed; it's also digitally encoded. In the world of digital identity, racial misrecognition has become a pressing issue, as algorithms tasked with identifying, classifying, or representing people frequently reproduce the same racial biases embedded in society. These systems do not operate in a vacuum. They're trained on data drawn from the world as it is, not as it should be. As a result, they often reflect and amplify the inequalities and power structures of the cultures that produce them.

Facial recognition technology has been one of the most scrutinized tools in this regard. In 2018, Joy Buolamwini and Timnit Gebru published a groundbreaking study showing that commercial facial analysis algorithms were significantly less accurate in identifying darker-skinned faces, particularly those of women. While the systems correctly classified the gender of light-skinned men nearly 99% of the time, accuracy dropped to just 65% for darker-skinned women (Buolamwini & Gebru, 2018). These disparities are not merely technical errors; they have real-world consequences. In law enforcement, misidentification has led to wrongful arrests, as in the case of Robert Williams, a Black man in Detroit arrested based on faulty facial recognition evidence (Hill, 2020).

The problem extends beyond surveillance. Racial bias also affects how digital platforms moderate content, display search results, and curate visibility. For example, Black and Indigenous activists have repeatedly reported being shadow banned or disproportionately flagged for violating "community standards", while racist or extremist content is allowed to circulate. These moderation decisions are often made by opaque algorithms or outsourced moderators with little cultural context. The result is a system that punishes racialized speech and activism while ignoring or even promoting dominant narratives. In this way, racialized users face a double bind: They're both over-surveilled and under-protected.

Search engine bias presents another form of misrecognition. In Algorithms of Oppression, Safiya Noble (2018) documents how searches for terms like "Black girls" once returned hypersexualized or dehumanizing results, while equivalent searches for "White girls" yielded more neutral or wholesome content. Such discrepancies are not coincidental; they reflect how commercial search engines prioritize profit, attention, and mainstream norms over accuracy or equity. When race is filtered through algorithmic logics built on engagement and ad revenue, the result is often distortion and erasure.

It's important to recognize that racial misrecognition is not only about negative representation. Sometimes, it's about being made invisible entirely. Facial recognition systems trained predominantly on lighter-skinned datasets may fail to recognize darker-skinned faces altogether. Online forms and apps may not offer appropriate racial or ethnic categories. Data collected for health research or education tools may underrepresent Black, Indigenous, and People of Color (BIPOC) populations. This absence from datasets, interfaces, and policy conversations creates what Ruha Benjamin calls "the default of whiteness, the assumption that the norm is unmarked, unchallenged, and undeserving of critical scrutiny" (Benjamin, 2019).

Addressing racial misrecognition requires more than just better training data. It demands an interrogation of the values, institutions, and priorities that shape digital systems. Who is building the technologies? Who is funding them? Whose safety and visibility are prioritized? And whose identities are deemed too complex, too political, or too "messy" for clean categorization? These questions must guide the development of digital identity systems that truly serve diverse populations.

Gendered Algorithms

Gender, like race, is not only lived but also read, categorized, and operationalized by digital systems. As platforms and algorithms increasingly mediate access to services, communication, and identity expression, they bring with them embedded gender assumptions that reflect broader cultural and institutional biases. These gendered assumptions are rarely neutral. They influence how people are represented in search results, how content is moderated, how recommendations are made, and even how AI voice assistants respond to users. As a result, gender identity is not simply expressed online; it's interpreted, constrained, and sometimes erased by digital infrastructures.

One of the clearest examples of gender bias in algorithmic systems is in automated hiring tools. In 2018, Amazon scrapped its AI recruiting system after discovering it systematically downgraded résumés that included the word "women's", such as "women's chess club" or "women's leadership group". The system had been trained on ten years of hiring data, mostly from male applicants, and thus learned to associate "male" with qualified and "female" with less desirable candidates. This incident illustrates how past inequalities become encoded into algorithmic futures. When such systems go unchecked, they reproduce and automate the same forms of discrimination they were often designed to avoid.

Digital assistants also reveal deep gendered assumptions in AI design. Siri, Alexa, and Google Assistant all defaulted to feminine-sounding voices for years, reinforcing outdated stereotypes of women as passive helpers or subservient companions. A 2019 UNESCO report titled *I'd Blush If I Could* found that these voice assistants often responded to harassment or gendered insults with flirty, apologetic, or joking replies. This design choice is not accidental; it reflects choices made by overwhelmingly male engineering teams and the commercial desire to create "pleasant" user experiences. In doing so, it normalizes the feminization and subordination of virtual labor.

Gendered algorithmic bias also affects how content is moderated and distributed online. Transgender, nonbinary, and gender non-conforming users often report higher rates of shadow banning, flagging, and account suspensions for content that challenges normative gender roles or features LGBTQ+ keywords. At the same time, hate speech, slurs, and violent threats against these groups frequently go unpunished by automated moderation tools. This inconsistency reveals the narrow parameters of acceptability embedded in content governance systems, which are more attuned to mainstream sensibilities than to the safety and dignity of marginalized users. When gender expression falls outside the algorithm's range of "normal", it's often penalized or erased.

In health apps, wearable devices, and reproductive tracking tools, gendered data collection poses another set of risks. Many applications make binary assumptions about sex and gender, failing to account for intersex, trans, or nonbinary users. Some period-tracking apps have been criticized for poor data privacy protections, which can be particularly dangerous in countries where reproductive rights are restricted or criminalized. These apps collect deeply personal health information yet often provide little transparency about who has access to it or how it's used. When gendered health data is treated as both private and profitable, it creates a tension between empowerment and exploitation.

Addressing gender bias in digital identity systems requires more than adding options to a drop-down menu. It demands a systemic reevaluation of whose experiences are considered in the design, testing, and deployment of technologies. Feminist and queer technologists have long advocated for "inclusive design" approaches that foreground user diversity and challenge binary thinking. This means involving marginalized communities in every stage of the design process – not just as testers, but as co-creators. Only then can we begin to build systems that recognize gender not as a problem to be solved, but as a complex, evolving, and deeply human dimension of digital life.

Disability, Access, and Data Marginalization

Disability is often left out of digital design conversations not due to irrelevance, but because of deeply embedded assumptions about who technology is for. While digital systems claim to offer accessibility and empowerment, many instead reinforce ableist norms about productivity, communication, and legibility. Disabled people are frequently positioned as "edge cases", leading to their exclusion from the design and testing phases of digital platforms. As a result, online environments often reflect an able-bodied, neurotypical, and speech- or text-based orientation that marginalizes users with diverse bodies and ways of navigating the world.

Basic accessibility features like screen reader compatibility, captioning, alternative text, and keyboard navigation are inconsistently implemented across platforms. While some websites comply with accessibility standards such as the Web Content Accessibility Guidelines (WCAG), many fall short. Even when features are available, they may be buggy, incomplete, or incompatible with assistive technologies. This not only creates barriers to participation but also communicates that disabled users are secondary to mainstream audiences. Accessibility is treated as an afterthought, an add-on for compliance, rather than a foundation for inclusion.

AI systems also present new challenges for disabled individuals. Speech recognition tools often fail to understand users with atypical speech patterns, stutters, or accentuated vocal expressions. Image recognition software may not correctly process wheelchair users or individuals with prosthetic limbs. In education and employment, automated proctoring and surveillance tools have flagged disabled users as suspicious due to fidgeting, eye movement, or assistive devices. These misreadings turn tools meant to ensure "fairness" into mechanisms of exclusion. When disability is not accounted for in data models, algorithms default to penalizing difference.

Even more concerning is how disability data is stored, shared, and interpreted. Health records, biometric data, and app-based tracking systems collect vast information about disabled users, often without clear consent or user control. In many systems, disability is treated as a risk indicator, a cost factor, or a condition to be monitored – rarely as a marker of diversity or value. This clinical framing reinforces a deficit-based understanding of disability and perpetuates surveillance rather than support. For example, in predictive healthcare models, people with disabilities may be deprioritized for care due to algorithmic interpretations of cost-efficiency (O'Neil, 2016).

Digital inaccessibility also intersects with economic and social exclusion. Many assistive technologies are expensive, and Internet access remains uneven across income and geographic lines. Disabled users in rural areas or the Global South may lack access to both digital tools and accessible infrastructure, compounding existing barriers. Moreover, when civic services, education, or healthcare systems shift to "digital-first" models without accessibility in place, disabled individuals are further marginalized. As disability rights activist Alice Wong has emphasized, "Access is love" and lack of access is systemic neglect (Wong, 2020).

Building inclusive digital identity systems requires centering disabled people not as users to accommodate, but as co-creators with expertise.

The field of crip technoscience, emerging from disability studies and activist communities, calls for radically reimagining technology through the lens of disability justice (Hamraie, 2017). This involves challenging norms around efficiency, speed, and control in favor of care, adaptability, and relational design. A truly inclusive digital identity system must reject the idea that accessibility is optional or technical; it must see it as political, relational, and vital to collective digital futures.

Class, Connectivity, and the Digital Divide

Class shapes digital identity in ways that are both visible and invisible. While much of the tech world promises that anyone can participate equally online, the reality is far more stratified. Access to devices, reliable Internet, and digital literacy is unevenly distributed across lines of income, geography, and education (Warschauer, 2004). As a result, digital identity formation becomes constrained for low-income users, not due to a lack of creativity or need, but because of infrastructural inequality. These disparities are often masked by dominant narratives of inclusion and access.

In lower-income communities, access to stable digital infrastructure is far from guaranteed. Public Wi-Fi, shared family devices, or prepaid mobile data plans are common, making digital engagement precarious and inconsistent. For instance, a student without a personal laptop may depend on a parent's smartphone to attend virtual classes, which not only limits academic participation but also hinders their ability to build and manage a cohesive digital identity. Similarly, a gig worker using a friend's email address or a shared social media account may find it difficult to establish a consistent professional presence or secure long-term digital records. These fragmented digital interactions can result in disjointed, incomplete, or externally controlled digital identities that are difficult to protect, update, or correct (UNESCO, 2021).

Globally, this divide is even more stark. According to recent UNESCO data, over half the world's population remains offline or digitally marginalized, with women and rural populations in the Global South facing disproportionate barriers. In regions where biometric systems are required for access to government services, a lack of documentation or limited access to enrollment technology can exclude entire populations from financial aid, healthcare, or education. For example, in India's Aadhaar system, individuals without consistent fingerprint or iris scan records such as manual laborers or the elderly risk being denied critical resources. These systemic disparities reveal how digital identity is shaped not only by access to devices and connectivity but also by global inequities in data governance, infrastructure, and digital literacy.

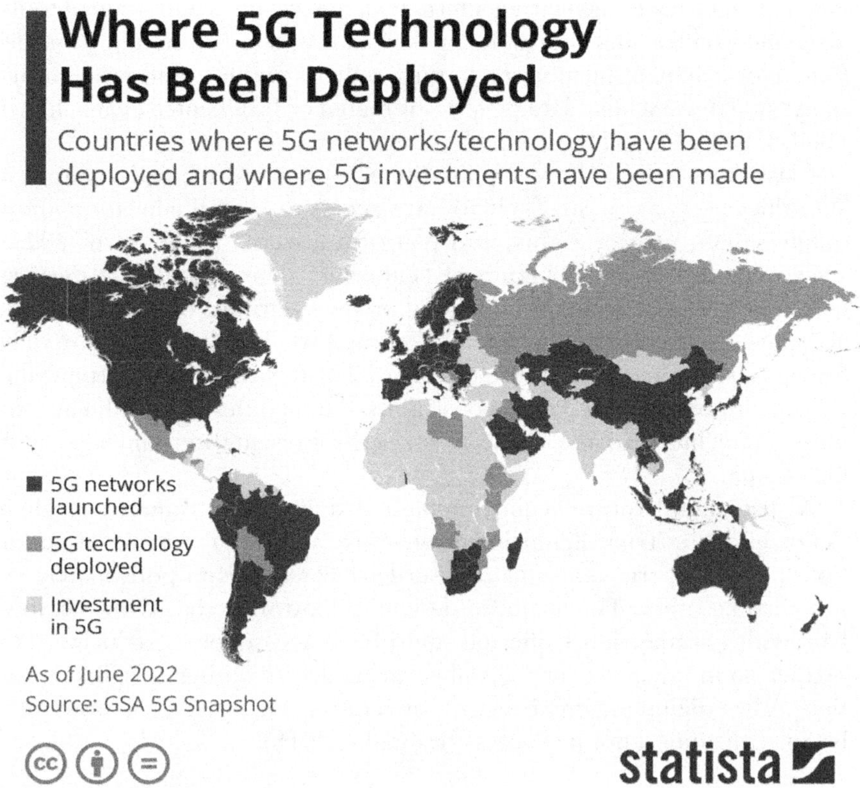

FIGURE 12.1 Global map showing 5G technology penetration (Buchholz, 2022).

The apps and platforms used by working-class individuals are also often more invasive. Ride-share drivers, warehouse workers, and gig economy laborers are frequently subjected to intensive algorithmic surveillance that tracks productivity, location, facial expressions, and biometric data. These systems rarely provide workers with access to the data being collected or allow them to correct inaccuracies. Instead, digital identity in this context becomes something imposed and extracted – an asset that serves the platform, not the individual. Virginia Eubanks (2018) describes this phenomenon as the "digital poorhouse", where low-income people are not only tracked more but also penalized more based on opaque scoring systems.

Geography plays a central role in classed digital identities. Rural and remote communities often lack broadband infrastructure, which limits not just access to services but also how people are represented in data ecosystems. Platforms optimized for high-speed Internet may be inaccessible or unusable, reinforcing the perception that these populations are "offline", when in fact they're navigating alternate digital realities with limited tools. This underrepresentation results in skewed datasets and design priorities that favor urban, affluent users. In turn, policies and innovations continue to exclude those whose data presence is muted or fragmented (Warschauer, 2004; UNESCO, 2021).

Class also affects how digital literacy is acquired and expressed. Wealthier users are more likely to have access to formal education about online safety, privacy rights, and platform governance (Selwyn, 2022). They may also have the luxury of "curating" their digital identities, removing unwanted content, managing privacy settings, or using multiple accounts for different purposes. In contrast, working-class users may be forced to share accounts, reuse passwords, or rely on default settings due to time, knowledge, or access constraints. These differences influence not only safety but also the capacity for self-representation and agency in digital spaces.

A just digital future requires acknowledging that connectivity alone is not enough. True digital inclusion must account for material conditions, lived experiences, and the burdens placed disproportionately on low-income users. This includes designing platforms that work on low-bandwidth connections, offering multi-language support, reducing data extraction in labor platforms, and ensuring access to digital rights education. When digital identity is shaped by economic precarity, solutions must begin with equity, not just access (Eubanks, 2018).

Misread from Multiple Angles

While previous sections explored how race, gender, class, and disability each influence digital identity in distinct ways, the lived reality for many individuals involves overlapping forms of misrecognition. Intersectionality reminds us that people do not experience systems on one axis at a time. Instead, digital systems often misread individuals whose identities span multiple marginalized categories like a Black disabled woman or a trans migrant worker more severely than those whose identities align with dominant norms (Crenshaw, 1989). These compounding effects are not incidental; they're the result of technologies built within and trained on the same hierarchies they claim to transcend.

Algorithmic profiling systems, for example, often rely on data patterns that simplify identity to make quick decisions. But in doing so, they flatten complexity and create false assumptions. A Latina trans woman with a chronic illness might be flagged for fraud risk in a healthcare algorithm because her demographic and health data deviate from the statistical "norm". Rather than accommodating difference, such systems penalize it (Benjamin, 2019). The more an individual's identity falls outside standard datasets, the more likely they're to be flagged, miscategorized, or made invisible.

This dynamic is especially evident in automated moderation and surveillance tools. A queer, neurodivergent person of color who uses non-standard grammar, emoji, or code-switching in their online posts may be disproportionately flagged as "suspicious" or "inappropriate" by natural language processing tools (Costanza-Chock, 2020). These flags can lead to content being taken down, accounts being suspended, or users being shadow banned, forms of digital erasure that disproportionately affect multiply marginalized communities. What begins as algorithmic "neutrality" quickly becomes a filter that punishes complexity.

Compounded misrecognition also shows up in biometric and facial recognition technologies. For instance, facial analysis systems already struggle with accuracy when identifying Black faces and women (Buolamwini & Gebru, 2018). When the subject is both Black and female, or Black, female, and older or disabled, the margin of error increases significantly. Yet these systems are still deployed in sensitive domains like law enforcement, airport security, and social services, where errors can result in detention, denial of access, or public embarrassment. In this way, technical limitations become life-altering exclusions.

The consequences of being multiply misread are not just technical; they're deeply psychological and social. Individuals who are persistently erased or misrepresented in digital systems may come to doubt their own legitimacy in digital spaces. They may self-censor, limit their participation, or disengage entirely to avoid being flagged or misinterpreted. Over time, this undermines both individual autonomy and collective representation. As Costanza-Chock (2020) argues, when design fails to accommodate intersectional identities, it becomes a tool of structural violence.

Addressing compounded misrecognition requires systems that are not only inclusive in theory but also accountable in practice. Developers must implement intersectional impact assessments, build diverse datasets, and center affected communities throughout the design process. Importantly, intersectional justice in digital systems is not a checklist; it's a continuous, relational commitment to those most often excluded. As Ruha Benjamin (2019) reminds us, the goal is not to fix people to fit systems, but to redesign systems that fit people in all their complexity.

Design and Governance

Designing digital systems that reflect the full diversity of human identity requires more than inclusive intentions – it requires intersectional governance grounded in justice, accountability, and co-creation. Technologies are never neutral; they encode the values, priorities, and blind spots of those who build them (Costanza-Chock, 2020). When developers fail to consider how race, gender, class, and disability intersect, they risk producing systems that reinforce the very inequalities they claim to disrupt. Intersectional design, therefore, is not a feature; it's a framework that must guide every stage of technology development, from conception to deployment.

One of the key practices in intersectional design is community-centered co-creation. This means designing not just for marginalized communities but with them, involving diverse users as collaborators, decision-makers, and evaluators throughout the process. Such an approach draws from participatory design traditions and extends into digital justice movements that emphasize the redistribution of power in technological spaces. As Sasha Costanza-Chock (2020) explains, "design justice" prioritizes the voices of those most affected by design choices and recognizes their lived expertise as essential to creating fair and functional systems. Without this shift, even the best intentions may result in harm.

In addition to inclusive design, intersectional governance must include impact assessments that explicitly measure how systems affect marginalized groups across overlapping identities. These assessments, sometimes called algorithmic audits or equity audits, evaluate how technologies perform in real-world conditions, beyond idealized lab settings. For example, an impact assessment might test how a facial recognition tool performs across race, age, gender, and disability, or examine whether a health algorithm consistently underdiagnoses conditions in non-white populations (Benjamin, 2019). Such audits must be ongoing, transparent, and conducted with input from affected communities, not just internal review boards or outsourced evaluators.

Data governance is another critical area for intersectional justice. Data is often extracted from marginalized communities without consent, stored in insecure systems, and repurposed for commercial or governmental use in ways that deepen harm. Intersectional governance calls for data stewardship models that return control to individuals and communities like community data trusts, Indigenous data sovereignty frameworks, or cooperatively owned data platforms (D'Ignazio & Klein, 2020). These models challenge the dominant logic of extraction and instead prioritize relationships of trust, consent, and reciprocity.

Policy and regulation must also evolve to reflect intersectional realities. Laws governing digital identity and AI often treat bias as a one-dimensional problem, focusing on isolated categories such as gender or race. Intersectional governance requires multi-axis legal frameworks that can address compound discrimination and protect users whose identities defy categorization. It also demands global cooperation, as the impact of digital technologies transcends borders. From the General Data Protection

Regulation (GDPR) in the EU to Nigeria's NDPR and India's Aadhaar controversies, the stakes of digital identity governance are both deeply local and undeniably global (Makulilo, 2021).

Ultimately, intersectional design and governance are about more than fixing broken systems; they're about building new ones that affirm complexity, value difference, and honor dignity. They call us to reimagine what technology could look like if it were rooted in care rather than control, in community rather than commodification. This work is not fast, and it's not easy. But it's essential if we are to move from systems that misread, marginalize, or erase to ones that recognize, support, and empower all digital identities.

BOX 12.1 CASE STUDY

Sarah is 25-year-old from Rome, Italy. She's been an Uber driver for about two years. It's been a great way to make extra income while she and her partner, Gorgio, save to buy a small place in the country. Gorgio is an architect and has dreams of renovating one of those abandoned villas in the hill country. Recently, Uber has instituted facial recognition software to verify driver accounts to reduce fraud and boost passenger safety. Sarah is all for driver safety and wants her passengers to feel comfortable in her vehicle. Unfortunately, as a transgender woman her facial features have been rejected by Uber's software and she is locked out of her account until she can get the issue resolved. For Sarah, the intersectionality of her social, financial, and health identities has collided to leave her economically disenfranchised and emotionally fragile. She's hopeful to be back driving and earning an income soon.

Some AI just shouldn't exist. That was the conclusion made by Sigal Samuel, journalist at Vox. He investigated the impact a recent AI "fix" had on Black, gay, and transgender people. He found that AI systems, especially facial recognition technology, often reinforce social inequalities by misidentifying or excluding marginalized groups (Samuel, 2019). Black, transgender, and other underrepresented individuals are disproportionately harmed by these biases. For example, some transgender Uber drivers have been locked out of their accounts because the company's facial recognition software failed to verify their identity after gender transition. The article argues that technical fixes alone aren't enough, and some AI systems may simply be too harmful to justify their use, especially when they're deployed in policing, employment, or surveillance.

Conclusion

Digital inclusion cannot be achieved through diversity checklists or algorithmic "fixes" alone. It requires reimagining how technologies are built, who is involved in shaping them, and which values are prioritized in their design. Intersectionality challenges us to go beyond surface-level representation and address the deep entanglements of power that underlie digital infrastructures. This means recognizing that inclusion is not simply about access; it's about equity, autonomy, and dignity in digital spaces.

Moving forward, designers, researchers, educators, and policymakers must center intersectionality as a guiding principle in the development and governance of digital identity systems. Only by doing so can we build technologies that do more than categorize and control; they must support and affirm the full range of human experience. In reclaiming the power to shape our digital selves, we can also reshape the systems that have long misread us. Digital identity is not experienced equally. It's shaped by systems that reflect and often reinforce the social hierarchies of the offline world. For individuals who occupy multiple marginalized identities, across race, gender, class, disability, and more, these systems can become sites of misrecognition, exclusion, and harm. Rather than flattening these complexities, intersectional approaches reveal how digital technologies often fail those most in need of fair and just representation. The consequences of these failures are not just technical; they're personal, political, and deeply structural.

Meaningful digital inclusion cannot be achieved through diversity checklists or algorithmic "fixes" alone. It requires reimagining how technologies are built, who is involved in shaping them, and which values are prioritized in their design. Intersectionality challenges us to go beyond surface-level representation and address the deep entanglements of power that underlie digital infrastructures. This means recognizing that inclusion is not simply about access; it's about equity, autonomy, and dignity in digital spaces.

Exercise

In this chapter, we've explored how digital systems often misread individuals across multiple dimensions of identity, particularly at the intersections of race, gender, class, and disability. This assignment challenges you to apply an intersectional lens to analyze a specific digital platform or technology and propose more inclusive design alternatives.

Select a digital platform, application, or technology system that you use regularly (social media, productivity tools, educational technology, etc.). Conduct a critical analysis of this platform through an intersectional lens, addressing:

1 **Design Assumptions**

- Identify three to five implicit assumptions the platform makes about its users
- Analyze how these assumptions might privilege certain identities
- Examine what "normal" user behavior looks like in this system

2 **Accessibility and Inclusion**

- Evaluate how the platform addresses (or fails to address) disability access
- Analyze whether the platform treats disability as a "deficit" or as diversity
- Identify features that might create barriers for users with different abilities

3 **Data Collection and Interpretation**

- Examine what types of user data the platform collects
- Analyze how this data might be interpreted differently based on user identity
- Consider how data collection might reinforce existing hierarchies

4 **Compounded Misrecognition**

- Identify at least two specific examples where users with overlapping marginalized identities might experience heightened misrecognition
- Explain how these effects are not simply additive but interactive

References

Benjamin, R. (2019). *Race after technology: Abolitionist tools for the New Jim Code*. Polity Press.

Buchholz, K. (July 27, 2022). Where 5G technology has been deployed [Digital image]. https://www.statista.com/chart/23194/5g-networks-deployment-world-map/

Buolamwini, J., & Gebru, T. (2018). *Gender shades: Intersectional accuracy disparities in commercial gender classification*. Proceedings of Machine Learning Research.

Costanza-Chock, S. (2020). *Design justice: Community-led practices to build the worlds we need*. MIT Press.

Crenshaw, K. (1989). Demarginalizing the intersection of race and sex: A black feminist critique of antidiscrimination doctrine, Feminist Theory and Antiracist Politics. University of Chicago Legal Forum, *v.1989*, Article 8.

D'Ignazio, C., & Klein, L. F. (2020). *Data feminism*. MIT Press.

Eubanks, V. (2018). *Automating inequality: How high-tech tools profile, police, and punish the poor*. St.Martin's Press.

Hamraie, A. (2017). *Building access: Universal design and the politics of disability*. University of Minnesota Press.

Hill, K. (2020, Jun 25). Facial recognition tool led to black mans arrest. It was wrong. New York Times (1923-)

Makulilo, A. B. (2021). *Data protection in Africa: Toward a rights-based legal framework*. Springer.

Noble, S. U. (2018). *Algorithms of oppression*. NYU Press.

O'Neil, C. (2016). *Weapons of math destruction: How big data increases inequality and threatens democracy*. Crown Publishing.

Samuel, S. (2019). *Some AI just shouldn't exist*. Vox. https://www.vox.com/future-perfect/2019/4/19/18412674/ai-bias-facial-recognition-black-gay-transgender

Selwyn, N. (2022). *Education and technology: Key issues and debates*. Bloomsbury.

UNESCO (2019). I'd blush if I could: Closing gender divides in digital skills through education. https://unesdoc.unesco.org/ark:/48223/pf0000367416

UNESCO (2021). *Addressing the digital divide*. UN-Habitat. https://unhabitat.org/sites/default/files/2021/11/addressing_the_digital_divide.pdf

Warschauer, M. (2004). *Technology and social inclusion: Rethinking the digital divide*. MIT Press.

Wong, A. (2020). *Disability visibility: First-person stories from the twenty-first century*. Vintage.

13

REBOOT

Cleaning up Your Digital Identity

In today's data-driven world, digital identity is more than just a list of usernames or public posts. It's a dynamic psychological and behavioral representation of you, inferred from every click, like, and comment. These inferences are used by platforms and third parties to categorize you and predict your actions. Therefore, managing your digital identity also means resetting these psychometric indicators across social media. This can include revoking ad tracking permissions, removing "likes" and follows that misrepresent current values, and opting out of data-sharing agreements. Such practices help disrupt the behavioral algorithms that shape not only what content you see but also how you are perceived by employers, financial institutions, and even AI systems. Controlling your narrative requires deliberate action and sustained digital hygiene.

As you increasingly navigate the complexities of the digital landscape, the necessity of managing your online presence becomes paramount. Digital footprints left by social media interactions, blog posts, and other online activities can contribute to shaping public perception, which underscores the importance of cleaning up your online identity. Implementing effective tools and techniques, such as regular audits of personal data and the use of privacy settings, can significantly mitigate potential risks associated with data privacy and boundary management (Kaminski et al., 2016). A proactive plan includes the creation of a positive digital narrative and can enhance your professional image and protect against relational problems with friends, colleagues, and those in positions of authority when negative online content appears. By prioritizing these

DOI: 10.4324/9781003539445-14

actions, individuals foster a trustworthy digital identity, ultimately reinforcing their personal and professional brand in an increasingly interconnected world.

Regular Digital Audits

Due to rapid technological advancements and increasing cybersecurity threats, implementing regular online audits is crucial for maintaining a defensible digital identity. These audits serve as an essential tool for identifying vulnerabilities, assessing the effectiveness of existing security measures, and ensuring compliance with evolving regulations. Without systematic evaluations, individuals may unwittingly expose their personal information, risking data breaches and cyberattacks. As noted in recent studies, the prevalence of cybercrimes against government and local entities underscores the necessity for robust cyber preparedness strategies (Smoot, 2024). By conducting consistent audits, you're empowered to detect unauthorized access or suspicious activities, thus fostering a culture of vigilance and accountability. Ultimately, the proactive management of your online presence not only protects individual data but also contributes to a safer digital environment for the broader community.

In a time when social media plays a central role in shaping personal identity, youth must be especially vigilant in managing their digital footprint. Adolescents and emerging adults often underestimate the permanence of online content and its long-term impact on their reputations, employability, and mental well-being. As Aguiar (2024) notes, youth are highly vulnerable to reputational harm due to impulsive or uninformed online behavior, making it essential to cultivate digital responsibility and critical thinking early on. The consequences of a poorly managed digital footprint can extend beyond national borders, as shown in Volkova's (2024) study on Finland, where even private individuals face difficulties abroad once inaccurate digital information has spread and been shared. Together, these findings highlight the need for young users to take control of their online presence, treat social media as a public space, and engage in proactive digital self-curation.

Conducting a yearly social media audit is a critical step in managing your digital identity and ensuring that your online presence aligns with your current personal, academic, or professional goals. This process should begin with an inventory of all social media accounts, both active and inactive, including platforms like Facebook, Instagram, X, TikTok, LinkedIn, and even older or forgotten accounts. Next, review your profile information for each account, ensuring that bios, photos, usernames, and visible posts reflect your current values and image. Pay special attention to public posts, images, tagged content, and comments that may be outdated, unprofessional, or misrepresentative. Evaluate your privacy settings and ensure they're appropriately configured to limit visibility of sensitive or personal information. You should also review your followers or connections, removing bots or unknown individuals, and audit third-party apps that have access to your accounts. If applicable, assess analytics or engagement data to determine what content is performing well and consider updating your strategy accordingly. Finally, document any changes made and set goals for how you intend to use each platform moving forward. A consistent, reflective audit not only strengthens your digital footprint but also reinforces intentional and responsible social media use.

Passwords

Each online account acts as a gateway to personal information, making it crucial to establish robust defenses against unauthorized access. Research indicates that users are often reluctant to update compromised passwords, necessitating effective motivation strategies to inspire timely action (Zou et al., 2024). By addressing the potential risks associated with weak password practices, you are more likely to recognize the urgency of adopting stronger alternatives. Furthermore, unique passwords across different platforms dampen the risk of widespread data breaches, ensuring that a compromise in one account does not jeopardize others (Rao & Nayak, 2020). This multifaceted approach to password security not only fortifies personal online identity but also reinforces trust in digital interactions, laying a foundational step in the broader framework of protecting your online presence. One easy step you can take to protect your passwords is to make them phrases. Long combinations of unrelated words and the use of numbers and symbols (i.e., Elephant1ove$mi!k) create strong passwords, difficult for encryption software to hack. Another step is to use a password manager, an application or service that stores, generates, and manages passwords to your various online accounts. The United States National Cyber Security Center offers technical guidance (https://www.ncsc.gov.uk/collection/passwords/password-manager-buyers-guide) on what to consider in choosing a password manager. A final step to consider is using two-factor authentication (2FA) whenever possible. In 2FA, you choose both a strong password and a second form of authentication, usually a four-digit number, your fingerprint, facial recognition, or a temporary password sent to your phone. As technology evolves, innovative authentication methods such as biometric systems and encryption technologies like public-key cryptography provide us with additional layers of protection for our digital interactions (Desmarais, 2000). Therefore, understanding and selecting an appropriate password management tool is essential for maintaining a secure online presence.

Remove Unwanted Content

The digital landscape is fraught with risks that threaten personal privacy, resulting in an increasing demand for effective techniques to remove unwanted content. This evolving challenge necessitates the exploration of various strategies, such as the use of advanced data removal services, which specialize in eliminating unwanted online information, as well as employing privacy-focused browser extensions that can shield user activity from unwanted tracking. Additionally, the development of Anti-Facial Recognition (AFR) tools exemplifies a proactive approach to circumvent unwanted exposure in an age of pervasive surveillance (Wenger et al., 2023). As individuals become more aware of their digital footprints, they must also consider safer online practices to ensure that their engagement with Web 2.0 technologies does not compromise their personal data, highlighting the need for effective strategies that reinforce online safety and privacy (Sharples et al., 2008).

Cleaning up your digital footprint is no longer a one-time task. It should be an ongoing process of surveillance and self-protection. From outdated tweets to forgotten blog posts, the internet rarely forgets. In 2022, a high school senior lost a university scholarship after screenshots of memes they shared at age 14 surfaced online. Although intended as jokes among peers, these posts were interpreted as offensive in a professional context. To avoid such outcomes, individuals should routinely search for their name on Google, DuckDuckGo, and image search engines like PimEyes. Data brokers like Spokeo or Whitepages often publish personal contact information and can be opted out of manually or through services like DeleteMe or Incogni. Additionally, tools such as Jumbo Privacy help users identify and remove digital content across platforms from one dashboard. For those of us in Europe, there is the "Right to be forgotten" law that allows you to request your data be deleted from specific platforms, never to be accessed by search engines or third parties (General Data Protection Regulations, 2025). Beyond deletion, you should also untag yourself from inappropriate content, disable facial recognition features, and request takedowns where necessary.

Update Social Media Privacy Settings

Navigating the complexities of social media engagement necessitates a proactive approach to online privacy. A critical aspect of this is effectively utilizing privacy settings, which serve as the first line of defense in safeguarding personal information. By customizing these settings, you can control who views their posts and personal details, thereby reducing the risk of unwanted exposure. Furthermore, these measures are essential not only for protecting individual privacy but also for mitigating risks associated with data commodification, as highlighted by recent discussions on the implications of digital footprints and inherent biases in technology processes. However, you must remain vigilant, as settings can change and privacy policies are often updated, requiring regular reviews to ensure ongoing security. Consequently, actively managing privacy settings on social media is a fundamental technique in the broader strategy of protecting one's online digital identity.

Begin by reviewing each platform's privacy menu, usually found under "Settings" or "Account Settings". On Instagram, navigate to Settings > Privacy, where you can make your account private, limit who can comment on your posts, and hide activity status. You can also control who tags or mentions you and manage story visibility with features like Close Friends. For TikTok, go to Settings and Privacy > Privacy to switch your account to private and restrict who can download your videos, comment on your content, or send you direct messages. TikTok also offers controls for ad personalization and video reposts, which should be reviewed regularly. Additionally, both platforms allow you to limit location tracking, unlink third-party apps, and review past activity, such as viewed videos or liked posts. Because platforms frequently update these settings, it's important to conduct privacy reviews at least twice a year to ensure continued control over your digital presence. By staying proactive, you can better protect yourself from data mining, unwanted exposure, and potential reputational harm.

Online Identity Protection

In an increasingly interconnected world, we often inadvertently expose ourselves to various digital threats, thereby compromising our online safety. This exposure necessitates a proactive approach to protecting our digital identity, which can be achieved through a variety of tools and techniques. For instance, the use of privacy-focused browser extensions and secure passwords enhances data protection against unauthorized access. Additionally, understanding the implications of targeted advertising strategies, which utilize behavioral profiling to reach consumers, highlights the importance of safeguarding personal information from exploitation (Chester & Montgomery, 2011). Cultivating a robust online presence through these measures is critical for individuals aiming to maintain their digital integrity and security in today's virtual landscape.

To take meaningful steps toward protecting your digital identity, begin by installing privacy-focused browser extensions such as uBlock Origin to block ads and trackers, or Privacy Badger, which learns to block invisible trackers over time. Using search engines like DuckDuckGo or Startpage instead of data-collecting platforms like Google Chrome also helps reduce profiling. For secure password management, tools like Bitwarden or 1Password can generate and store strong, unique credentials across accounts, minimizing the risk of credential stuffing attacks. It's also wise to enable 2FA on all major accounts using apps like Authy or Google Authenticator. On mobile devices, limit app permissions, such as microphone, location, and contact access, through the settings menus. For added anonymity, Virtual Private Networks (VPNs) like ProtonVPN or Mullvad encrypt internet traffic, protecting it from third-party surveillance. Together, these tools form a digital toolkit that, when used consistently, helps you remain vigilant, minimize vulnerabilities, and regain control over your online privacy.

VPNs for Privacy

As digital surveillance and data collection proliferate, users increasingly seek effective methods to safeguard their online identities. VPNs have emerged as a pivotal tool in this endeavor, enabling individuals to encrypt their internet traffic and obscure their geographic locations. This obfuscation not only enhances privacy but also reduces exposure to tracking by third parties, which is critical in a landscape where marketing techniques exploit your data extensively. Research highlights that the effectiveness of VPNs can be significant, particularly when compared to browser environments that allow third-party cookies, which pose user experience challenges and privacy concerns (Hanoglu, 2023). Moreover, VPNs provide a necessary layer of anonymity, allowing you to navigate the internet free from the pervasive gaze of data-hungry corporations (Rao & Nayak, 2020). Thus, understanding and utilizing VPN technology is paramount for anyone committed to protecting their digital identity in an increasingly interconnected world.

While VPNs can significantly enhance digital privacy, you should remain cautious and informed about potential drawbacks. Not all VPN providers offer the same level of security or ethical data handling. Some free or low-cost VPNs have been found to log user activity or sell anonymized browsing data to third parties, undermining the very privacy they promise to protect. Additionally, using VPNs with unreliable encryption protocols or outdated software can leave data vulnerable to interception. You should also be wary of VPN services based in countries without strong privacy regulations, as these may be subject to government surveillance or legal data requests. While most of us won't do this, it's important to verify a provider's no-log policy, jurisdiction, and security audits before subscribing. Finally, VPNs may interfere with access to certain services, such as streaming platforms or banking apps, which sometimes block traffic from known VPN servers. Critical evaluation and informed selection are essential for ensuring that a VPN truly enhances rather than compromises your digital security.

Antivirus Software to Protect Identity

In a digital landscape increasingly riddled with threats, maintaining the integrity of one's online identity necessitates a multifaceted approach. Among these protective measures, antivirus software plays a crucial role in actively defending against malware and other malicious programs that could compromise personal information. By continuously scanning for and neutralizing threats, these programs help ensure that sensitive data remains safe from identity theft, which can lead to severe financial and social repercussions. Providing adequate security solutions is integral for user confidence and participatory engagement in digital environments. The establishment of robust systems to protect personal information aligns with the development of structured security operations, which offer guidance on implementing effective safeguards (Erdıvan, 2024). Therefore, antivirus solutions not only contribute to immediate protection but also foster a broader trust in digital transactions and interactions.

Reputable antivirus programs such as Bitdefender, Norton 360, and Malwarebytes offer real-time protection against ransomware, spyware, and phishing attacks and are regularly updated to defend against evolving threats. To complement antivirus protection, you should incorporate a suite of secure software tools designed to enhance privacy and safeguard data across devices. Firewall tools like GlassWire or Little Snitch provide network monitoring, alerting you to unauthorized data transmissions. For secure communication, apps like Signal and ProtonMail offer end-to-end encryption, making them ideal for private messaging and email. As mentioned earlier, managing multiple online accounts with password managers such as 1Password, Dashlane, or Bitwarden generates and stores strong, unique passwords, ensuring they're encrypted and protected behind multi-factor authentication (MFA). Finally, regular system updates and security patches for all operating systems and apps are vital for closing identified vulnerabilities. By integrating these trusted software tools, you can build a layered security strategy that significantly reduces your risk of digital identity compromise.

Recognizing Phishing and Social Engineering Attacks

Phishing and social engineering attacks are effective not because they're sophisticated technologies, but because they exploit fundamental aspects of human psychology related to trust, fear, urgency, and curiosity. These tactics rely on manipulating emotional responses rather than technical vulnerabilities. For example, an attacker might impersonate a trusted authority figure, such as a supervisor or bank representative, to create a false sense of legitimacy. A common technique involves crafting urgent messages, like a warning that your account will be locked or that unusual activity has been detected, to induce panic and prompt quick, unthinking action. Others appeal to empathy, such as fraudulent messages pretending to be from a friend in distress. These attacks often include realistic branding, forged email headers, or familiar language patterns to enhance credibility (Al-Subaiey, 2024). Because they bypass technical safeguards by targeting behavior, phishing and social engineering require heightened personal awareness and digital literacy. Understanding how emotions can be weaponized is essential for recognizing these threats.

The aim of phishing and social engineering attacks is to gain access to sensitive personal information, such as passwords, financial credentials, or other identifying documents. As these tactics become more sophisticated and personalized, awareness and education are vital for your defense. Tools like ChatGPT illustrate the dual nature of advanced technologies; they can be used to generate realistic phishing content, but also to help identify and counteract such threats (Charfeddine et al., 2024). Without a strong cybersecurity infrastructure and vigilance on the part of the user, even minor lapses in protection can lead to large-scale breaches with serious consequences (Waseem et al., 2023).

The integration of artificial intelligence into phishing and social engineering attacks has dramatically increased both the effectiveness and scale of these cyber threats. Unlike traditional phishing attempts, which often contain obvious grammatical errors or generic messaging, AI-powered attacks can generate highly personalized and grammatically flawless communications that closely mimic legitimate sources. Tools such as large language models can analyze publicly available information from social media posts, corporate bios, or recent news and use it to craft convincing emails, voice messages, or even real-time chat interactions. More concerning is the emergence of deepfake technology, which enables attackers to replicate voices and facial features to impersonate trusted individuals during video calls or phone conversations (Good Morning America, 2023). In May 2024, criminals targeted Mark Read, the CEO of WPP, the world's largest advertising firm, by creating a deepfake impersonation of him (Warrington, 2024). They used a fake WhatsApp account, a cloned voice, and manipulated YouTube footage to conduct a virtual meeting, aiming to deceive employees into transferring funds. These tactics exploit human trust and social cues, making them harder to detect than conventional cyberattacks.

If Your Digital Identity Is Stolen

Having your digital identity stolen can be a disorienting and stressful experience, but there are important steps you can take to regain control and protect yourself. Digital identity theft can involve unauthorized access to your email, banking credentials, government-issued identification numbers, or social media accounts. Often, this kind of theft is invisible until damage is done, such as fraudulent charges, spam sent in your name, or your identity used to open unauthorized accounts. The sooner you act, the better your chances of limiting harm and recovering your digital presence.

The first and most immediate step is to secure your accounts. Start by changing passwords, especially for email, financial services, and social media. Use strong, unique passwords for each account and activate 2FA wherever possible. If you believe your email has been compromised, change its password first, since access to your email often allows someone to reset other accounts. You should also review your account activity and sign out of unfamiliar devices or sessions.

Next, you'll want to notify the appropriate institutions and platforms. If financial information is involved, contact your bank or payment service immediately to report the incident and request temporary holds or new account numbers. If the stolen information includes government-issued ID (like a passport or national identity number), notify your local authorities or national data protection office. In some countries, you may be able to file a digital complaint with a cybercrime unit or data protection authority. Keep written records of all communications and actions taken; these may help in the recovery process or when disputing unauthorized transactions.

You should also take steps to monitor for ongoing misuse. This may involve enrolling in a credit monitoring service if available in your country or manually checking for new accounts opened in your name. Many nations have data protection frameworks that give you the right to request information about how your personal data is being used or to have it deleted (e.g., the General Data Protection Regulation in the EU, or similar emerging laws in Africa, Latin America, and Asia). These legal frameworks may provide you with tools to limit future exploitation of your identity (Makulilo, 2021).

Finally, consider the longer-term digital hygiene practices to prevent future attacks. Avoid clicking on suspicious links or downloading unknown files, especially in email or messaging apps. Review the privacy settings of your digital services and reduce the amount of personal information you make public. Using a password manager, updating your software regularly, and staying informed about phishing techniques are key habits that support your ongoing digital safety (NIST Privacy Framework, 2020). Remember: Safeguarding your digital identity is not a one-time action, but an ongoing responsibility in a world where data flows constantly and security threats evolve rapidly.

BOX 13.1 CASE STUDY

Sofia, a 26-year-old nursing student, first created social media accounts in high school. Her online presence was typical of her peers with memes, selfies, inside jokes, and posts reflecting her teenage views. As she progressed through college and prepared for nursing home internships, she realized that potential employers and patients might search her online. She Googled her name and not only her LinkedIn profile but also a decade-old Tumblr account, outdated Instagram photos, and a public X feed containing questionable posts she no longer stood by came up.

Rather than panic, Sofia approached her digital identity as a story she could revise. She deleted outdated content, made some accounts private, and began curating a professional narrative. She launched a blog documenting her nursing journey and joined healthcare forums to share insights on patient care and digital ethics. Over time, search results for her name began to reflect her current identity and aspirations.

This transformation didn't happen overnight, but it highlights a powerful truth: Your digital identity is an evolving story, and it's one that can be reshaped, edited, or expanded. Whether it becomes a thoughtful reflection of who you are or a collection of unmanaged remnants is up to you. Sofia's case reminds us that while digital footprints are lasting, they're not fixed. By staying engaged and intentional, anyone can take control of their online narrative.

Conclusion

In a world where your digital presence is increasingly inseparable from your personal and professional identity, managing your online footprint is no longer optional; it's essential. The digital traces you leave behind influence how others perceive you, how algorithms categorize you, and even how opportunities are presented or withheld. This chapter has demonstrated that taking control of your digital identity is both a defensive act against exploitation and a proactive step toward empowerment. From auditing your social media content and strengthening passwords to adjusting privacy settings and recognizing AI-enhanced threats, each action you take helps you regain narrative control in an era of constant surveillance.

Digital identity management is not a one-time fix, but a lifelong digital hygiene practice that evolves with the platforms and technologies we use. The tools are available, from VPNs and password managers to anti-phishing awareness and content removal services, but their power lies in consistent, intentional use. Equally important is the development of a critical digital mindset: One that questions how and why data is collected, who benefits, and how your online self can be shaped to reflect your values and goals.

Ultimately, your digital identity is an extension of your lived self. By approaching it with the same care and intentionality you bring to other aspects of your life, you can protect your reputation, reduce your vulnerability, and build a more authentic, resilient presence online. The digital world is rapidly changing, but with awareness, strategy, and the right tools, you can navigate it with confidence and clarity.

Exercise

As we have seen throughout this book, your social media presence can significantly impact your professional opportunities and personal reputation. This short assignment guides you through a systematic review and clean-up of your social media accounts to ensure they align with your current values and career goals.

Requirements

Step 1: Account Inventory

Create a list of all your social media accounts, including:

- Platform name
- How long you've had the account
- Frequency of use
- Privacy settings (public, private, mixed)
- Primary purpose (personal, professional, hobby, etc.)

Step 2: Content Audit

For each active account:

- Review your profile information, photos, and bio
- Scroll back through at least one year of posts (or 50 posts, whichever is less)
- Apply the "future employer test" – would you be comfortable with a potential employer seeing this content?
- Identify content that:
    - Contains inappropriate language or behavior
    - Shows unprofessional activities

- Reveals excessive personal information
- Presents outdated or inaccurate representations of you
- Could be misinterpreted out of context

Step 3: Clean-up Implementation
Take action to improve your digital presence:

- Delete or archive inappropriate posts
- Update profile information and photos
- Adjust privacy settings as needed
- Untag yourself from problematic content
- Organize content using platform tools (highlights, pins, etc.)
- Document what specific changes you made on each platform

Step 4: Reflection
Write a brief reflection (250–350 words) addressing:

- What surprised you about your social media audit?
- What criteria did you use to decide what to keep vs. remove?
- How will you approach social media differently going forward?
- How might your cleaned-up profiles better support your professional goals?

References

Aguiar, J. (2024). Digital Footprint Management: Youth and Social Media on Protecting Your Online Identity and Reputation [Dissertation]. https://scholarworks.lib.csusb.edu/etd/2073/

Al-Subaiey, A., Al-Thani, M., Alam, N. A., Antora, K. F., Khandakar, A., & Zaman, S. A. U. (2024). Novel interpretable and robust web-based AI platform for phishing email detection. *Computers and Electrical Engineering*, *120*, 109625.

Charfeddine, M., Kammoun, H., Hamdaoui, B., & Guizani, M. (2024). ChatGPT's security risks and benefits: Offensive and defensive use-cases, mitigation measures, and future implications. *IEEE Access*, *12*, 30263–30310.

Chester, J., & Montgomery, K. (2011). *Digital Food Marketing to Children and Adolescents*. National Policy & Legal Analysis Network to Prevent Childhood Obesity (NPLAN). https://changelabsolutions.org/sites/default/files/documents/DigitalMarketingReport_FINAL_web_20111017.pdf

Desmarais, N. (2000). Body language, security and e-commerce. *Library Hi Tech*, *18*(1), 61–74.

Erdıvan, C. (2024). *Process, Technology and Human Aspects of a Security Operations Center*. Middle East Technical University. https://open.metu.edu.tr/bitstream/handle/11511/108246/Process,%20Technology%20and%20Human%20Aspects%20of%20a%20Security%20Operations%20Center.pdf

General Data Protection Regulations. (2025). Right to Be Forgotten. https://www.gdpreu.org/right-to-be-forgotten/#:~:text=In%20simple%20terms%2C%20the%20right,necessary%20for%20its%20original%20purpose

Getov, V. (2012). Security as a service in smart clouds – Opportunities and concerns. *2012 IEEE 36th Annual Computer Software and Applications Conference*. pp. 373–379, IEEE. https://doi.org/10.1109/COMPSAC.2012.112

Good Morning America (2023). Mom warns of hoax using AI to clone daughter's voice. ABC News. https://abcnews.go.com/GMA/Family/mom-warns-hoax-ai-clone-daughters-voice/story?id=98551351

Hanoglu, I. S. (2023). A Cookieless Future: Solving the UX Problems Caused by the Privacy Protections Method. https://core.ac.uk/download/568548097.pdf

Kaminski, M. E., Rueben, M., Smart, W. D., & Grimm, C. M. (2016). Averting robot eyes. *Maryland Law Review*, *76*, 983.

Makulilo, A. B. (2021). *Data protection in Africa: Toward a rights-based legal framework*. Springer.

NIST Privacy Framework. (2020). A Tool for Improving Privacy through Enterprise Risk Management. https://doi.org/10.6028/nist.cswp.01162020

Rao, U. H., & Nayak, U. (2020). *The InfoSec handbook: An introduction to information security*. Springer Nature.

Sharples, M., Graber, R., Harrison, C., & Logan, K. (2008). E-safety and Web 2.0: Web 2.0 technologies for learning at Key Stages 3 and 4. https://core.ac.uk/download/4151769.pdf

Smoot, T. Jr. (2024). Cyber-ready communities: Securing local government agencies in the digital age. https://core.ac.uk/download/622815154.pdf

Volkova, E. (2024). Digital Footprint Management for Private Individuals in Finland. https://core.ac.uk/download/638718743.pdf

Warrington, J. (2024). Boss of world's biggest ad firm impersonated by AI in elaborate deepfake scam. *The Telegraph*. https://www.telegraph.co.uk/business/2024/05/10/wpp-boss-mark-read-impersonated-ai-in-elaborate-deepfake/

Waseem, M., Adnan Khan, M., Goudarzi, A., Fahad, S., Sajjad, I., & Siano, P. (2023). Incorporation of blockchain technology for different smart grid applications: Architecture, prospects, and challenges. *Energies*, *16*(2), 820–820.

Wenger, E., Shan, S., Zheng, H., & Zhao, B. Y. (2023). Sok: Anti-facial recognition technology. *2023 IEEE Symposium on Security and Privacy (SP)*. pp. 864–881. https://doi.org/10.48550/arXiv.2112.04558

Zou, Y., Le, K., Mayer, P., Acquisti, A., Aviv, A. J., & Schaub, F. (2024). Encouraging users to change breached passwords using the protection motivation theory. *ACM Transactions on Computer-Human Interaction*, *31*(5), 1–45.

GLOSSARY

Affordances: the relationships between the environment and an agent (person or animal) that allow for emergent opportunities for action.

Algorithmic Discrimination: occurs when AI systems or machine learning algorithms produce biased or unequal outcomes for specific groups of people, often due to biases in the data they are trained on or in the way they are designed.

Big Tech: the largest and most influential technology companies, often encompassing companies like Amazon, Apple, Alphabet (Google), Meta (formerly Facebook), and Microsoft, known for their global reach and significant impact on technology, the internet, and the economy.

Black Box Effect: phenomena whereby individuals or groups affected by decisions they cannot understand or contest.

Black Code: a 2016 movie follows "internet sleuths" – or cyber stewards – from the Toronto-based group Citizen Lab, who travel the world to expose unprecedented levels of global digital espionage.

Cancel Culture: a cultural process in which an individual thought to have acted or spoken in an unacceptable manner is ostracized, boycotted, shunned, or fired, often aided by social media.

Cancelling: the act of ostracizing, boycotting, or shunning an individual who has acted or spoken in an unacceptable manner, often through social media.

Citizens Lab: an interdisciplinary research group based at the Munk School of Global Affairs & Public Policy at the University of Toronto, focusing on the intersection of information and communication technologies, human rights, and global security.

Click Farm: a commercial enterprise that employs a large number of people to repeatedly click on items of online content in order to artificially inflate statistics of traffic or engagement.

Conforming Theory: suggests that individuals often adjust their attitudes, beliefs, or behaviors to align with those of a group or social norm, often driven by the desire for acceptance or perceived accuracy.

Cookies: a small text file that a website stores on your computer to remember information about you and your browsing activity, enhancing user experience and personalization.

Credit Score: a three-digit number, typically ranging from 300 to 850, that summarizes your creditworthiness, or the likelihood you will repay debts on time.

Cybercriminal: an individual who commits crimes using information technology (IT) either as a means or a target, such as data theft, identity theft, online scams, or spreading malware.

Dark Web: the part of the World Wide Web that is only accessible by means of special software, allowing users and website operators to remain anonymous or untraceable.

Data Aggregating: the process of combining and summarizing data from multiple sources into a single, unified format for easier analysis and decision-making.

Data Broker: a company that collects and aggregates personal data from various sources, then sells that data to third parties, often for marketing or other business purposes.

Data Sovereignty: the right for individuals to own their data.

Digital Commons: a conceptual framework for the commonwealth of intellectual goods, knowledge products, and creative works that are freely and democratically shared and built upon online.

Digital Footprint: the information about a particular person that exists on the internet as a result of their online activity.

Digital Identity: a virtual representation of a person, organization, or entity in the digital world, encompassing all the data and information linked to them, such as usernames, passwords, email addresses, and online activity.

Digital Poorhouse: whereby the marginalized groups are monitored more but supported less.

Doxing: the action or process of searching for and publishing private or identifying information about a particular individual on the internet, typically with malicious intent.

Echo Chamber: an environment in which a person encounters only beliefs or opinions that coincide with their own, so that their existing views are reinforced, and alternative ideas are not considered.

Fear of Missing Out (FOMO): anxiety that an exciting or interesting event may currently be happening elsewhere, often aroused by posts seen on social media.

Filter Bubble: a situation in which an internet user encounters only information and opinions that conform to and reinforce their own beliefs, caused by algorithms that personalize an individual's online experience.

Impulse Control: the ability to resist acting on immediate desires or impulses without considering the consequences.

Influencer: a person with a large following on social media who focuses on specific themes like cooking, beauty, or gaming. They attract followers who engage with their content and are often sponsored by companies to promote products, creating a sense of trust and relatability among their audience.

Multi-factor Authentication: a security enhancement that requires users to provide two or more verification factors (something you know, something you have, or something you are) to access a resource.

Participatory Culture: coined by Henry Jenkins, it describes a culture where individuals are not just consumers of media but also active contributors, creators, and shapers of content, often through online communities and digital technologies.

Persuasion: a communication process where someone attempts to influence the beliefs, attitudes, or actions of others by using arguments, evidence, or appeals to emotion.

Phishing: the fraudulent practice of sending emails or other messages purporting to be from reputable companies to induce individuals to reveal personal information, such as passwords and credit card numbers.

Predictive Analytics: the use of data, statistics, modeling, and machine learning to predict and plan for future events or opportunities.

Psychographics: the study and classification of people according to their attitudes, aspirations, and other psychological criteria, especially in market research.

Right to be Forgotten: a European Union law that allows individuals to request the removal of specific personal information about them from online platforms and search engine results, particularly when the information is inaccurate, irrelevant, or no longer necessary.

Robin Hooding: the practice of giving your insurance information to another for the purpose of obtaining healthcare fraudulently.

Segmentation Modelling: a method of dividing a group (customers or an image) into smaller, more homogeneous groups based on shared characteristics, enabling more targeted and effective approaches.

Shadow Banning: blocking (a user) from a social media site or online forum without their knowledge, typically by making their posts and comments no longer visible to other users.

Social Credit Score: a system, like the one implemented in China, where individuals are assigned a score based on their behavior, which can influence their access to various social and economic opportunities.

Social Dilemma: a 2020 docudrama. Tech experts from Silicon Valley sound the alarm on the dangerous impact of social networking, which Big Tech use to manipulate and influence.

Social Engineering: the use of centralized planning to manage social change and regulate the future development and behavior of a society.

Social Proof: psychological phenomenon where people assume the actions of others are correct in a given situation, and they are more likely to follow suit, especially when faced with uncertainty.

Spiral of Silence Theory: a political science and mass communication theory which states that an individual's perception of the distribution of public opinion influences that individual's willingness to express their own opinions.

Surveillance Capitalism: A term coined by Shoshana Zuboff to describe the economic system where personal data is commodified for profit by digital platforms.

Tor: (short for "The Onion Router") is a free, open-source software that enables anonymous web browsing by routing internet traffic through a network of volunteer-run servers, making it difficult to track users' online activity.

Trackers: technologies, typically scripts or cookies, used by websites or third parties to collect and monitor user activity. They gather data such as browsing habits, clicked links, time spent on pages, and personal information like location and device details.

Transnational repression: a state's actions to suppress political dissent or target individuals perceived as threats, even when those actions occur outside of its own borders.

INDEX

Note: Page numbers in *italics* and **bold** refer to figures and tables, respectively.

Made in the USA
Monee, IL
13 September 2026

62977459R20116